The Role of Economic Advisers in Israel's Economic Policy

Daniel Schiffman • Warren Young •
Yaron Zelekha

The Role of Economic Advisers in Israel's Economic Policy

Crises, Reform and Stabilization

Springer

Daniel Schiffman
Department of Economics and Business Administration
Ariel University
Ariel, Israel

Warren Young
Department of Economics
Bar Ilan University
Ramat Gan, Israel

Yaron Zelekha
Faculty of Business Administration
Ono Academic College
Kiryat Ono, Israel

ISBN 978-3-319-60680-4 ISBN 978-3-319-60682-8 (eBook)
DOI 10.1007/978-3-319-60682-8

Library of Congress Control Number: 2017943317

Printed on acid-free paper

This Springer imprint is published by Springer Nature
The registered company is Springer International Publishing AG
The registered company address is: Gewerbestrasse 11, 6330 Cham, Switzerland

To my wife Bruria and our sons Ariel and Itiel

Daniel Schiffman

To my wife Sara, our daughters Shani and Naty and their families

Warren Young

To my wife Orly and our children Noa, Omer, and Yoav

Yaron Zelekha

Acknowledgments

We thank our colleagues, students, department chairs, deans, and administrators for creating and maintaining a supportive environment for our research endeavors.

Daniel Schiffman and Yaron Zelekha thank the Aharon Meir Center for Banking at Bar Ilan University for financial support.

We also wish to thank the following individuals for their assistance in obtaining archival materials: Prof. Russell Boyer of the University of Western Ontario and the Hoover Institution, Stanford University; Patricia McGuire and Tracy Wilkinson of the King's College Archive Centre, Cambridge University; Will Hansen and Megan O'Connell of the David M. Rubenstein Rare Book and Manuscript Library, Duke University; Rami Shtivi and Malki Pomeranc of the Begin Heritage Center Archives; Carmit Cohen and Alice Baron of Israel State Archives; and Marina Michaeli of the Israel Broadcasting Authority Film Archive.

Chapter 4 was originally published as "Richard Kahn and Israeli Economic Policy, 1957 and 1962," *History of Economic Thought and Policy* 1-2014, 31–73. We thank the editors of *History of Economic Thought and Policy* for permission to reproduce this article, which has been revised for inclusion in this volume.

Daniel Schiffman thanks the Royal Economic Society for a grant that facilitated his research in the Kahn papers at the King's College Archive Centre, Cambridge University.

Daniel Schiffman thanks Prof. David Papineau for granting him permission to quote from the Kahn Papers and answering his inquiries regarding Richard Kahn's family, and Rabbi Yehuda Fishman for providing the text of the eulogy delivered at Kahn's funeral.

Warren Young thanks the late Allan Meltzer and Marvin Goodfriend of Carnegie Mellon University for their ongoing support of this project.

Finally, we thank Johannes Glaeser and Sivachandran Ravanan of Springer for their professionalism and dedication. It was truly a pleasure to work with them to bring this project to fruition.

Acknowledgments

[illegible]

Contents

Chapter 1
Introduction: The Impact of Economic Advisers in Israel

> I realize how unusual it is for outside advisers to be given as active a role in the formulation of policy as we eventually had. (Fischer 1995, 3)

Economic research on the role of economic advisers, while now widespread, has not been fully able to resolve why and when advisers can affect economic policies in the countries they advise. While some may succeed completely or partially in their policy advice, others may fail, again partially or completely. Our focus here encompasses these possible scenarios in a specific national context, that is, foreign economic advisers in Israel.

The present volume utilizes the *unique historical fact* that well-known *academically based* international advisers took part—albeit with varying degrees of efficacy—in the development of Israel's economic policies over the period 1948–2007. The involvement of international (and local) advisers can be, inter alia, explained by the fact that all of Israel's prime ministers and ministers of finance during this period *lacked formal training in economics* and thus also turned to independent advice, aside from the advice of their own civil servants. Moreover, Israel faced tremendous economic challenges that attracted high-level international advisers.

The aim of this book is to survey the recommendations of international (and in specific cases local) advisers that took part in the development of Israel's economic policy from 1948 to 2007 and analyze their recommendations vis-à-vis:

1. Policymakers' own (including their political parties') interests
2. Actual policies that were implemented

It should be stressed that we will not be dealing here with the role of international organizations (such as The World Bank and IMF), except insofar as their policy advocacy interacted with that of foreign advisers. All of these characteristics, (1) the intensity and reputation of the advisers, (2) the absence of any formal training or experience in economics of prime ministers and ministers of finance, (3) the impact of international entities, and (4) the tremendous economic challenges

D. Schiffman et al., *The Role of Economic Advisers in Israel's Economic Policy*,
DOI 10.1007/978-3-319-60682-8_1

that Israel faced, create a baseline for examining when, and if, international advisers could have had an influence on Israel's economic policy.

The book is organized as follows. Below, we outline our focus based upon the agency information-theoretic approach and possible scenarios and hypotheses that we have developed. Chapters 2–7 present the *purposive* sample, that is, an *overview* of case studies of the role of some well-known academically based international advisers who took part in the development of Israel's economic policies: Kalecki, Mikesell, Lerner, Kahn, Friedman, Stein and Fischer, *along with the input of local economic advisers, as the case may be*. Detailed case studies will be presented in the relevant chapters, and will be based on archival research, and include new historical facts regarding the impact of the international and local advisers. Chapter 7 presents a variation on the theme by discussing the 2003 economic crisis and the recovery program that was implemented.

We present the *purposive* case studies in the context of the possible scenarios and our *grounded* hypotheses accordingly (Glaser and Strauss 1967; Strauss 1987; Strauss and Corbin 1990, 1994, 1998; Clarke 2005; Charmaz 2006).

1.1 Theory

The problem of *policymakers* and their willingness to use well-known international (or local) *advisers* is driven by two basic issues in decision-making theory: (1) the *agency problem* of conflicting interests between the policymaker's political and personal interests and the public interest represented by the international adviser and (2) the *information problem* of the informed adviser versus the uninformed policymaker, who therefore faces a risk of losing control regarding the direction of the policy recommendation.

First, there is the *agency problem* of potential conflict between the policymaker's political and personal interests and the public interest as represented by the international adviser. Since a well-known international adviser is more probably unbiased, as compared to the policymaker, he is better suited to promote what he perceives as the public interest. However, the adviser's perception of the public interest may deviate from that of the policymaker, who may mix a nonprofessional understanding of the public interest with personal or party political interest. Indeed, Dur and Swank (2005) find that the quality of the policy recommendation is inversely related to the difference between the policymaker's and adviser's perceptions of the public interest. They show that unbiased advisers make the greatest effort to collect quality information and utilize it in an objective manner. This implies that biased advisers may manipulate information accordingly. Eliminating manipulation of information, however, requires that the preferences of the policymaker and the adviser be aligned. Policymakers usually appoint advisers with preferences that are less extreme than their own. Moreover, as the policymaker finds it more difficult to align his preferences with that of the adviser, there will be a trade-off between the quality of the recommendation and the quality of the information that the recommendation is based on. In this regard, Samuelson (1978, 38) criticized the ability of economists as advisers in general, emphasizing the agency problem in particular by asserting: "It is a sad finding that, for the most part, I can predict on what side of an issue every economist present in the room will be." Samuelson's criticism makes it clear that policymakers do indeed have the option of appointing advisers after examining their preferences which they can easily identify.

Second, there is the *information problem* driven by informed advisers versus an uninformed policymaker. This problem may lead the policymaker to face the risk of *losing control* over the direction of policy recommendations. Since information about the consequences of policies (both the current policy as well as the policy recommended by the adviser) is usually hard for policymakers to verify, informed advisers are able to manipulate information or frame their recommendations. Thus, informed advisers often acquire control of decisions at the expense of policymakers (Aghion and Tirole 1997).

Below, we briefly present a *theoretical* outline of the adviser-policymaker relationship as described above:

Let A = adviser, P = policymaker.

Agency problem:

A's interest ≠ P's interest
A's interest = his perception of the public interest
P's interest = political interests mixed with his perception of the public interest

(Acemoglu and Robinson 2013)

Information problem:

A's information > P's information
A's cost of failure < P's cost of failure

Due to P's lack of information regarding consequences of policies, A can manipulate information in framing his policy recommendations so that P loses control over the direction of policy (Aghion and Tirole 1997).

Furthermore, we should stress that one of the most robust findings in empirical research is the importance of political leaders in explaining economic outcomes. Within this framework, Jones and Olken (2005) show that leadership transitions negatively affect economic growth, while Besley et al. (2011) show that having a more educated leader positively affects economic growth. We suggest that one way of interpreting the results of Besley et al. (2011) is to argue that some leaders are more competent than others and hence better able to make sensible economic policy, for example, by their willingness to use advisers. However, the exact mechanism at work explaining how educated leaders matter remains opaque. Our suggestion is that as the leader is more educated, his willingness to use advisers increases.

An additional important question in this regard is the parameters by which we can evaluate the success of the international adviser. We suggest three possible criteria for success (arranged in order from the strictest to the least strict):

(a) Significant success—implementation of the adviser's recommendations (Edwards 2005; Seers 1962)
(b) Limited success—serious consideration of the adviser's views but no implementation (Bronfenbrenner 1963)
(c) Minor success—contribution to helping government officials attain greater clarity on economic issues, but without serious consideration or implementation (Seers 1962)

Seers claims that most economic advisers fail to make significant contributions and attributes this failure to either personal deficiencies,[1] technical errors,[2] or political errors.[3]

1.2 Possible Scenarios and Hypotheses

The literature described above, and our *initial reading and review of the case studies themselves*, leads to *three possible scenarios*, which we will examine *purposively* using the Israeli case studies accordingly:

Crisis—in a crisis environment, the policymaker's balance of interests changes, and the public interest may overcome any other interest. The alternative of advancing the public interest may then ensure the continuation of the policymaker's own position. Therefore, it is expected that the policymaker will adopt the recommendations of the adviser, whether they were requested by him in the first place or whether the recommendations were initially imposed.

Convergence (ad hoc)—a limited difference emerges between the policymaker's original policy and interests and the adviser's perception of the public interest. In such an environment, the adviser's recommendations can serve to strengthen the *policy decided on a priori by the policymaker*. Under these circumstances, and as a direct outcome of Samuelson's critique (1978), the adviser from the "relevant" side of the issue (as Samuelson put it) will be probably approached first by a government *that wishes to strengthen its public image*. Therefore, the adviser will appear successful in convincing the policymaker to adopt his recommendations. However, close examination of current policy, and scrutiny of the policymaker's interests, *will reveal that the adviser did not really affect the policy implemented.*

Divergence—significant differences between the policymaker's *original* policies and interests and the adviser's perception of the public interest may emerge. In such an environment, the adviser's recommendations can only undermine the

[1]For example, the adviser may be insufficiently sociable and therefore fail to establish rapport with his hosts.

[2]For example, the adviser may fail to learn enough about how the economy actually works and/or fail to assess major noneconomic factors.

[3]For example, the adviser may ignore the tendency of the public to misinterpret his public statements and attribute to him political positions that he does not hold.

Table 1.1 Scenarios and hypotheses

Scenario	Interests	Hypotheses
I. Crisis	Good policy (advancing the public interest) is good politics	P follows A's advice even in the absence of (IMF-style) conditionality
II. Convergence	P's original policy/interests ≈ A's perception of the public interest	A recommends the policy already chosen by P This creates the illusion of influence by A
III. Divergence	P's original policy/interests diverge significantly from A's perception of the public interest	P ignores/rejects A's advice

policies *already decided on* by the policymaker and thus contradict his interests. Therefore, it is expected that the adviser's recommendation will be ignored, at least until the policymaker's interests change. Moreover, under these circumstances, the adviser will probably offer to advise the government (perhaps even on a pro bono basis) without being asked.

We summarize the possible scenarios and hypotheses in tabular form (Table 1.1).

However, another dimension enters the analytical framework outlined above. Given the nature of the interaction between the politician and his economic adviser, there may be shifts between the alternate scenarios. Thus, convergence may shift to divergence depending on changes in political circumstances. On the other hand, divergence may become crisis, again, given certain political situations. Moreover, partial convergence may also occur, depending on the objectives of the politicians who receive the advice.

References

Acemoglu, D., & Robinson, J. (2013). Economics versus politics: Pitfalls of policy advice. *Journal of Economic Perspectives, 27*, 273–293.

Aghion, P., & Tirole, J. (1997). Formal and real authority in organizations. *Journal of Political Economy, 105* (1), 1–29.

Besley, B., Montalvo, J. G., & Reynal-Querol, M. (2011). Do educated leaders matter? *Economic Journal, 121*, F205–F227.

Bronfenbrenner, M. (1963). Balm for the visiting economist. *Journal of Political Economy, 71*, 293–297.

Charmaz, K. (2006). *Constructing grounded theory: A practical guide through qualitative analysis*. New York: Sage.

Clarke, A. (2005). *Situational analysis: Grounded theory after the postmodern turn*. New York: Sage.

Dur, R., & Swank, O. (2005). Producing and manipulating information. *Economic Journal, 115*, 185–199.

Edwards, S. (2005). *Establishing credibility: The role of foreign advisors* (NBER WP 11429).

Fischer, S. (1995, November). Recollections of the United States role in the Israeli stabilization program. International Monetary Fund.

Glaser, B., & Strauss, A. (1967). *The discovery of grounded theory*. Chicago: Aldine.
Jones, B. F., & Olken, B. A. (2005). Do leaders matter? National leadership and growth since World War II. *The Quarterly Journal of Economics, 120* (3), 835–864.
Samuelson, P. (1978). Policy advising in economics. *Challenge, 21*, 37–38.
Seers, D. (1962). Why visiting economists fail. *Journal of Political Economy, 70*, 325–338.
Strauss, A. (1987). *Qualitative analysis for social scientists*. Cambridge: Cambridge University Press.
Strauss, A., & Corbin, J. (1990, 1998). *Basics of qualitative research: Grounded theory procedures and techniques* (1st and 2nd ed.) New York: Sage.
Strauss, A., & Corbin, J. (1994) Grounded theory methodology: An overview. In N. Denzin and Y. Lincoln (eds.) *Handbook of qualitative research* (1st ed.). New York: Sage.

Chapter 2
Economic Crisis and Policy Prescriptions: The Kalecki and Mikesell Reports, 1950–1952

2.1 Kalecki's "Report"

Not long after Israel attained independence, the Ben-Gurion government came under political attack from the center-right opposition parties—Herut, the General Zionists, and the Progressives. The center-right opposition denounced the government's quasi-socialist policies and advocated the abolition of exchange and price controls, along with the introduction of a floating exchange rate. In response to these pressures, the government turned on an ad hoc basis to the well-known economist, Michal Kalecki, and indeed he recommended not only the retention of exchange controls but also the retention of price controls (Young and Lee 1993). Not surprisingly, Kalecki's advice was at first implemented, although it seems that he was approached in the first place to strengthen the public and international image of policy decisions *that had already been made*.

The politicization of policy recommendations by international advisers in Israel is, thus, first exemplified by Kalecki's September 1950 "Report on the main current economic problems of Israel." At first "confidential," the report was subsequently circulated in 1951 by the Ministry of Finance, which had, in 1950, invited Kalecki to compile it (Gross 1990, 79n24).[1] Indeed, it is a prime example of a government's identifying with and subsequently distancing itself from policies advocated by international advisers, whose policy views are known in advance. In order to understand the context and influence of Kalecki's report—or lack thereof—we must recall here the international and domestic political environment and constraints affecting Israel, its political leadership, and its economic policymakers at the time.

After Israel declared independence in May 1948, the provisional government implemented de facto austerity measures—rationing and price controls. After the

[1]At the time, Kalecki was working at the UN, on leave from his position at the Oxford Institute of Economics and Statistics.

D. Schiffman et al., *The Role of Economic Advisers in Israel's Economic Policy*,
DOI 10.1007/978-3-319-60682-8_2

general election of January 1949, the first elected government implemented a de jure austerity program in March 1949. In early 1949, the extensive needs of the new state became evident with a $100 million loan granted to Israel by the US government-backed Export-Import Bank and a $250 million appeal for funds by the United Jewish Appeal (the leading American Jewish philanthropic organization). These sums were only a part of the estimated $800 million the country needed for its economic development, settlement, and absorption of immigrants, at least according to Oscar Gass, an American Jewish economist who negotiated the Export-Import Bank loan while serving as adviser to the Ministry of Finance.[2]

Public disillusionment with austerity and controls—especially exchange controls—and black markets in both goods and foreign currency brought some politicians and economists to claim that these policies were not only responsible for differentials between formal and black market rates of exchange but also a distortion if not breakdown of the price system and capital flight. Prime Minister David Ben-Gurion and his cabinet, on the other hand, were initially unwilling to undertake major policy changes. They looked for support to Kalecki's "confidential report" of September 1950.

What then were the main points of Kalecki's report? First, he attacked the idea that abolishing exchange controls would be a panacea; rather, he advocated keeping existing controls, including price controls. Secondly, he recommended fiscal policies to reduce inflationary pressure. As he put it (1950, para.7; 1951 [1993], 98–99):

> It is useful to consider briefly a theory which is often propounded in Israel. It is frequently maintained that all problems could be solved at one stroke by abolishing foreign exchange restrictions and full decontrol at home [domestic controls] ... This viewpoint, I think is an entirely unrealistic one ... The measures recommended below go in exactly the opposite direction. It is advocated that the greatest possible effort should be made to reduce imports and to increase exports and thus to rely as little as possible on import of foreign capital, while maintaining the strictest possible exchange restrictions. These measures for improving the current balance of payments will require a much larger degree of government supervision and interference then has hitherto been the case.

In his report, Kalecki actually came out *against investment for modernization of Israel's industries*. He claimed that while "a considerable savings in imports" could be achieved by such investment, because there was "unused capacity" and "no scarcity of labor" in the country at the time, "modernization is a luxury that the Israeli economy cannot afford for the time being" (1951 [1993], 102–103). In order to expand exports of these industries, he recommended "export premiums." He justified this recommendation by asserting that "from the point of view of saving foreign currency, which is the scarcest factor in the Israel economy, it is much more reasonable to pay export premiums, however unnatural such a subsidization of obsolete methods of production might appear" (1951 [1993], 103).

In other words, he was against *both* private capital imports *and* private investment, which he thought should be regulated. Rather, he advocated state-organized

[2]As we shall see below, Gass was later appointed by Ben-Gurion to head the Economic Advisory Staff (1953–1955), comprised of a number of foreign economic advisers, including Abba Lerner.

investments so as to maximize exports and finance imports of industrial goods and machinery. As he put it in his report, in Israel, "there exists, I believe," a tendency "to exaggerate the possibilities of foreign direct investment" (1951, para.43 as cited in Gross 1990, 82).

Initially, based on its Weltanschauung, the Israeli government actually "preferred certain assumptions and recommendations" in his report (Gross 1990, 81). By mid-1951, however, there was "severe erosion of public support" for the economic policies of the government, as evident in the July 1951 election results (more about this below). Moreover, by the end of 1950, the government realized that in order to continue receiving US aid, such as the 1951 $64.5 million grant to Israel approved by Congress, it had to undertake economic reform. At the time, many—including the British Foreign Office, the US State Department, and even the US Joint Chiefs of Staff—regarded Israel as a socialist state, in danger of becoming a Communist one (Bullock 1985, 648); a contemporary account in *Fortune* magazine reported that "some allege" that Israel "is a Moscow-drifting socialist mess" (Lehrman 1952, 89). At the same time, and in spite of Kalecki's position and the initial ideological predilection of the Israeli government, *Fortune* also reported that from 1949 to the end of 1951, private foreign investment in Israel amounted to some $180 million, $65 million of which was investment by American firms (Lehrman 1952, 90).

2.2 Kalecki's "Report" and the "New Economic Policy"

In the early 1950s, Israel was characterized by almost complete government intervention in the economy. The ruling party was the socialist Mapai ("Workers of the Land of Israel Party"), under the leadership of Prime Minister David Ben-Gurion. Mapai used statist policies to consolidate political control over the economy and undermine the liberal and centrist opposition parties (Herut, the General Zionists, and the Progressives), which drew their support from small businesses and the commerce and service sectors (for details, see Zelekha 2011, 26–28).

The government effectively controlled capital investment, credit allocation, and foreign currency. Prices were fixed by the government, wages (and wage differentials) were fixed by the Histadrut (the General Federation of Trade Unions, which was dominated by Mapai), and a legal maximum was set on interest rates. The government also imposed rationing and austerity as a means of maintaining economic control: Everything from foreign currency to food was rationed, and black markets flourished until they brought about the collapse of the rationing/price-fixing system in 1952 (Patinkin 1956, 1960a, b).

From mid-1951 onward, public discontent with existing economic policies increased. Moreover, "the faith of the leaders of economic policy in the potential of intervention by the state" had "weakened, as did their mistrust of the price mechanism," and it thus "became obvious that a change in policy was due" (Michaely 1975, 23). Israel's international position was deteriorating: External foreign exchange reserves dwindled from $117 million in 1949 to $34 million in 1951 (Michaely 1975, 34–35), and the trade deficit (measured in current US dollars) rose by an alarming 27.3% in 1951, driven by a 29.9% rise in imports (Michaely 1975, Appendix A, Table A-10).

Political instability and policy disagreements brought about the July 1951 general election (Gross 1990, 79). While Mapai's Knesset representation stayed roughly constant,[3] the centrist General Zionist Party almost tripled its Knesset representation, from 7 to 20 Members of Knesset, thus becoming the Knesset's second-largest party. Most of the General Zionist gains came at the expense of the rightist Herut and the leftist Mapam parties rather than Mapai. Nevertheless, Mapai understood that it would have to satisfy the electorate's demand for a change in economic policy (Etzioni 1959). Thus, Kalecki's report, which legitimized the status quo, would have to be jettisoned.

After a lengthy negotiation, Ben-Gurion formed Israel's third government with the religious parties in October 1951. The General Zionists, who opposed controls and austerity, and the Soviet-leaning Mapam (the third-largest party) were excluded. In February 1952, realizing that Kalecki's policy recommendations did not suit its revised politico-economic position, the government reversed its economic policy and announced a "New Economic Policy" (henceforth NEP)[4] consisting of the following measures: (nominal) devaluation, import liberalization,[5] increased capital flows, abandonment of most rationing and price controls, absorption of excess demand by raising the domestic price level, and reducing credit and the budget deficit.[6]

The NEP was implemented gradually over 1952–1954, within a favorable political climate: After the third government broke up over the issue of religious education, Ben-Gurion formed the fourth government with the General Zionists and Progressives in December 1952.[7] The NEP was rather successful. Relative import prices almost tripled (Michaely 1975, 48). Imports (in current US dollars) declined by 7.7% in 1952 and 7.1% in 1953 before rising by 2.2% in 1954, and the trade deficit (in current US dollars) narrowed by 14.5% in 1952, 14.3% in 1953, and 9.5% in 1954 (Michaely 1975, Appendix A, Table A-10). External reserves fell to $31 million in 1952 before rising to $39 million in 1953 and $81 million in 1954 (Michaely 1975, 35). Michaely (1975, 48) sums up the NEP as follows: "Altogether, the NEP of 1952–1954 and related developments may be considered an

[3]Mapai lost one Knesset seat, but its Arab satellite party gained three.

[4]The choice of the Soviet-sounding name "New Economic Policy" was rather ironic.

[5]For a detailed analysis of the import liberalization, see Michaely (1975, 27–57).

[6]Mapai economists justified the NEP on the basis of the new possibilities created by the (expected) reparations agreement with West Germany (by January 1952, both the Bundestag and the Knesset had empowered their respective governments to begin official negotiations), but the election results clearly played a role (Etzioni 1959).

[7]The composition of Moshe Sharett's fifth government (January 1954–June 1955) was virtually identical.

outstanding example of the substitution of the price mechanism for regulation through quantitative restrictions."

It is not surprising, therefore, that in retrospect, Kalecki recalled that "in only one case my advice was not ignored but taken account of. This happened in Israel … Instead of simply ignoring my advice, the Israeli government did exactly the opposite" (as reported in Laski 2004, 124). Kalecki's advice *was only partially implemented early on when it suited the government's purpose. Later, the government distanced itself from* ***all*** *of his policy recommendations when the NEP was subsequently implemented.*

2.3 Austerity, Crises, Policies, and the Mikesell "Report"

In 1951, Israel's exports of goods and services covered less than 20% of its imports, the import surplus reaching $360 million. Both in 1950 and 1951, the import surplus exceeded grants and long-term loans, governmental and private. As a result, at the start of 1952, short-term debt rose to $100 million, and the government faced serious difficulties covering impending debt repayments. In effect, the Israeli government had run out of foreign currency *and was facing default on its short-term debt.* In early 1952 then, the US government, for its part, became very concerned that if Israel defaulted on its external debt, it would face difficulties obtaining funds from US Jewry via the sale of the recently established financial tool, Israel Development Bonds. Moreover, a default could potentially exacerbate the Arab-Israeli conflict. On the other hand, the US government was not keen to provide aid to enable Israel to cover its short-term debt, which might, in turn, bring about an increase in imports of consumer goods. Rather, the US favored aid that would be used for producing investment goods, so as to enable Israel to attain *economic independence*.

From the mid-1951 onward, "the faith of the leaders of economic policy in the potential of intervention by the state" and directing the economy by government fiat had "weakened, as did their mistrust of the price mechanism," and it thus "became obvious that a change in policy was due" (Michaely 1975, 23). In February 1952, economic policy was reversed, and the government adopted a "New Economic Policy" based upon (nominal) devaluation, liberalization of current account transactions, increased capital flows, abandonment of most rationing and price controls, absorption of excess demand by raising the domestic price level, and cutting back on credit and the budget deficit.

After low inflation rates in 1950 and 1951, due to price controls, *suppressed* inflation became evident after February 1952, when, as noted, price controls and rationing were abolished and the currency devalued. The inflation rate rose to 70% in mid-1952. An additional factor generating consumption and import demand was the rise in real wages brought about by the pressure of Israel's then very politically powerful General Federation of Trade Unions (Histadrut). While real wages declined somewhat with the increase in consumer prices resulting from the devaluation in February 1952, by mid-1952 they returned to their 1951 levels and continued to rise. And, despite the massive inflow of immigrants (the population of Israel doubled between 1948 and 1952, from some 800,000 to 1,600,000), per capita real consumption rose between 1950 and 1952. Thus, the level of per capita consumption rose in the early 1950s, due in part to the strength of the Histadrut and in part due to government policies which, after February 1952, *did not constrain private consumption expenditure*. In other words, rising per capita consumption and its impact on the trade balance, and not only mass immigration, prevented Israel from decreasing its reliance on foreign assistance and attaining economic independence during the period in question (Patinkin 1960a, Chap. 5).

By the end of April 1952, then, Israel's financial position had deteriorated to what was described as a "financial emergency" by its foreign minister, Moshe Sharett. This was due to its considerable short-term debt, which by then had reached $124 million. In an exchange of documents between the US and Israel, US Secretary of State Dean Acheson announced his decision to send an economic expert to Israel so as to survey its financial difficulties. Raymond Mikesell of the University of Virginia—a noted economist who had been US Treasury Representative in the Middle East in 1943–1944, assistant to Harry Dexter White [architect of the Bretton Woods Agreements along with Keynes] in 1944, economic adviser to the Joint Anglo-American Cabinet Committee on Palestine in 1946, and subsequent consultant to US government agencies—was chosen to assess Israel's financial problems and propose solutions (Mikesell 1995, 211). Concomitantly, in early May 1952, Congress authorized a grant to Israel of $70 million to assist it to become self-supporting, finance its import bill, and pay overdue short-term debts.

On 18 June 1952, Sharett met Acheson and, on 1 July, President Truman to discuss Israel's economic problems. According to the memorandum of the Sharett-Acheson meeting, Sharett said "that he wished the assistance of the US Government. The problem is to find a way to refund Israel's short-term debts, which, he stated, amount to about $124 million." To this, Acheson reportedly replied: "What must be determined is whether Israel's financial policy will be effective or whether Israel will continue policies which would recreate the present situation" (Doc. 446, Secretary's Memoranda, *FRUS*, 1952–54, IX, 1).

A fortnight later, on 30 June 1952, the Acting Secretary of State, Undersecretary Bruce (Acheson was in Berlin) sent a detailed memorandum on behalf of Acheson to President Truman regarding his scheduled meeting with Sharett. Bruce wrote: "Possibilities suggested by the Foreign Minister included an Export-Import Bank loan or use of the United States Treasury Stabilization fund. The need for such aid has not yet been proven, nor has it yet been possible to evaluate its effect upon our policy of impartiality in the Near East" (Doc. 453, *FRUS*, 1952–54, IX, 1). During July 1952, Mikesell was in Israel. His main recommendation was the immediate implementation of a detailed and comprehensive foreign exchange budget and the mechanisms by which to implement it.

It should be recalled here that despite extensive negotiations between West Germany, Israel, and the World Jewish Congress, and concomitant acrimonious political debate in Israel during 1951 and 1952, the first reparation and restitution agreement between West Germany, Israel, and the Committee representing Holocaust survivors was only signed in September 1952. The agreement provided 3 billion DM in reparations to the Israeli government on behalf of European Jews who did not survive the Holocaust and 450 million DM in direct restitution payments (one-time and monthly) to Holocaust survivors scheduled over a 12-year period (Rosensaft and Rosensaft 2001).

On 12 August 1952, Israel's ambassador to the US, Eban, wrote US Secretary of State Acheson regarding Israel's agreement to the recommendations of the Mikesell Report, among other proposals dealing with its foreign exchange and short-term debt crisis. Because of its importance in understanding the impact of the Mikesell Report, we cite Eban's letter to Acheson in detail below. Eban wrote (Doc. 469, *FRUS*, 1952–54, IX, 1):

> In paragraph 4 of his Note of April 30, 1952 the Secretary of State announced his decision to dispatch a representative to Israel for the purpose of surveying the current financial and economic problems of the country. In reply, the Ambassador of Israel conveyed his Government's willingness to receive such a representative and to provide the fullest available information on its foreign exchange income and expenditures, its internal budgets and fiscal procedures. The Government of Israel further agreed to make such information available for the duration of United States economic assistance to Israel.
>
> During the month of July 1952, Dr. Mikesell, the representative of the United States appointed pursuant to the Secretary of State's Note of April 30, 1952, carried out a rapid survey in Israel of the country's short-term debt position on the basis of information made available by the Government of Israel …
>
> In the course of examining its financial problems in recent months, both before and during Dr. Mikesell's mission, the Government of Israel became aware of the need to institute substantial revisions in its economic and fiscal policies, as well as in some of its administrative procedures. Early in 1952, the prime minister announced a series of economic reforms, calculated to combat inflation and to restore financial equilibrium. This policy, which involved an intensification of austerity programs and a stricter control of all foreign currency expenditures, has borne marked results; yet it cannot, in the nature of things, have yielded its full effect within so brief a time. At this stage, the Government of Israel has decided to adopt further detailed measures to promote financial recovery and to avoid recurring threats to its financial structure …
>
> The Government of Israel is now in the course of preparing a foreign exchange budget for the twelve months' period beginning July 1, 1952. Every effort will be made to have this budget ready by September 15, 1952. The foreign exchange budget will constitute a working basis for Israel's foreign currency operations throughout the year …

Over the months of July and August 1952 while visiting the Finance Ministry in Jerusalem at the invitation of Finance Minister Eshkol, Oscar Gass—later to be the director of the Economic Advisory Staff[8] appointed by Prime Minister Ben-Gurion—was engaged in the first effort at drafting a framework foreign exchange budget for Israel, based upon the principles outlined in the Mikesell Report. In a covering letter dated 12 September 1952, Gass wrote to Eshkol regarding his "Memorandum" entitled "Outline of notes and observations for a foreign exchange budget of the Israel economy" for the period 1 July 1952–30 June 1953: "I think you will pardon my perhaps wearisome repetition that what

[8]The Economic Advisory Staff (EAS) operated from May 1953 to July 1955. Its senior staff was comprised of five US economists, including Abba Lerner, who is the subject of Chap. 3.

is submitted herewith is certainly of no value if it is conceived as an episode in the continuous, hard work of improving budgetary processes."

The Eisenhower Administration took office in January 1953, with Dulles becoming secretary of state. In early March 1953, Foreign Minister Sharett and Finance Minister Eshkol met with the US ambassador and members of the US Technical Cooperation Administration (TCA) in Tel Aviv. Sharett presented Israel's problems in refinancing its short-term debt and its need for "special assistance." In his comment on the meeting, US Ambassador Davis wrote that despite Israel's "progress in implementing" the Mikesell Report via its foreign exchange budget, US "influence might now be shifted ... to that of attaining broader policy objectives," that is, "broader economic reforms needed here." As he put it: "Time has now come for" the US "to exert influence toward attaining" economic reform (Doc. 582, *FRUS,* 1952–54, 9:1, 10 March 1953). In May 1953, Dulles visited Israel in the course of a wider visit to the Middle East. On 13 May, Stassen, who was director of the Foreign Operations Administration—and had accompanied Dulles—met in Tel Aviv with Finance Minister Eshkol. At the meeting, Eshkol reviewed the $380 million debt problem facing Israel at the time. The next day, 14 May, Dulles and Stassen met in Tel Aviv with Sharett and Eshkol, who emphasized the need for a refunding loan. Later that day, they met with Prime Minister Ben-Gurion in Jerusalem. During the economic "conversation," Stassen "speaking on behalf" of Dulles stated that such assistance would be contingent on provision of "full details on the composition of the debt and of Israel's future plans with respect to its balance of payments goals and its efforts to achieve greater economic stability" (Doc. 11, *FRUS* 1952–54, 9:1. 14 May 1953).

A month later, on 26 June 1953, there was a meeting between the US ambassador; Mikesell, who had returned to Israel; Gardner Patterson of Princeton University, who was assigned along with Mikesell to monitor the implementation of the 1952 Report's recommendations; TCA representatives; Finance Minister Eshkol; and members of his staff. According to the minutes of this meeting, "US representatives pointed out the need for examining expenditures under government control on basis of priorities as to foreign exchange earnings, or saving, potentialities and optimum utilization of human and material resources." More importantly, with regard to the debt problem, they reiterated the "statement of Dulles and Stassen that fundamental responsibility for this problem lies with government of Israel." Mikesell and the Embassy-TCA representatives also "presented elements of policy outlined" by Dulles in his telegram 1139, regarding "guidelines" for operating the US grant program in Israel. Because of its importance, we reproduce verbatim the main points of the Dulles telegram (Doc. 628, *FRUS* 1952–54, 9:1):

1. Primary objective of Aid Mission should be hastening viability of Israel. In administration of program we should seek to achieve maximum influence on the economic policies of GOI and maximum impact on economy as a whole, recognizing relationship internal conditions to external viability.
2. Following specific objectives should be sought by means outlined in (1) above:

(a) Achievement and maintenance of internal economic stability through encouraging GOI to adopt appropriate fiscal and monetary measures designed to retard inflation, bring about most effective use of resources and reduce need for external aid.
(b) Adoption and maintenance (through periodic revision when necessary in light of foreign exchange position) of exchange budget …
(c) The allocation of the maximum amount of resources to investment designed to make Israel self-supporting in shortest possible time;
(d) *This necessarily means minimizing consumption;*
(e) Investment in industry should be made only after careful analysis of direct and indirect foreign exchange costs and with special encouragement to *private* capital investment; internal and external.

[our emphases]

According to the protocol of the meeting on June 26 prepared by Mikesell (Doc. 631, *FRUS* 1952–54; 9:1, 26 June 1953) [our emphasis]:

In reply to United States representatives' statement of policy objectives outlined in Department telegram 1139, Eshkol spoke disparagingly of experts and their advice. He also defended Israel's deficit financing policies in past and stated United States should help Israel in dealing with past debts. Eshkol implied that Israel would continue to borrow as much as possible in future for rapid development of economy in a manner determined by statesmen motivated by faith in Israel and not by experts, bookkeepers and statisticians, and urged the United States to approach *Israel's problem in that light*. Eshkol's response appeared to be based on conviction either that Israel will receive a United States Government refunding loan or alternatively 1954 funds will be available in free dollars for debt management by [direct] approaches to Washington …

The protocol of this important meeting then outlined suggestions for a possible US response to Eshkol's reply to US policy objectives. Once again, because of its importance, the relevant part of the protocol's *recommendations*—reflecting the US position—is reproduced below:

… the implementation of policy objectives of Department telegram 1139 requires firm administrative approach to Government of Israel backed up with threat of aid curtailment … In view of recent developments, furtherance of policies set forth in Department telegram 1139 … requires a reconsideration of past policy of not allowing Israel under any circumstances to default on its external obligations for following reasons:

1. The present policy of preventing default has become known to Israelis and the threat of withholding assistance cannot be employed effectively as a means of achieving our objectives;
2. Borrowing capacity of Israel and hence propensity to expand indebtedness will remain high so long as firm United States policy against default is known to exist;
3. Government of Israel will not make maximum effort to handle debt problem through *private* channels so long as it is convinced that United States Government will not allow default;
4. Continued failure of Government of Israel to take realistic steps toward viability may require shock of default or partial moratorium as only means of bringing about reforms …

Some 25 years later, the Columbia University labor economist Eli Ginzburg, who visited Israel in 1953, recalled (1977, 1–2):

> I remember that the two distinguished American economists, Raymond Mikesell and Gardner Patterson, consultants to the United States Treasury, who had been posted to help the Israeli government bring its fiscal affairs into order so as to minimize potential American subsidies, were of the opinion that, since the Arabs had been able to subsist largely on figs and olives and other local products during the years of the Mandate, there was no reason that the Jews could not do likewise. I never succeeded in explaining to them that the Zionist ethos which had provided the momentum for the creation of the state had more ambitious goals which included the establishment of a society that would provide a haven for millions of Diaspora Jews, while combining a socialist ethic with a modern high income economy. Their assignment was to protect the American taxpayer.

In any event, *despite* Finance Minister Eshkol's disparaging remarks regarding "experts, bookkeepers, and statisticians," by September 1952, as noted above, a first attempt for drawing up a foreign exchange budget for 1952–1953 had been made. Moreover, starting with the 1953–1954 government budget, a supplemental foreign exchange budget (based on the recommendations of the Mikesell Report) was drawn up by the Bureau of the Budget, a newly established office within the Ministry of Finance. This foreign exchange budget was only discontinued in 1964 (Barkai and Liviatan, vol. 2, 2007, 69).

References

Acheson, D. (1952). Doc. 446, Secretary's Memoranda, *FRUS*, 1952–54, IX, 1.

Barkai, H., & Liviatan, N. (2007). *The Bank of Israel, Selected topics in Israel's monetary policy* (Vol. 2). Oxford: Oxford University Press.

Bruce, D. (1952). Doc. 453, *FRUS*, 1952–54, IX, 1.

Bullock, A. (1985). *Ernest Bevin, Foreign Secretary*. Oxford: Oxford University Press.

Davis, M. (1953). Doc. 582, *FRUS*, 1952–54, IX, 1.

Dulles, J. (1953). Doc. 628, *FRUS* 1952–54, IX, 1.

Eban, A. (1952). Doc. 469, *FRUS*, 1952–54, IX, 1.

Etzioni, A. (1959). Alternative ways to democracy: The experience of Israel. *Political Science Quarterly, 74*, 196–214.

Ginzburg, E. (1977). *Israel and American Jews: The economic connection*. New York: American Jewish Committee.

Gross, N. (1990). Israeli economic policies: 1948–1951: Problems of evaluation. *Journal of Economic History, 50* (1), 67–83.

Kalecki, M. (1950 [1951, 1993]) *Report on the main current economic problems of Israel*. Jerusalem: Israel Ministry of Finance, September (circulated 1951; reprinted in J. Osiatynsky. *Collected works of Michal Kalecki*, Vol. 5. Oxford: Oxford University Press].

Laski, K. (2004). Three ways to … high unemployment. In Z. Sadowski & A. Szeworski (Eds.), *Kalecki's economics today* (pp. 111–124). London: Routledge.

Lehrman, H. (1952). Israel without ideology. *Fortune Magazine, 46*, 89–100.

Michaely, M. (1975). *Foreign trade regimes and economic development: Israel*. New York: NBER.

Mikesell, R. (1953). Doc. 631, *FRUS*, 1952–54, IX, 1.

Mikesell, R. (1995). Israel's short term debt crisis of 1952–53: A memoir. *Economic Quarterly, 42* (April), 208–220 [in Hebrew].

Patinkin, D. (1956). Money and price developments in Israel: 1949–53. In R. Bachi (Ed.), *Scripta Hierosolymitana: Studies in economic and social science 3* (pp. 22–52). Jerusalem: Magnes Press, Hebrew University.

Patinkin, D. (1960a). Economic progress in Israel. *Economic Quarterly, 7*, 22–28 [in Hebrew].

Patinkin, D. (1960b). *The Israel economy: The first decade*. Jerusalem: Jerusalem Post Press.

Rosensaft, M., & Rosensaft, J. (2001). The early history of German-Jewish reparations. *Fordham International Law Journal, 25*, S1–S45.

Stassen, H. (1953). Doc. 11, *FRUS*, 1952–54, IX, 1.

Young, W., & Lee, F. (1993). *Oxford economics and Oxford economists*. London: Macmillan.

Zelekha, Y. (2011). *Reforming consumption patterns*. Bnei Brak: Ono Academic College and Hakibbutz Hameuchad Publishers [in Hebrew].

Chapter 3
Adviser and Activist: Lerner on the Israeli Economy, 1953 and Afterward

3.1 Introduction

Abba Lerner's contributions as a *theoretical* economist are well known and have been dealt with in many places. In this chapter, we focus on a specific aspect of his contribution as an *applied* economist qua economic *adviser* in Israel and commentator on the Israeli economy, over the period 1953–1974. Below we provide a brief account of the activities of the Economic Advisory Staff (EAS) in Israel, of which Lerner was a member, over the period 1953–1955. Sections 3.2 and 3.3 focus on Lerner's specific contributions—first, as an adviser and, later, as a commentator—to policy debate in Israel between 1953 and 1974. The second section deals with his views on the role of the central bank and its independence, the trade balance and exports, and the problem of Israel's economic independence. Section 3.3 focuses on Lerner's views on inflation, wages, and the cost-of-living allowance in Israel. Section 3.4 outlines Lerner's views of economic institutions and policy in Israel *in retrospect* and addresses his prescient criticism of them. It also provides some intellectual context for Lerner's approach to the Israeli economy, that is to say his earlier work, and broad knowledge of theory and institutions (Lerner 1944).

On 12 May 1953, Prime Minister Ben-Gurion announced the formation of the Economic Advisory Staff (EAS), a group of US experts who would assist Israel in solving its economic problems—financial, production, and development. Oscar Gass—a US government economist during World War II and economic adviser to the Israel Ministry of Finance—was appointed director of the EAS. The other senior members were Bernard Bell, deputy director of the EAS and former chief economist of the Export-Import Bank; Bertram Gross, former secretary of the Council of Economic Advisers; Marion Clawson, former director of the

D. Schiffman et al., *The Role of Economic Advisers in Israel's Economic Policy*,
DOI 10.1007/978-3-319-60682-8_3

Department of the Interior's Bureau of Land Management; and the subject of this paper, Abba Lerner, professor of economics at Roosevelt University in Chicago.[1]

The EAS operated from May 1953 to July 1955 and produced dozens of reports on industry, agriculture, macroeconomics, housing, labor, and project evaluation (among other topics). To date, no comprehensive study of the EAS has been undertaken. In his paper on the role of government economists in Israel, Kleiman (1981, 552) sums up the accomplishments of the EAS as follows:

> In its search for economic expertise the government turned also to seek advice abroad. The list of foreign economists consulted included such luminaries as M. Kalecki ... but their opinions were often disregarded as not suiting local conditions. More successful was the establishment, in 1952 [sic], of an Economic Advisory Staff outside the regular governmental bureaucracy. Headed by Oscar Gass, formerly the Jewish Agency's economic adviser in the United States, the EAS managed to recruit some top level experts from abroad, and included among its members Abba P. Lerner and M. Clawson, the well-known agricultural expert ... A number of young economists, either newly migrated from Western countries or recently graduating in Israel, served their apprenticeships on its supporting staff. The EAS had considerable influence both on current decisions and on professional standards. (Its most lasting effect, perhaps, was in the sphere of investment project evaluation, where it seems to have foreshadowed some later theoretical developments in the field.) But the government found the EAS's independence inconvenient, and did not renew its contract after 1955.

Arye Gaathon, Israel's leading expert on economic planning and a member of the EAS from July 1953 to July 1955, recalled as follows (cited in Tischler 1975, 132–135):

> In 1955 the government did not renew the contract with EAS because of its criticisms of economic policy and arguments with Gass.[2] Some see this as a failure of the EAS, but I think that its activities were not without utility. It stimulated interest in the basic economic problems of the economy, that is to say, for those involved in the national economic policy discourse—members of parliament, government ministers and journalists. Their reports and memoranda also contributed to understanding the workings of the economy, albeit not enough to correct the actions of the government and other operational institutions in the economy.

In April 1955, Lerner accepted Eshkol's offer to move to the Ministry of Finance upon the dissolution of the EAS at the end of July. Lerner served as an economic adviser and a member of the new Advisory Committee on Research and Policy in the Ministry of Finance, and, as we shall see, he wrote important memoranda and participated in major policy debates while there.

---

[1]Lerner had been approached by Gass almost a month before, with an invitation to join the EAS and a contract to begin work in July 1953. During 1945–1947, Gass and Lerner had been involved with the Academic Committee for the Hebrew University (Salo Baron Papers, Stanford University, Box 34, Folder 1).

[2]Indeed, in late March 1954, David Horowitz, the former director-general of the Ministry of Finance and first governor (designate) of the Bank of Israel, complained to Prime Minister Sharett about the EAS, which he dubbed "the Gass Team." As Sharett wrote in his personal diary: "[Horowitz] is prepared to endure the 'Gass Team' without Gass, but if Gass is removed, then he [Horowitz] advocates breaking up the group and installing each of its individual members in the relevant Ministries-Bell to the Finance Ministry, [Bertram] Gross to the Ministry of Labor, Clawson to Agriculture, Abba Lerner to the Central Bank" (Sharett 1954, entry for 31 March 1954).

3.2 The Central Bank and Its Independence, the Balance of Trade and Exports, and Economic Independence

3.2.1 Central Bank Independence

The story of the establishment of the Bank of Israel (henceforth BOI) has been the subject of much recent interest, and a number of surveys have also dealt with Lerner's role in it (see, e.g., Gross 1990, 2007; Krampf 2009, 2010, 2014, 2015).

Toward the end of 1952, Finance Minister Eshkol asked David Horowitz, formerly director-general of the Finance Ministry, and Eliezer Siegfried Hoofien, director-general of Bank Leumi, to expedite preparations for the establishment of a central bank (which Horowitz had begun under Eshkol's predecessor, Eliezer Kaplan) and draft the necessary legislation (*New York Times* 1952). Horowitz and Hoofien recommended that authority over monetary policy be vested in the governor alone. Eshkol adopted this recommendation, although it curtailed his own authority as finance minister, and brought Prime Minister Ben-Gurion on board. By the end of January 1953, the government had designated Horowitz as the central bank's first governor, and the preparations for its establishment were quickly moving forward. Eshkol also appointed Horowitz as an economic adviser to the government and formed a strong personal connection with him (Goldstein 2010). On 12 May 1954, the cabinet voted in favor of the Bank of Israel Bill. It was passed by the Knesset on 24 August 1954 and came into effect on 1 December 1954, when the BOI opened for business.

In April–May 1954, at a late stage in the legislative drafting process, Lerner and Gass engaged in an acrimonious debate with Horowitz regarding the BOI's prospective structure and functions. In a 26-page report dated 27 April 1954 (henceforth referred to as "Report"), which was sent to Horowitz, Eshkol, and others, Lerner (1954b) argued that the draft legislation was characterized by "serious weaknesses." These related to (i) "division of labor," (ii) "limitation of monetary policy," (iii) "wage stabilization," (iv) "interrelations of functions," (v) "central bank objectives," and (vi) "supremacy of the government." Gass authored a three-page covering memo that briefly summarized Lerner's Report (Gass 1954, henceforth referred to as "Summary").

Lerner's main criticisms were as follows:

(a) The BOI lacks the independence to control the money supply because the Treasury determines which government securities may be used to back the currency and the issue size of these securities.
(b) "Undue personalism"—all executive powers are vested in the governor, with the [Advisory] Board and [Advisory] Committee relegated to an advisory role. As Gass (Summary) put it, "It seems likely that the insufficiency of independence given to the Bank is a result of the feeling that too much of this responsibility is laid on one man." Lerner recommended that "as a permanent rule it would be much more satisfactory to have the authority for the most

important decisions in the hands not of a single man but in the hands of a small Board, consisting of, say three full-time men—the Governor, the Vice Governor and a full-time Chairman of the Board, and two part-time members of the Board. With the Governor responsible to the Board, it would be easier to give the Bank full control over monetary policy with complete independence from the Treasury in the creation (and retirement) of currency."

(c) Lerner attacked "the tendency that appears in many parts of the Bill to saddle the Bank with functions that do not fall strictly within the special field of monetary policy …" The incorporation of the Banking Code into the BOI bill leads people to erroneously conflate banking supervision with monetary policy. These functions must be kept completely separate; to ensure this, the government should establish a separate banking supervision agency. Furthermore, the central bank should not be charged with "management on behalf of the government of its foreign exchange account and foreign exchange regulations"; this function properly belongs in the Treasury.

(d) The BOI is granted "unnecessarily wide and arbitrary [regulatory] powers." Should a bank charge a higher interest rate than permitted by the governor, he may declare an emergency takeover, suspend the bank, or close it. Similarly, the governor is authorized to set capital requirements in an "unspecified and presumably arbitrary manner." It seems that the BOI bill is designed to restrict entry, limit competition, and ensure that the banking system carries out the government's directed credit program, all in the name of protecting depositors. Israel should replace directed credit with direct, open subsidies to favor industries (where necessary), permit free competition in the banking sector, and establish an FDIC-style deposit insurance system.

Lerner concluded that the BOI bill must be reconsidered. Yes, it had been approved by experts, but these experts "were either not really specialists on central banking or did not take the time to go into the bill in detail." A Fed or IMF expert should be brought to Israel for a month in order to facilitate a "full and open discussion." Yes, this would delay the passage of the law, "but it seems far more important to have a really good law than to have it a few months sooner." Lerner reported: "In the course of the preparation of this memorandum, I have discussed it with Mr. Hoofien, who felt that delay would be helpful, and with Mr. Horowitz, who felt that it would not be."

Gass (1954) added (Summary 27.4.54, 2–3):

> In suggesting [a Fed or IMF expert], we do not mean to say that there are no people in Israel who could apply the lessons to be learned from a study of the constitutions of Central Banks that have recently been established. It is quite likely that the local talent is superior to that of the expert who might be sent. It is rather that the fundamental issues that have to be settled would probably be aired more thoroughly if such an expert comes here for this particular job and the expression of the different views held by different people here were stimulated by a debate carried on around the expert.

Gass concluded by saying:

> But whether or not such an expert is invited, we think it essential for the basic principles to be threshed out in the most thorough manner possible before the Bank of Israel Law is enacted. It would be most undesirable to sacrifice substance for the benefits which might be anticipated from the early opening of an *inadequately-designed institution.* [authors' emphasis]

Horowitz (1954) took umbrage at both Lerner's Report and Gass' covering memo. He attacked their critique in a 25-page reply (Horowitz, "Comments on the Memorandum by Gass and Lerner of the EAS, on the Bank of Israel Law"—henceforth Reply, 2 May 1954) (to which he attached supplementary material written by the Finance Ministry's legal adviser and the supervisor of banks) that was also sent to the prime minister and finance minister. Horowitz first cited extensively from what he referred to as "a 1951 Federal Reserve Board of Governors report on international aspects of Treasury-Central Bank relationships" (Horowitz Reply, 2 May 1954, 1–3), which in his view ostensibly supported his position. He then asserted that based upon the Board of Governors' report, the discussions that took place during the drafting of the bill, and the specific characteristics of the Israeli case, the Lerner Report and Gass Summary were seriously flawed in three respects (Horowitz Reply, 2 May 1954, 3):

(a) Lack of adequate knowledge of precedents and administrative details of central banking in general
(b) Not taking into account the special characteristics of the Israeli case
(c) Lack of knowledge of the existing legal framework in Israel regarding banking, especially the banking law, the companies law, and the interest law

Regarding Lerner's specific suggestion to bring in an expert from the Fed or IMF, Horowitz replied that four experts, recommended by the Financial Advisory Directorate of the UN, had previously considered questions relating to the structure and function of a central bank for Israel. These experts were Edward Bernstein (IMF), Robert Triffin (Yale), Arthur Bloomfield (New York Fed), and Louis Rasminsky (Bank of Canada), all of whom, according to Horowitz, had supported his views regarding the bill, as against those of Lerner and Gass (Horowitz Reply, 2 May 1954, 4–5).

In an EAS memorandum dated 10 May 1954, Lerner (1954c) replied to Horowitz's "broadside" (Lerner, "Memorandum: the Bank of Israel bill"—henceforth Rejoinder, 10 May 1954). He listed four fundamental issues not dealt with by Horowitz in his reply: (i) the basic function of the central bank, (ii) the issue of rules vs. discretion, (iii) the degree of authority to be invested in the governor, and (iv) long- vs. short-term considerations regarding inflation as against deflation. Lerner also repeated his view that even the input of an expert cited by Horowitz as supporting his position—such as Bloomfield of the New York Fed—would result in improving the proposed BOI bill (Lerner Rejoinder, 10 May 1954, 2–3).

Now, interestingly enough, almost half of Lerner's Report *actually related to wage policy in Israel.* In this context, Lerner proposed establishing a "wage authority" alongside the Finance Ministry and the central bank, so as to enable "wage stabilization" (Lerner Report 27 April 1954, 4–10). In order to do so, he noted that "the lines on which this can be done … are sketched in my *Economics of Employment* [1951] Chapters 13–16" (Lerner Report 27 April 1954, 4 note 1). According to Lerner, the objective of the wage authority and wage policy would be "to keep the average wage rising (with productivity etc.) at the rate necessary for stable prices, while providing for desirable changes in relative wage rates" (Lerner Report, 27 April 1954, 7). In his critique of Lerner's Report, however, Horowitz wrote (Horowitz Reply, 2 May 1954, 14):

> Pages 1–10 provide a theoretical discussion of the importance of wage policy in Israel and the reasons for the establishment of three authorities: Treasury, Central Bank, and Wage Authority and a discussion of the interaction and coordination between them. We do not have any comments to make on this theoretical part of the memo as no specific recommendations or conclusions are provided therein regarding the Central Bank, and it is not our province to discuss the need for or ability to establish a Wage Authority.

Like Horowitz, Eshkol was not swayed by Lerner's Report. As Eshkol stated in the cabinet meetings of 12 and 26 May 1954, the roles of the proposed BOI were to develop the country via directed credit to agriculture and industry and to regulate the banks. Because Eshkol did not want the BOI to be too independent, he advocated a purely advisory Board and Committee, rather than a Board of Directors with real executive powers. The four General Zionist ministers and Minister of Justice Pinchas Rosen (Progressives) opposed Eshkol on this matter; Horowitz and Hoofien, of course, continued to back Eshkol (Lammfromm 2014, 157–158). Eshkol and Horowitz prevailed in the cabinet, and the debate moved on to the Knesset.

In the Knesset, Lerner's advocacy of a monetary board was embraced by all 32 members of Parliament from the right-liberal parties—the Progressives, the General Zionists, and Hapoel Hamizrachi; one MK charged Eshkol with deliberately concealing Lerner's Report from the Knesset (Krampf 2015, 153). But once again, Eshkol and Mapai prevailed. The final BOI law, which was passed in August 1954, was essentially identical to the draft that Lerner had criticized.

3.2.2 *Interest Rate, Credit, and Loan Policy, 1948–1957*

One of the major constraints regarding determination of the rate of interest and the operation of the credit market and credit policy in Israel resulted from the existence of laws and ordinances that set a maximum legal rate of interest until 1957. These vestiges of Ottoman Law and British Mandate ordinances of 1887, 1929, and 1932 set the maximum annual rate of interest at 9% (BOI Report 1955, 199). Over the period 1948–1952, the maximum rate reflected a "reasonable equilibrium" given the "economic conditions existing at the time." Over the subsequent period up to the establishment of the BOI in December 1954, on the other hand, disequilibrium in the credit market at the "ceiling" of 9% interest per annum was prevalent (BOI Report 1955, 199–200). Moreover, "the reasons for the high level of the rate of interest in Israel" were "to be found in those economic factors" determining the "supply and demand for credit" over the period 1952–1955, which included expectations of price rises, a low savings rate, a strong tendency for large-scale investment, bank credit restrictions, and higher than "ceiling" interest on marginal credit (BOI Report 1955, 200–202). According to the BOI, the problem it faced in 1955 was that as a result of prevailing economic conditions, it was unable to bring down the short-term interest rate "by economic means" and thus had to examine "the possibilities of dealing with this matter in other ways" (BOI Report 1955, 203). After consideration of its legal options under the 1954 BOI law, it came to the conclusion that, for the time being, it was "advisable to maintain the application of the Ottoman Law of Interest ..." (Report 1955, 204). In any event, the BOI restricted credit over the period 1954–1956 (Halperin 1965, 26). At this point, however, it must be recalled that under the BOI Law of 1954 (section 56A), the governor could set the bank's maximum rate, but only after consultation with the BOI Advisory Council *and with the permission of the government*. Thus, it is not surprising that after the 1957 "new interest law" was passed in the Knesset, it was the minister of finance who published the new differential interest rate structure for commercial bank and government loans, not the governor of the BOI (Rubner 1960, 89). The interest rate "ceiling" de jure was only abolished by the 1970 maximum interest rate decree.

In 1966, Lerner strongly advocated repeal of the interest law, on the grounds that it "belongs to the Middle Ages," is routinely violated and is in effect a nontransparent subsidy for the politically well connected. If subsidies are justified, they should be given directly, so that recipients can utilize them for any purpose that they wish (*Davar* 1966).

Lerner also served on the Public Committee on the Indexation of Government Loans, which was popularly known as the Lehman Committee (appointed by Finance Minister Eshkol on 15 April 1954). In its report of 2 January 1955 ("Report of the Public Committee on the Indexation of Government Loans," 2 January 1955), the Committee recommended that nonagricultural loans be indexed at rates between 50 and 70%, linked to either the dollar or the CPI. In his "reservations," Lerner advocated full indexation of all loans of more than 12 months (4 January 1955, "Reservations by Abba P. Lerner to the Report of the Lehman Committee on Securing Stability of Value of Loans from the Development Budget"; see also Shiffer 1999). Lerner also advised the newly established National Insurance Institute (NII) on how to invest its reserves in order to preserve their real value while maintaining sufficient liquidity to make payouts on time. In a memorandum prepared at the NII's request,[3] Lerner recommended that the NII invest all of its reserves (except for limited working capital) in 1-, 5-, and 10-year CPI-indexed government bonds. He saw the NII's reserves as an important anti-inflationary tool, as long as the government succeeded in collecting National Insurance contributions effectively, while refraining from borrowing the NII's reserves to finance current expenditures (*Davar* 1954; *Jerusalem Post* 1954b).

[3]We are unable to locate the original memorandum.

3.2.3 Balance of Trade and Exports

Given its importance to the Israeli economy, as noted in Sect. 3.1 above, an additional issue Lerner focused upon was the problem of Israel's trade balance. Lerner (1955b) presented his ideas on this topic in a detailed EAS memorandum dated 5 July 1955 entitled "Export subsidies and unemployed resources." He started by saying (Lerner Memo 5 July 1955, 1):

> Israel cannot afford to finance the induced [increases in] imports [resulting from an increased level of effective demand] out of foreign exchange reserves, even when there are some. It may however, be possible to finance them by increased exports brought about by export subsidies.

Sections 1 and 2 of his memo presented a theoretical analysis of how this could be achieved (Lerner Memo 5 July 1955, 2–14). Sections 3 and 4 dealt with "the practical conclusions" of his analysis. Lerner stated that these could not be "produced without considering our perspective foreign balance situation … in light of expected reductions in foreign aid." He wrote: "Israel must learn to tighten its belt … so as to reduce the cost of production of exports" via "the cutting of the wage" in dollar terms (and to a smaller extent in real terms). He went on to say that the import surplus in Israel "measures not how far we are from economic independence but rather how much foreign aid we are getting and using (i.e. not accumulating it in foreign balances)." Thus, given his "assumptions as to foreign aid and import surplus, apart from the accumulation and using up of the foreign balance," reserves would fall by a total of $220 million over the period to the projected end of German restitution payments. This would not be catastrophic if nonessential consumption goods were eliminated or investment goods imports for completed investment projects terminated. In his view, "the long-term problem is to direct resources during the period when foreign aid is available into investments which can be completed by the time the foreign aid is reduced and which will then take the place of foreign aid in earning the foreign exchange needed for essential imports" (Lerner Memo, 5 July 1955, 15–17).

Lerner then turned to how the "cost of living allowance system" in Israel "by preventing any adjustment which would make the export industries feasible by reducing the dollar wage (and to a lesser degree the real wage) is responsible for the induced unemployment as the only remaining instrument for protecting or improving the foreign balance." He went on to observe that "in Israel the level of unemployment that is politically and socially feasible would not reduce money wage rates, so that it would not make exports more profitable for private enterprisers or more feasible for collectivist managers who must cover their costs" (Lerner Memo 5 July 1955, 19).

Lerner finally turned to the relation between exports, investment for export, and the exchange rate. He distinguished between the short period problem of "adjustments to a given foreign balance position" and the "long period problem of influencing the foreign balance position by investment for exports." He concluded by saying that Israel's differential exchange rate structure would have to undergo revision. Despite the "practical and potential difficulties" preventing "a unitary rate of exchange" at the time, he said that "we must try, in devising new economic programs, to get as closely as possible to the accounting of Dollars and [Israel] Pounds at the same ratio for all economic decisions, long period and short period" (Lerner Memo 5 July 1955, 22).

3.2.4 Economic Independence

Lerner publicized his proposals on Israeli economic policy in a series of public lectures which he delivered in 1954. In October of that year, he published a Hebrew-language article in the influential and widely circulated *Economic Quarterly*, under the title "Stability and economic independence" (1954d). This article was based on two lectures, one at the forerunner of Tel Aviv University and one at the Tourism Club in Jerusalem.

Lerner outlined a plan for attaining economic independence, defined as growth and development without reliance upon foreign assistance. Lerner's plan was based on the following premises:

- Israel was receiving foreign assistance and net foreign investment to the extent of 50% of its national product.
- Foreign aid would be phased out over the next 10 years. Israel needed to make a planned, gradual adjustment to this new reality.

Lerner's general proposals were as follows:

- At the end of the period, Israel would have to cut imports in half and expand its exports sixfold. This would require doubling import prices to local consumers and cutting export prices by half—in other words, Israel would have to accept a worsening of its terms of trade.
- At the end of the period, Israel would have to accept a 10% cut in real wages and personal incomes.
- These adverse outcomes could only be avoided by an increase in labor productivity or by "working harder."

Lerner elaborated as follows: A 7.5% cut in real income would be necessary to cut export prices by 50% and raise exports by a factor of six. A further cut of 2.5% in real income would be necessary in order to achieve import substitution on the order of 13.6% of the original amount of imports. Thus, the total 10% cut in real income resulted from the worsening of the terms of trade. Furthermore, to cut export prices by 50%, there were three policy options:

(a) A 50% cut in wages and personal incomes
(b) The use of export subsidies and import tariffs to halve export prices and double import prices
(c) A devaluation of 50% with wages and domestic currency incomes left unchanged

From an economic point of view, according to Lerner, it did not matter which option was chosen, so the choice would have to be made based on political considerations. Lerner recognized that all three options were likely to meet stiff political opposition. Therefore, he proposed an alternative: Israelis should simply work more hours for the same wage. Thus, the goal of halving export prices could be accomplished with a smaller cut in real income.

Lerner's plan aroused both academic and political controversy. In practical terms, its chances of realization were always very slim. The ruling coalition government headed by Ben-Gurion's Mapai party, while ostensibly committed to the ideology of economic independence, was not willing to pay the political price of implementing Lerner's plan. Specifically, it was not prepared to take the measures required in order to ensure that the public sector and the public at large would "work harder" and pay more for fewer imports.

3.3 Prices, Wages, Inflation, and the CLA in Israel

3.3.1 Prices, Wages, Inflation, and CLA

In December 1953, the Histadrut (Israel's federation of trade unions) and the industrialists signed an agreement to extend the cost-of-living allowance (CLA) for one more year, with higher maximum payments. The agreement was a clear victory for the Histadrut. At first, the industrialists had sought to abolish the CLA. When the Histadrut resisted, they fell back to the position that the CLA payment period should be lengthened from 3 to 6 months. Once again, the Histadrut resisted, and the industrialists were forced to back down. Lerner was not pleased with this development. In a February 1954 lecture on inflation at the forerunner of Tel Aviv University, he condemned "the vicious circle of the rise in prices and wages," the government's inability to stick to a policy until it bears fruit, and its unwillingness to listen to foreign advisers: "… none of the Government's steps since the establishment of the New Economic Policy in February 1952 had been strong enough to reach the policy's goal. They were all interrupted in the middle, and we suffered from the inevitable bad consequences of each step, with little benefit from any of the expected results. We wonder what are the reasons for keeping foreign advisers whose opinions we do not follow" (*Jerusalem Post* 1954a).

In a memorandum dated 30 March 1954 to Finance Minister Eshkol and other cabinet ministers, Lerner (1954a) expressed concern at the possible inflationary impact of the new agreement. According to Lerner, it raised "the inflationary potential of the CLA in a degree which may be considered a change from quantity into quality." He continued:

> In reaching equilibrium via rising prices, an essential part is played by the lag of wages behind prices. With the new arrangement this not only disappears, it is reversed … a 10% increase in the COL index results in an increase in wages and costs in general of more than

> 10%. This would result in an increase in domestic prices of more than 10% and a further and still greater increase in wages, so that everything is set for a really grand inflation …

Lerner went on to explain that with a constant price/cost markup, prices and wages will rise in the same proportion. Devaluation would then be required so as to keep exports from falling.

He continued to set out the possibility of rising prices resulting from rising costs and the necessity of curtailing economic activity in the same proportion as the rise in prices. The resulting unemployment would bring about an increase in the budget deficit and credit expansion so as to prevent a further increase in unemployment. Lerner then said: "If this is so the check to inflation from holding down the supply of money or the total level of expenditure cannot be relied upon and the new CLA agreement constitutes a pressing invitation to inflation." He concluded: "Since I first pointed out this phenomenon … I have found an almost unanimous reluctance to accept the arithmetical proposition that an increase in the COL index caused wages to rise more than proportionately."

In an EAS memo dated 16 May 1955, Lerner (1955a) analyzed the BOI's annual report on money supply expansion in 1954/1955. There he focused on the Israeli CLA system as a major contributing factor to the "inflationary process in Israel" and a constraint on achieving economic independence. As he put it, "The automatic increases in wages via the CLA … are an essential part of the picture," and their removal would move "the country in the direction of economic independence" (Lerner Memo 16 May 1955, 3). However, he went on to say (Lerner Memo 16 May 1955, 8):

> The rapidity of movement towards economic independence will be determined by the degree to which the government finds itself able to expand exports and restrict imports without setting in motion a cost inflation. The cost inflation comes about when the people refuse to go along with the government and react by raising wage rates and profit margins (markups).
>
> In a democratic country the government cannot move the people more rapidly to economic independence than the people consent to go. The people show that they are not willing to go further by insisting on increases in wages and in markups. In some unsophisticated countries it may have been possible to squeeze the consumption of the people by means of inflation. This is not possible in Israel so that inefficiency, injustice, and disorganization are its only fruits. Credit expansion must therefore be limited to the level that permits the available goods and services to be sold at the current prices, while the contraction of goods and services (by expanding exports and producing imports) must be limited to the degree that the people's consent can be won.

3.3.2 Lerner on the Wage Controversy and CLA, 1955–1956 and Afterward

Labor relations were very contentious in the mid-1950s. Two core issues dominated the public discourse on labor relations: the basic wage level and the wage differential between professionals and unskilled workers. In December 1954, Finance

Minister Eshkol obtained from the Histadrut a freeze in the basic wage. In 1955, there was great agitation, especially by the public sector unions, to lift the wage freeze; Eshkol refused. In 1954–1955, there was a concerted campaign, led by the Israel Medical Association (IMA), to increase the wage differentials between professionals (including managers, attorneys, engineers, architects, academics, and physicians) and unskilled employees. Eshkol and the Histadrut adamantly opposed this campaign, because it undermined Mapai's policy of egalitarianism between the proletariat and the professional class (Bareli and Cohen 2008a, b).

To settle the professional wage issue, the government formed the Guri Committee in November 1954; it issued its interim recommendations in June 1955 (prior to the general election of 26 July) and its final recommendations in August 1955 (following the general election). The core of the final recommendations was that the government should give raises to its professional employees for "responsibility and effort at work" (*Maariv* 1955). Eshkol declared that the government should "delay momentarily" the implementation of the Guri recommendations (Lammfromm 2014, 176). But Eshkol did not prevail. On 11 September 1955, the government adopted the Guri recommendations and promised wage increases to professionals at an estimated cost of IL 5 million.[4] Ben-Gurion (who had rejoined the government as minister of defense in February 1955) became personally involved in settling the labor dispute with the physicians, and they agreed to end their slowdown. On 29 September, the Aranne Committee on physicians' wages, which had been formed at Ben-Gurion's behest just 1 week earlier, submitted its recommendations.

Meanwhile, trouble was brewing on the security front. On 27 September 1955, Nasser announced the Czech-Egyptian arms deal, which plunged Israel into a mood of national emergency. At the same time, Ben-Gurion saw a new opportunity to acquire weapons from France, and there was a spike in immigration, especially from North Africa. Eshkol and Ben-Gurion concluded that now was a time for fiscal rectitude. They resolved to resist all demands for new wage increases and to postpone the implementation of the Guri recommendations.

The new government was finally formed on 3 November 1955, with Ben-Gurion as prime minister once again (replacing Sharett) and the left-wing parties Ahdut HaAvoda and Mapam replacing the General Zionists. It immediately faced pressure from labor unions (especially those representing agricultural workers, teachers, and construction workers) and from Ahdut HaAvoda and Mapam to unfreeze the basic wage. The professionals demanded the implementation of the September 1955 agreement; the Progressive Party even threatened to leave the coalition over this issue.[5] But Eshkol and Ben-Gurion did not budge.

---

[4]This estimate excluded the anticipated cost of raises for teachers, nurses, and career military personnel.

[5]This was apparently an empty threat, considering that the Progressives had only 5 of the 80 coalition MKs.

It was in this context that Lerner appeared before the Mapai Economic Forum and proposed the following (*Davar* 1955):

(a) Cut nominal wages to 180% of the 1951 basic wage.
(b) Protect purchasing power of the poor, according to a formula based on family size and not the basic wage as is the current practice. Instead of the CPI, use a price index that covers only a small number of necessities.
(c) Establish a wage board that will decide on wage increases and decreases in certain sectors according to supply and demand, while maintaining a constant average wage.

Lerner attacked the CLA for failing to protect real wages; failing to prevent basic wage increases; wasting capital imports (by simulating higher imports as a counterweight to inflation); reducing export competitiveness; causing wage compression, which in turn creates a disincentive for labor effort and employee training; distorting the tax system by means of exemptions; and distorting the CPI, thus undermining public confidence in it.

On 11 November 1955, Eshkol was quoted as follows: "My clear understanding is that a general increase in basic wages is the biggest gift we could give to Abdel Nasser … the CLA that compensates the worker in a real way for price increases" not only raises the nominal wage but also "preserves and even increases the real wage … The wage increase will immediately raise prices which will in turn harm exports, widen the trade deficit and undermine the currency's stability" (*Al Hamishmar* 1955). Eshkol's position was supported by Ben-Gurion, Sapir, Golda Meir, and BOI Governor Horowitz. However, the Histadrut leaned toward accepting, or even advocating, a basic wage increase; Mapai's own wage committee recommended a 5–15% basic wage increase. Histadrut officials also argued that it was unrealistic to expect the professionals to waive the wage increase that had been promised to them in September.

On November 24, Lerner joined Eshkol at a press conference. Eshkol emphasized that wage increases will harm workers and bring about devaluation and other adverse consequences; this was not understood by those who demanded wage increases. He also called for reconsideration of the Guri recommendations. Lerner stated that in order to move toward economic independence, nominal wages should not just be frozen—they must be reduced for a long period. This will make possible a long run wage increase (*Jerusalem Post* 1955).

Lerner (1955c) expressed his views on wages and the CLA more formally in a memorandum to Eshkol dated 27 November 1955, entitled "Inflation: will it wreck the Israel economy in 1956? An analysis and an outline of a policy." Lerner opened by saying "there seems to be an insufficient recognition of the degree of inflation that would be set off by what seems like a relatively moderate increase in the basic wage." He went on to list a number of "interesting elements" for "the present drive for an increase in basic wages" such as "government deficits and credit expansion," "pay increases to some professional groups" and the salary linkage between these and other groups, and "various election promises." However, he observed that "any increase in wages will appear as increased costs which will be passed on in higher prices. The resulting increase in the CLA will again increase wages and cost and prices in a continuous process" (Lerner Memo, 27 November 1955, 1).

Later in his memo, he wrote (Lerner Memo, 27 November 1955, 7):

> Once more, we come up against the fundamental fact that the CLA is a swindle. It underwrites the reality of promises to give the worker more than there is, and it cannot possibly give reality to such promises except by blackmailing the government under the threat of cost inflation via CLA into providing more consumption out of foreign aid funds which have been solemnly consecrated to investment and the absorption of immigrants.

Lerner then returned to his advocacy of the establishment of a "wage authority" that would be "responsible for preventing [wage] inflation," going so far as to advocate "lowering the price level by cutting the money wage" under the aegis of the "wage authority" and enabling wage adjustments "in accordance with 'indices of attractiveness' regarding movements in relative wages," as he had proposed in part 4 of his 1951 book *Economics of Employment* (Lerner 1951) (Lerner Memo, 27 November 1955, 9–12). Specifically, he suggested:

(a) Cut nominal wages to 180% of the 1951 basic wage or alternatively 70% of the 1 November 1955 basic wage.
(b) Raise the average wage by 1% every 4 months. Raise sectoral wages every 4 months by 0, 1, or 2%, according to the "indices of attractiveness."

Finally, Lerner sent out a six-point program based upon "the policy of reduction of the price level for preventing inflation while moving towards economic independence." The points were as follows (Lerner Memo, 27 November 1955, 12–13):

1. Reduction of the ratio of prices to wages
   (a) by anti-monopoly measures
   (b) by measures to increase efficiency.
2. The overall reduction of money wage rates and the abolition of CLA.
3. Establishment of a Wage Authority to adjust particular money wage rates over time subject to a 1% increase in the average wage every 4 months.
4. Special vigilance to forestall possible delays in reduction of prices in proportion to the reduction in costs.
5. Reform of income tax
   (a) smaller allowances for earners and larger allowances for dependents.
   (b) lower marginal rates in middle brackets.
   (c) higher rates for very large incomes.
6. Protection of minimum income for everybody by income tax allowances and relief payments tied to a price index of a basket of necessities.

Lerner believed that now was a politically opportune time to implement a wage cut:

> The existence of a labor coalition government provides an unusual opportunity for achieving the benefits for the Community as a whole from the adoption of the policy of Reducing the Price Level (by a wage cut). This is because it would be easier for a labor government to resist the untrue but inevitable demagogic claims that a general wage cut is "anti-Labor" and would mean lower real wages than would result from any other policy (except one of eating" up investment capital) (Lerner Memo, 27 November 1955, 10).

On 29 November 1955, Lerner joined Ben-Gurion and Eshkol at a joint meeting of Mapai ministers and Histadrut officials, at which it was decided to postpone the wage decision for 2 weeks. The *Jerusalem Post* (30 November 1955), which reported the meeting, also summarized Lerner's new memorandum.[6] On 7 December, it was reported that Eshkol had cited Lerner's memo in negotiations with left-wing parties and at press conferences. Eshkol was quoted as saying: "Dr. Lerner is more extreme than I am" (*Hatzofeh* 1955).

Meanwhile, Lerner published a series of four articles on wages and inflation in the *Jerusalem Post* (6–9 December), entitled "High costs: runaway inflation," "Wage cut will stop inflation," "Israel is on a 'wage standard'," and "Raising wages without inflation," respectively. Obviously, Lerner hoped that these articles would influence the Mapai party machinery.

In December 1955, two compromise proposals were under serious consideration:

(a) The government proposal—Keep the basic wage frozen. Give the professionals 50% of what they had been promised in September 1955.
(b) The Becker proposal (by MK Aharon Becker, head of Histadrut Trade Union Department[7])—Keep the basic wage frozen. Increase the CLA in the higher salary brackets and make it tax exempt (for details, see Table 3.1 below). Reduce the income tax for lower salary brackets.

Lerner was intensively involved with the Becker proposal: He was present when Becker presented it to Eshkol, Interior Minister Yisrael Bar Yehuda, and representatives of five political parties (including Mapai) on 23 December, and he discussed it in two meetings with the Histadrut Trade Union Department on 25 and 29 December (*Jerusalem Post*, 25, 26, and 29 December 1955).

Mapai sought to hammer out a unified Histadrut position with the left-wing coalition parties Ahdut HaAvoda and Mapam. The negotiations led to a stalemate, which generated great uncertainty. In the end, the wage issue was placed before the Mapai central committee. On 8 January 1955, the Mapai central committee voted 39-13 with 9 abstentions to give all workers a limited, stepped wage increase of at least 5% (in Lerner's estimation, the increase would be in the range of 4–8%). Five days later, the Histadrut Executive Committee ratified this decision, despite the objections of Eshkol and Ben-Gurion. According to the JTA report (JTA 1956),

[6]The *Post*'s (anonymous) reporter exaggerated Lerner's views by attributing to him the following dire warning: "Wages must be reduced by 25%, or inflation, followed by disastrous devaluation, will be inevitable next year." Lerner never wrote this. In his memorandum, Lerner warned that a basic wage increase would precipitate "a runaway inflation" (Lerner memo, 27.11.55, 1). He strongly recommended a 25% cut under the auspices of the wage authority and emphasized its potential positive effects but did not explicitly predict rapid inflation in the event of non-implementation (Lerner memo, 27.11.55, 11–13). Rather, he qualified his recommendations as follows: "I would stress not so much the desirability of accepting these particular lines of operation as the necessity for the Wage Authority to adopt some criteria for regular and rational decision on these matters" (emphasis in original; Lerner memo, 27.11.55, 12).

[7]Becker was effectively second in the Histadrut hierarchy; only the secretary-general ranked higher.

Table 3.1 The Becker Proposal

Monthly salary (IL)	CLA under current policy	CLA under Becker proposal
<80	Full, tax exempt	Full, tax exempt
80–125	Partial, taxable	Full, tax exempt
>125	None	None

> The decision … was taken by a majority vote in the executive in which the Mapai party carried over the opposition of all the minority parties which wanted larger increases. Prior to the adoption of the resolution, Mr. Eshkol warned the Histadrut leaders that "a raise in pay and bank notes will not raise the standard of living, but will bring inflation". This he added, might not be felt immediately, but it would be felt in a few months' time. The only way to combat inflation, he asserted, was to increase production and exports.

Earlier, Eshkol had said that he would consider raising subsidies (financed by a cut in the development budget) in order to counteract the inflationary effects of the wage increase. He also said that it would be necessary to lengthen the CLA payment period from 3 to 6 months and have it apply only to a price increase of at least 3% (*Davar* 1956).

In the wake of the defeat in the Mapai central committee, Lerner became convinced that the only way to avert what he saw as an impending disaster was to make his case directly to the public. On 10 January 1956, Lerner published an open letter (1956b) in several newspapers.[8] Lerner's goal was to mobilize public support against a basic wage increase and in favor of the Guri recommendations, thus breaking the linkage between basic and professional wages that pervaded the prevailing political discourse. He believed that given sufficient public support, Ben-Gurion and Eshkol would be willing to take tough but necessary measures to fight inflation.[9]

Lerner began by vociferously denouncing the left-wing coalition parties and their allies within Mapai:

> One half of the Mapai Center is for the wage increase because they are afraid of demagoguery from the left, or because they are afraid of admitting that promises made before the elections were unwise and irresponsible, or because they are afraid that *others* will not be able to understand that a general wage increase brings harm and not benefits to workers and the State. The two left-wing parties support a general wage increase in part because they have not got out of the habits of an irresponsible opposition … and in part because they, too, are afraid that their supporters would not understand the difference between the money wage and the real wage …

He then justified his unusual decision to appeal directly to the public:

> I know that in writing this letter to the Israel public, through the press, I am departing from the proper role of a foreign expert. I should write memoranda to the office where I am employed, shrug my shoulders, collect my exorbitant (by Israel standards) salary and go back to America. But I have a more than professional interest in Israel, and I am writing this letter, in my personal capacity, because of my belief that the Israel public can understand the issues and is not really pushing towards the abyss of inflation, in the way that some leaders claim.

[8] The English version which we cite (Lerner 1956b) was dated 8 January.

[9] Since there was nothing new in Lerner's substantive argument, we will not quote it here. Instead, we will focus exclusively on Lerner's political arguments.

Lerner proceeded to break with Ben-Gurion and Eshkol by endorsing the Guri recommendations and argued that the public would not oppose their implementation:

> I do not believe that it is the public that resent high officials or doctors getting more pay than a semi-skilled laborer or would be outraged if the Government kept the solemn promise of salary increases to doctors and other higher grade professionals …

Lerner ended his letter with an (American style) appeal to the public to directly contact its elected officials, including the minister of finance, and Histadrut leaders:

> I am therefore appealing to serious men in all parties to let their leaders know that courageous leadership to save the country from inflation would have support.
>
> Pick up a pen or a telephone and tell your trade union secretary or your party leader, and tell the Minister of Finance, too …
>
> that in order to prevent inflation you would be willing to cooperate in postponing wage increases in general.
>
> … [and] that you do not want to blackmail the Government into breaking its solemn promises to the professionals …
>
> If enough of you do this today, the inflation may yet be stopped.

Lerner's letter had immediate political repercussions: The Ahdut HaAvoda party wrote to Eshkol and Ben-Gurion on 9 January demanding that Lerner be fired for "staining [our reputation]" (1956). Both Eshkol and Ben-Gurion refused to fire Lerner. They pointed out that Lerner had spoken as a private individual and did not purport to represent the government; as such, he had the right to freedom of expression (Ben-Gurion 1956a; *Davar* 1956).[10] However, both Ben-Gurion and Eshkol were critical of Lerner's rhetoric.[11] More importantly, the IMA's chairman used Lerner's letter to justify rejecting Ben-Gurion's offer of 50% of the Guri-recommended wage increase. He told Ben-Gurion that even Lerner, who supports a general wage freeze, recognizes the justice of the professionals' demand for a salary adjustment (*Maariv* 1956). Ben-Gurion retorted: "Lerner's paragraph has nothing in it to confer merit upon the physicians' decision. Prof. Lerner is an expert in economics, not in public psychology of the Jewish people" (Ben-Gurion 1956b).[12,13]

---

[10]According to a source within the Finance Ministry, because Lerner was employed on a special contract, he was not bound by standard civil service regulations (*Davar* 1956).

[11]The Finance Ministry source stated: "It would have been better if [Lerner] had left out one or two sentences in his public letter, because of their excessively sharp [tone] and lack of justification, and also because of their irrelevance to the core issue" (*Davar* 1956).

[12]Ben-Gurion implied that he rejected Lerner's advice only because Lerner had opined on political matters in which he had no expertise; had Lerner stuck to economics, Ben-Gurion would have accepted his advice. But this should not be taken at face value. As a rule, Ben-Gurion rejected expert advice when he thought he knew better (Knesset speech reported in *Jerusalem Post* 1953), and in this case, he had made up his mind to reject the Guri recommendations regardless of Lerner's opinion. As an experienced negotiator, Ben-Gurion knew that the IMA would never accept the argument "I know better than Lerner," so he attributed his rejection of Lerner's advice to Lerner's lack of expertise on "public psychology."

[13]After the physicians struck from February 7 to 20, the government agreed to pay the professionals two-thirds of the increase recommended by the Guri Committee.

Lerner continued to speak out publicly. On 20 January, he told the Tel Aviv Commercial Club that it is possible to mitigate the inflationary effects of the 4–8% wage increase by increasing productivity and fighting cartelization. In so doing, the government should not be afraid to let some firms go bankrupt and to allow efficiency dismissals. The government does not have the option to fight inflation via subsidies, because it needs all (potential) surplus funds for development and defense. He commended the Histadrut for its responsibility "to a large degree" on wage and institutional issues but reiterated the need for a wage authority (*Herut* 1956).

On 2 July, Lerner met with Ben-Gurion and reiterated his support for a 25% wage cut, as detailed in his 27 November 1955 memorandum to Eshkol (Ben-Gurion Diary, 2 July (1956c)). Two facts are worth noting: (a) Lerner said nothing about the need for a wage authority. (b) At this stage, Ben-Gurion apparently had a sincere interest in hearing Lerner's advice, but (of course) he did not commit to implementing it. He concluded his diary entry as follows: "I asked [Lerner] to submit a brief written summary [of] what to do in order to achieve economic independence under the existing practical conditions, to the extent that he knows the human reality in Israel."[14,15]

On 19 July 1956, Lerner (1956a) circulated a memo entitled "The economic rehabilitation of Israel," in which he argued that devaluation must be exploited to increase exports and increase investments for export or import substitution. In order to avoid shifting increased import costs to production costs, subsidies should be utilized to compensate employers for wage increases and self-employed business owners for the decline in their real incomes. Lerner noted that subsidies were, at the time, financed by capital imports, which resulted in lower investment. While admitting that this could not be prevented, he still justified the "consumption" of capital imports for subsidies on the grounds that there was a lack of sufficient initiative for productive investment under extant circumstances. To promote investment required elimination of price and income distortions, that is, the reduction of real expenditures. Therefore, devaluation would be beneficial, even if Israel continued to consume capital imports in order to maintain "real" consumption, so long as the consumption of capital imports served to reduce production costs via these subsidies (summarized by Gaathon (1956), Gaathon Papers, Israel State Archives 1831/2-Peh, 108–119).

On 14 August 1956, Lerner held a press conference, at which he distributed "a farewell letter" entitled simply "Letter to Israel." In the letter (1956c), which was published in the newspapers and is preserved in the Lerner Papers (Box 13, Folder 2, 30–33), he made the following major points:

(a) Ben-Gurion and Eshkol know what must be done and will implement the necessary reforms "even in the face of irresponsible demagogic opposition."

[14]We choose to take Ben-Gurion's words at face value. Ben-Gurion never would have met with Lerner had he been uninterested in Lerner's advice.

[15]It is not known whether Lerner ever prepared the document that Ben-Gurion requested.

But in order to do so, they must receive sufficient public support: "A successful democracy needs good citizens even more than it needs good ministers."

(b) The CLA is "the focal point of almost every economic problem." Even union leaders are beginning to understand this. At the press conference, Lerner pointed out that the CLA would be fine if Israel's inflation were of the demand-pull variety. But since Israeli inflation is cost-push, the CLA is disastrous.
(c) "Compromises are being put forward for saving [the CLA] from abolition by watering it down," such as lengthening the payment period from 3 to 6 months and making the CLA payable only on CPI increases of at least 5% (instead of the current 1.2%). "Such compromises do nothing significant to correct the evil."
(d) The psychological effects of the CLA are more pernicious than the technical aspects of its operation. What we have is "a system that promises that rising prices will not be permitted to reduce real wages or to negate wage increases." Currently, there is an "implicit promise to keep wages 10–12% ahead of prices." When this unrealistic promise is not kept, the workers feel cheated.
(e) The only way to raise real wages is to achieve productivity growth. Productivity growth can be achieved if efficiency dismissals are permitted: "Without the efficiency dismissals, all talk about increasing efficiency as an alternative policy is dishonest and indecent."
(f) Unfortunately, the response to his first open letter of January 1956 was abysmally low. Only 100 people had written letters to oppose the basic wage increase,[16] although (in Lerner's estimation) at least 10,000 people were opposed: "Democracy does not work if everyone depends on someone else and in Israel the power of the individual in expressing and forming public opinion is a basic infant industry that has to be developed. I am therefore asking every reader who agrees with my analysis and who has an earnest interest in the welfare and security of Israel to recognize that it is not someone else but he himself who must act."

Lerner asked each of his readers "to explain the issue to the people he meets in a national campaign of economic education" and to send the enclosed chain letter "within three days … to four of his acquaintances, and to the Minister of Finance, so as to keep the chain going until appropriate action is induced." Lerner's chain letter consisted of six points, which can be summarized as follows: I [the writer] support abolishing the CLA and permitting efficiency dismissals, on two conditions—(i) everyone else agrees to give up the CLA; (ii) "wage stabilization and efficiency dismissals [are] not misused for increasing profits …"; instead, the profit-to-wage ratio will be reduced via anti-cartelization measures.

On 18 August 1956, Lerner departed from Israel. At the airport, he told the *Jerusalem Post*: "In every democratic state, the citizen is 'the boss,' and he has to know that he can influence the government. In Israel, public-mindedness has to be

[16]Israel's first lady, Rachel Yannait Ben Zvi, was reportedly one of Lerner's few public supporters (*Davar*, 27 January 1966).

reshaped … If the public does not voice its opinions, civil servants will get the habit of doing only as they think fit and suits them. The citizen has to take an active interest in the work of civil servants" (*Jerusalem Post* 1956).

Lerner returned to his academic position at Roosevelt University in Chicago. In 1957, he published an article in which he attacked Israel's CLA system and especially the role of the Histadrut in preventing wage adjustments that would have enabled Israel "to move toward economic independence" (Lerner 1957, 76). Lerner had refrained from criticizing the Histadrut while in Israel.

Lerner spent the 1965–1966 academic year in Israel, where he served as dean of the Faculty of Social Sciences and chair of the Department of Economics at Tel Aviv University. He published a letter to the editor in the *Jerusalem Post* entitled "C-o-l increase is a deceptive gift," which reiterated points that he had previously made in the Hebrew press (*Davar* 1966; *Maariv* 1966). After restating his earlier anti-CLA arguments, Lerner advocated "the suspension of further CLA increases until either the price level or productivity has caught up with the increase in the basic wage" (*Jerusalem Post* 1966). It is clear that by this time, Lerner acknowledged the political impossibility of abolishing the CLA. Lerner also reminisced about his role in the wage controversy of 1955–1956: "I never truly and honestly believed that it was possible to bring about a wage cut. But I sometimes think that my proposal, which received a lot of publicity, helped to reduce the increase in salaries" (*Davar* 1966).

In his later writings on the Israeli economy, dealing with its second decade (1958–1968), Lerner criticized the combination of planning and lack of reliance upon the price system in Israel, which caused significant misallocation of resources and prevented the attainment of economic efficiency. He maintained that while government intervention prevailed in all markets and sectors, Israel lacked overall economic direction. Lerner also analyzed the problem of inflation. Contrary to the prevailing conventional wisdom in Israel at the time, he attributed this phenomenon not to excess demand inflation but to the structural distortions of the economic system, that is, cost (wage) inflation. He reiterated his earlier recommendations with regard to wage policy: Wages should be linked to labor productivity, thus keeping production costs and prices stable. The government, together with the Histadrut, should set relative wage levels in the various sectors in order to ensure labor mobility from sectors with excess supply to those with excess demand (Lerner 1970, 1971).

In July 1974, Lerner visited Israel in conjunction with the translation of his book *Flation* into Hebrew. The volume, while originally published in 1972, had been revised after the 1973 oil shock and reissued in English in 1974. During his visit, *Maariv* reported that he had "changed his earlier views that the CLA in Israel accelerated inflation." Now, Lerner believed that a *uniform increase in wages via the CLA would be preferable to a wave of differential wage demands that would exceed the increase in wages via the CLA* (emphasis ours; Gutterman, *Maariv* 1974).[17]

[17]Lerner kept a copy of this article in his personal papers (Lerner Papers, Box 13, Folder 3).

3.4 Lerner's Views in Retrospect: Prescience, Institutional Functions and Failures, and the Context for His Critiques

Lerner's criticism regarding the BOI was prescient in several important respects. First, his fears about the BOI's regulatory behavior turned out to be correct. The BOI granted special privileges to the largest banks in return for their cooperation with the government/BOI-directed credit program (Krampf 2014, 2015, 187). Concentration in the banking sector increased sharply: The share of bank branches owned by the three largest banks rose from 23.5% in 1951 to 31% in 1956 to 55% in 1961 (Krampf 2015, 187). To this day, Israel still suffers from excessive concentration in the banking sector. Directed credit expanded rapidly after Lerner's advice to abolish it went unheeded; the share of directed credit in total bank credit was 30–40% in the 1960s and 40–50% in the 1970s (Barkai and Liviatan 2007, 67). It reached 65% in 1985 before finally being phased out over 1985–1998 (Ben Bassat 2002). Second, the current BOI Monetary Committee, which was introduced in the 2010 BOI Law at the behest of then-Governor Stanley Fischer, strongly resembles the monetary board that Lerner envisioned. The current monetary committee consists of the governor, the deputy governor, another BOI official, and three representatives of the public (typically academic economists). Third, Lerner's advice to introduce formal deposit insurance was not taken. Currently, Israel is one of the few Western countries that lack formal deposit insurance; fortunately, it has not experienced any large-scale bank failures. Only in 2015 did the BOI and Ministry of Finance announce a plan to introduce formal deposit insurance.

What stands out regarding Lerner's economic analysis during his stay in Israel over the period 1953–1956 is his emphasis on the relationship between the various facets of economic activity and institutions such as wages, the CLA, inflation and economic independence—which he proposed dealing with via a "wage authority"—and his concern for the structural and functional independence of the central bank, as against the views of some at the time, who, in our opinion, saw it as another government institution subject to constraints such as monetary accommodation and the interest law. In order to understand Lerner's views regarding the "wage authority" and central bank independence, we must recall two institutional factors that characterized the US economy over the decade of 1942–1951 *that may have influenced them.*

The first was the existence of the National War Labor Board (NWLB) over the period January 1942 to December 1945, replaced by the National Wage Stabilization Board (NWSB) in 1945. The former, including regional war labor boards, executed the War Stabilization Act authorized by the US Congress and implemented by presidential executive order in October 1942. *The NWLB was part of the overall program of economic stabilization covering prices, rents, wages, salaries, profits, rationing, and subsidies.* In June 1943, the regional war labor boards were applying "wage brackets" that set maximum and minimum wage rates for key occupations based upon existing rates in labor market regions across the US. The NWSB, established in December 1945, existed until February 1947 and operated a limited wage stabilization program over the period of transformation from a wartime to a peacetime economy (Shister 1945; Workman 2000).

We *conjecture* that the NWLB was the basis for Lerner's idea of a "wage authority," as expressed in his 1951 book *Economics of Employment* (Lerner 1951) and in his memos while a member of the EAS and adviser to the finance minister of Israel.

The second institutional characteristic of the decade 1942–1951 was the reality that the Federal Reserve was essentially a "branch" of the US Treasury, only recovering its "independence" after the Treasury-Fed "Accord" of April 1951. This is not the place for an extensive discussion of the events leading up to this important episode in US monetary history (for the best account, see Hetzel and Leach 2001). Suffice it to say, however, that the chronology of transition from "nonindependence" to renewed "independence" of the Federal Reserve *may have impacted Lerner's view regarding the importance of the independence of the central bank in Israel, as manifest in his emphasis on it in his report on the proposed BOI bill in April 1954.*

What is interesting to note here is that Horowitz's extensive citation from a Federal Reserve Board of Governors' report to counter Lerner's approach to the central bank in Israel is problematic to say the least. Horowitz, in his May 1954 reply to Lerner's report (and the Summary memo by Gass), dated the Federal Reserve report on Treasury-central bank relations internationally as having appeared in 1951. The actual report, entitled "The Treasury-central bank relationship in foreign countries: procedures and techniques," first appeared in November 1950, *before* the Treasury-Fed Accord. *Moreover, while taken as gospel by Horowitz,* the Federal Reserve Report was prefaced by the following caveat (FRASER, Eccles Papers, Box 49, Folder 15, item 1):

> The following report was prepared by the Staff of the Board of Governors of the Federal Reserve System. It does not necessarily represent the views of the Board. It is based on available information obtained in part from published documents and in part from personal contacts with foreign central banks developed over a period of years. The accuracy of the information has not been checked by the officials of the foreign countries concerned and is not guaranteed by the Board.

Lerner's *applied* economic analysis as an adviser and economic commentator on the economic problems of Israel, then, *may have* flowed *both* from the headwaters of his *theoretical* economic work and the influence of events and institutions that in turn *may have* shaped his views regarding the interaction between them. This can be seen *especially with regard to the problem of Federal Reserve (Central Bank) independence* (House Committee on Banking and Currency 1968). Indeed, in his review of Milton Friedman's volume *A Program for Monetary Stability* (1959), Lerner wrote (1962, 213):

> He [Friedman] has an excellent discussion of the necessary relationships between the Central Bank and the Government (or the Treasury), showing how a Central Bank can be most useful if it is neither completely subservient to the Government—as the Federal Reserve was recently when it had to peg the rate of return on government bonds [1942–1951]—nor so completely independent as to be able to nullify the activities and

> the policies of the Treasury. Particularly neat in this area is his treatment of the proper relationship of the Treasury to the Federal Reserve in the management of the National Debt, where he makes a good case for the Government's limiting itself to quite short- and quite long-term borrowing and the undesirability of its trying to tailor the kind of loan to the state of the markets.

In summing up Lerner's legacy regarding the Israel economy and its institutions, especially the BOI, the following three points may be made. First, Lerner's recommendations regarding the structure and functions of the BOI and the role of its governor were finally implemented in the 2010 BOI law. Second, Lerner's argument that placing bank supervision under the aegis of the BOI creates a conflict of interest with setting independent monetary policy remains relevant to the present day. This is best illustrated by the ongoing debate in Israel regarding questions as to who should be responsible for supervision and regulation of credit card companies and, as result of capital market reforms, retirement and providence funds? Third, the debate over the contradictory roles of the BOI—its responsibility for foreign exchange management as against its responsibility for monetary policy—is best manifest in its attempts to influence the shekel-dollar exchange rate via open market purchases of $70 billion over 2008–2016 and its concomitant maintenance of low interest rates, which in turn destabilized housing prices in Israel.

Appendix

Lerner's First Open Letter: 8 January 1956

Reproduced with the permission of the *Jerusalem Post*; published January 10, 1956 under the title "Wage Rise Will Mean Disastrous Inflation: PROF. LERNER APPEALS TO PUBLIC." Emphasis (via bold type) in original.

Editor, *The Jerusalem Post*

Sir—

There is great danger that the Israel economy will rush into a ruinous inflation on the wave of a general increase in money wages. The surprising thing is that such a panic action could come about after weeks of intense deliberation. It is as if, at the end of a theatre performance, a thorough discussion by the audience of the dangers of panic were followed by unsuccessful negotiations in which each person insisted on being the first to go out, and it was solemnly decided to solve the deadlock by crying "Fire!"

In the discussion on wages that has been raging, all serious participants have recognized:

(1) **that a general increase in wages by itself would lead to increased prices and inflation and would not give anything real to the workers.**

(2) **that accompanying measures that could result in increasing real wages (by increasing the total product or increasing the share of it going to labor) would be at least as effective without an increase in the money wage.**
(3) **that in any inflation such measures are ineffective and the total national product and the share going to wages are both reduced, so that the worker must suffer a reduction in his real wage.**

From this, it follows that anyone who cared for the real conditions of the workers should be against a *general* wage increase. Yet there is now the great danger that we will have a "compromise" general wage increase which will bring ruin to all.

That this should be the policy of Communists is understandable. They can say to themselves (in accordance with Lenin's strategy of disrupting capitalist societies by debauching their currency), "We will pretend to be friends of the workers and ask for higher wages for them. When this results in inflation and in lower real wages, we will turn their anger against the Government, and over the ruins of the Israel economy we will march forward to the social revolution."

While the important protagonists of a general wage increase in Israel are not Bolshevik-Leninists but Zionists, the reason for their position no less distressing. One half of the Mapai Centre is for the wage increase because they are afraid of demagoguery from the left, or because they are afraid of admitting that promises made before the elections were unwise and irresponsible, or because they are afraid that *others* will not be able to understand that a general wage increase brings harm and not benefits to workers and the State.

The two left-wing parties support a general wage increase in part because they have not got out of the habits of an irresponsible opposition (for whom claims that cannot be met are better than claims that can be met—revolution is superior to reform) and in part because they, too, are afraid that their supporters would not understand the difference between the money wage and the real wage (even though they have for years been telling them how past increases in money wages have been negated by increases in prices).

It is this fear and cowardice on the part of leaders who hide behind their followers, that is putting the Israel economy in dire danger. It is therefore possible for the situation to be saved if such followers as are not as ignorant or as intimidated as these leaders think would make themselves heard before it is too late.

I know that in writing this letter to the Israel public, through the press, I am departing from the proper role of a foreign expert. I should write memoranda to the office where I am employed, shrug my shoulders, collect my exorbitant (by Israel standards) salary and go back to America. But I have a more than professional interest in Israel, and I am writing this letter, in my personal capacity, because of my belief that the Israel public can understand the issues and is not really pushing towards the abyss of inflation, in the way that some leaders claim.

I believe the public recognizes that wage increases lead to price increases—it has had plenty of experience of this. The Israel worker does not want a wage increase that turns to dust in his hands and in a general agreement not to push, where he would not be left behind, he would be willing to cooperate.

I do not believe that it is the public that resents high officials or doctors getting more pay than a semi-skilled laborer or would be outraged if the Government kept the solemn promise of salary increases to doctors and other higher grade professionals (that were found necessary for justice and efficiency after long and careful study) even in the absence of a general wage increase. It is only some doctrinaire leaders who are so addicted to what the Russians called "bourgeois equalitarianism."

I am therefore appealing to serious men in all parties to let their leaders know that courageous leadership to save the country from inflation would have support.

Pick up a pen or a telephone and tell your trade union secretary or your party leader, and tell the minister of finance, too,

1. that in order to prevent inflation you would be willing to cooperate in postponing wage increases in general, although you could not stay behind if wages are being raised all over.
2. that you do not want to black-mail the Government into breaking its solemn promise to the professionals, especially since the black-mail would take the form of demanding a general wage increase that would bring inflation on everybody.

If enough of you do this today, the inflation may yet be stopped.

Yours, etc.

Prof. Abba P. Lerner

Jerusalem, January 8.

This letter has also been sent to other newspapers.

Lerner's Second Open Letter: August 1956

From Lerner Papers, Library of Congress, Box 13, Folder 2, 30–33.

Letter to Israel by Abba P. Lerner August 1956

After working for three years as an economic adviser to the Government of Israel and before returning to my University in America, I feel I can do a service by saying a few last words to the Israel equivalent of Mr. John Q. Public.

During my stay I have seen a great deal of progress not only in economic conditions (although some of these may be questioned as sacrificing future economic security to present comfort) but in the spread of understanding of the difficult steps that will have to be undertaken if the economy is to reach economic independence—i.e. if it is to be protected from the destruction that otherwise would accompany the fall in foreign aid that is expected in a few years' time.

The spread of this understanding is of the utmost importance because without it the government and the other centers of power in a democracy are unable to do what needs to be done. And this is why I think it is useful for me to speak to the public even though it is not what I am paid to do and even though there are some people who would prefer me to be silent.

The minister of finance, the prime minister, and some of the other men in charge of economic policy are aware of what needs to be done and are fully prepared to sponsor the policies necessary for economic health even in the face of irresponsible demagogic opposition. The existence of a labor government makes it more possible for even unpleasant medicines to be applied because the public would less easily be persuaded by the demagogues that such a government is motivated by hatred of the working man and woman. But without the support of the public, the necessary medicine cannot be applied. A successful democracy needs good citizens even more than it needs good ministers.

The focal point of almost every economic problem is the Cost of Living Allowance System (CLA). The economist sees that it prevents the achievement of the relationship between costs and prices in Israel and costs and prices abroad which must be achieved if Israel is to reach the harbor of economic independence, and that it induces instead inevitable, repeated and fruitless devaluations. The man in the street sees that it leads to inflation, with its injustices and damage to the efficiency of the economy. And the worker is increasingly aware that it is a swindle because it cannot keep its promise of keeping wages ahead of prices. He has been learning from experience that every time the CLA raises wages in order to catch up with prices, it only pushes the prices up again. Prices may still be held down by subsidies out of money needed for defense or development,—but in that case it is the subsidies and not the CLA that should be praised (or blamed).

Although this understanding of the harmfulness of the CLA is more and more widely felt, there is still a strong defense for it for several reasons:

1. It is properly felt that if there is a runaway price inflation, to which wages must, of course, be adjusted, the CLA method is more orderly and may be less disturbing than a less systematic readjustment. But this does not apply where the inflation is being overcome, as in recent years, when the CLA can only work against the stabilization.
2. It is correctly seen that the inflationary effect of the CLA may be absorbed by increased productivity and by increased use of foreign aid to subsidize consumption—as has happened in recent years. But this cannot happen if there is a wage increase, such as that of 1956, and there is no corresponding sudden increase in productivity, or in funds available for subsidies, to provide the real increase in consumption. The CLA cannot then succeed in keeping wages ahead of prices (except for a possible short interval during which the country is being impoverished by capital consumption in the form of the eating up of goods that are sold for less than their replacement costs). This means that the increase in wages will not be a genuine increase in real wages, and that the attempt by the CLA to keep wages ahead of prices will only cause inflation. From this inflation the workers will lose much more than they can gain from any possible temporary enjoyment of capital consumption.
3. Trade Union leaders, perhaps thinking of periods of rapid inflation, have the indestructible habit of considering the CLA "the greatest achievement of

organized labor" even when everybody else, including the workers themselves, can see that this is not true when some progress towards stability is being achieved.

In spite of these protestations in favor of the CLA even many trade union leaders are conceding that something must be done about it. Compromises are being put forward for saving it from abolition by watering it down. Thus, it is being proposed that CLA increases should take place only every 6 months instead of every 3 months, and only when prices are increased by 5% instead of by 1–1/5% (3 points on a base of about 250 points).

Such compromises do nothing significant to correct the evil. The 10–12% general wage increase will certainly raise costs and prices by more than 5%. The 6 months rule would mean theoretically that the secondary repercussions would be only half as fast as on the 3 months rule. But much more important than the mechanical operation of the CLA according to the rules of the game is the psychological effect of a system that promises that rising prices will not be permitted to reduce real wages or to negate wage increases. The psychological effect is that any failure of these promises to be fulfilled—whether because of time lags, or because of suspected distortion of the index or because of anything else—is seen as some form of cheating. It is then felt to be proper to engage in "counter-cheating" by upgrading, by phony allowances, by fictitious ("automatic") efficiency premiums, etc., in attempts to maintain real wages or real wage increases.

In 1951 the "New Economic Policy" included a CLA system that was calculated to reduce real wages in a mechanical way by giving CLA on only a part of the basic wage, as prices were raised by devaluation and decontrol. Nevertheless real wages continually and gradually increased because of the "counter-cheating."

It was possible for this "counter-cheating" to be successful between 1951 and 1955 because of increased productivity and because of increased (hidden) subsidies to consumption, but at present there is no source available to enable the increased basic wages to keep ahead of prices. There was no sudden increase in productivity of 10–12% in June 1956 and the defense situation means that subsidies to consumption are more likely to be reduced than to be increased. Consequently, the attempt by CLA and "counter-cheating" to keep wages ahead of prices can now lead only to a continuing and accelerated inflationary race between wages and prices.

It is the glimpsing of this that is responsible for the current concern about CLA. But a full recognition of the situation must involve also a recognition that compromises like the 6 months rule or the 5% rule completely fail to solve the problem. Only the complete abolition of the CLA can remove the implicit promise to keep wages 10–12% ahead of prices. Only a completely free system of fixing wages annually would permit the realities to be recognized. Wages could then be set at levels compatible with the ability of the economy to provide the goods that the wages are to buy. The CLA, in any form, in conjunction with the 1956 wage increase, constitutes a promise that the workers will be able to buy more than the economy is able to provide and this promise can only be a false promise. The resulting inflation is only the inevitable result of workers trying to obtain that which has been promised them but which does not exist.

The contention that a 10–12% increase in wages, in real terms, could come out of profits cannot be treated seriously without considering whether this means out of profit consumed or out of profits reinvested. To claim that it could come out of reduced consumption by capitalists is simply dishonest, while to increase wages, and thereby consumption, out of the invested profits would constitute disastrous economic sabotage.

It is possible for real wages to be increased, and therefore for the promise of increased real wages to be kept, if there is increased efficiency and increased production. But the test of whether such suggestions are anything other than empty talk is whether men displaced by increased efficiency can be dismissed so that costs can be cut and the labor saved (as well as materials, machines, etc. saved) can be used elsewhere to produce the increased real wages. Without the efficiency dismissals, all talk about increasing efficiency as an alternative policy is dishonest and indecent. With them it can be hoped that increased efficiency will produce what the CLA can only promise.

I have been convinced that the men and women of Israel are able to understand all that I have said, that there is wide agreement with it, and that the great majority could be made to accept the policy. Some labor leaders are lagging and will continue to lag behind the public. But that is only because they cannot forget their share in the credit for the "famous victory" of the CLA as an alleviation of runaway inflation or because they tend to act as if they were representing a particular group of workers against exploitation by the economy at large. All others are realizing more and more that unless there is an increase in real output of consumption goods all promises of general increase in real wages are bound to be false promises.

Nevertheless, it is not possible for the minister of finance and the other leaders with genuine social responsibility, to do what needs to be done if the citizen does not show his support. Some months ago, I published a letter suggesting that those who agreed with my view that the 1956 wage increase was a bad thing and a fake promise should make themselves heard. Well only about 100 made themselves heard and the wage increase took place. Judged by the sample of those who spoke to me about it, there must have been at least 10,000 who would have written letters if they had realized that it was not somebody else who was meant; and very many times that number are in agreement, but do not write letters. Of every 100 people who expressed earnest agreement with me, and were asked if they had written a letter, about 99 said, "Who, me?"

Democracy does not work if everyone depends on someone else and in Israel the power of the individual in expressing and forming public opinion is a basic infant industry that has to be developed. I am therefore asking every reader who agrees with my analysis and who has an earnest interest in the welfare and security of Israel to recognize that it is not someone else but he himself who must act. I am asking him to explain the issue to the people he meets in a national campaign of economic education and to begin by sending a letter to four of his acquaintances, and to the minister of finance, containing the 6 points of the following sample chain letter.

Abba P. Lerner

Dear Moshe:

1. I'm worried about the dangers of inflation and economic collapse and I think it is up to citizens like you and me to show those leaders who have the courage for social responsibility that we are prepared to support necessary measures even if they appear to be temporarily painful.
2. It is clear to me that the Cost of Living Allowance cannot keep wages ahead of prices and can only help to cause inflation and destruction.
3. I am for giving up the CLA for annual determination of total wage rates; and for permitting efficiency dismissals as a means for achieving the increased productivity which alone can provide both economic security and higher income levels.
4. It is understood, of course, that I would not give up my CLA unless everyone else gives it up too, and that the wage stabilization and efficiency dismissals would not be misused for increasing profits, but that, on the contrary, that profits would be reduced in relation to wages by effective measures for fighting cartels and increasing competition.
5. I am sending this letter to three other acquaintances and to the minister of finance for whose information I mention my occupation.
6. If you think I am right, it is your duty to do the same, namely, to explain the matter to your friends and to begin by sending a letter containing these 6 points (including this one) within three days, to four acquaintances of yours and to the minister of finance, so as to keep the chain going until appropriate action is induced.

Yours for responsible citizenship,

Name____________________

Address__________________

Occupation________________

References

Ahdut HaAvoda-Poalei Zion Knesset Faction. (1956, January 9). *Letter to Ben-Gurion*. Ben-Gurion Archives.

Al HaMishmar. (1955, November 11). Newspaper Report [in Hebrew].

Bank of Israel. (1955, May). Annual Report 1955. Jerusalem.

Bareli, A., & Cohen, U. (2008a). Distributive justice and a rising middle class: Conflict between MAPAI and white-collar professionals before the 1955 general elections in Israel. *Israel Affairs, 14*, 255–276.

Bareli, A., & Cohen, U. (2008b). The middle class versus the ruling party during the 1950's in Israel: The 'engine-coach car' dilemma. *Middle Eastern Studies, 44*, 489–510.

Barkai, H., & Liviatan, N. (2007). *The Bank of Israel* (Vol. 1: A monetary history). Oxford: Oxford University Press.

Ben Bassat, A. (2002). The obstacle course to a market economy in Israel. In A. Ben Bassat (Ed.), *The Israeli economy, 1985–1998: From government intervention to market economics*. Cambridge, MA: MIT Press.
Ben-Gurion, D. (1956a, January 10). *Letter to Ahdut HaAvoda-Poalei Zion Knesset Faction*. Ben-Gurion Archives.
Ben-Gurion, D. (1956b, January 16). *Letter to Z. Avigdori*. Ben-Gurion Archives.
Ben-Gurion, D. (1956c, July 2). *Diary*. Ben-Gurion Archives.
Board of Governors, Federal Reserve System. (1950, November). The Treasury-Central Bank relationship in foreign countries-procedures and techniques. Washington, DC, FRASER, *Eccles Papers*, Box 49, Folder 15, item 1.
Davar. (1954, August 16). Prof. Lerner recommends depositing National Insurance payments with government.
Davar. (1955, November 3). Newspaper report [in Hebrew].
Davar. (1956 January 9, 11). Newspaper reports [in Hebrew].
Davar. (1966, January 27). Newspaper report [in Hebrew].
Gaathon, A. (1956, July 19). Summary of Lerner memo entitled The economic rehabilitation of Israel. In *Gaathon Papers*, Israel State Archives 1831/2-Peh, pp. 108–119.
Gass, O. (1954). Evaluation of proposed Israel Central Bank bill. Summary of Lerner Report 27.4.54, ISA 5617-13/Gimmel, pp. 160–162.
Goldstein, Y. (2010). Eshkol and the 'new economic plan' in historical perspective: The price and return to the recession policy as a solution to the economy's problems – The first attempt. *Economic Quarterly, 57*, 241–253 [in Hebrew].
Gross, N. (1990). Israeli economic policies: 1948–1951: Problems of evaluation. *Journal of Economic History, 50* (1), 67–83.
Gross, N. (2007). Economic policy in Israel as viewed by leading officials of the Bank of Israel, 1954–2000. In N. Liviatan & H. Barkai (Eds.), *The Bank of Israel* (Vol. 2: Selected topics in Israel's monetary policy). Oxford: Oxford University Press.
Gutterman, R. (1974, July 9). Professor Lerner changes his mind, *Maariv* [in Hebrew].
Halperin, A. (1965). Interest rates payable on bank credit facilities. *Quarterly Banking Review, 16*, 22–28 [in Hebrew].
Hazofeh. (1955, December 7). Newspaper report [in Hebrew].
Herut. (1956, January 22). Newspaper report [in Hebrew].
Hetzel, R., & Leach, R. (2001). The Treasury-Fed Accord: A new narrative account. *Federal Reserve Bank of Richmond Economic Quarterly, 87*, 33–55.
Horowitz, D. (1954). Reply to Lerner report on Bank of Israel bill, 2.5.54. ISA 5617-13/Gimmel, pp. 86–110.
House Committee on Banking and Currency. (1968, December). Compendium on monetary policy guidelines and federal reserve structure. Washington, DC: US Government Printing Office.
Jerusalem Post. (1953, June 9). State too busy for public relations.
Jerusalem Post. (1954a, February 4). Lerner Lecture at Tel Aviv School of Law and Economics.
Jerusalem Post. (1954b, August 13). Lerner testifies before the Investment Committee of the National Insurance Institute Council.
Jerusalem Post. (1955, November 25, December 6–9, December 25–29). Newspaper reports.
Jerusalem Post. (1956, August 19). Newspaper report.
Jerusalem Post. (1966, June 9). Newspaper report.
Jewish Telegraphic Agency. (1956, January 17). Histadrut executive decides to press for five percent general increase.
Kleiman, E. (1981). Israel: Economists in a new state. *History of Political Economy, 13* (3), 548–579.
Krampf, A. (2009). The coining of the expression 'economic independence' in the Israeli economic discourse. *Iyunim Betkumat Yisrael, 19*, 1–34 [in Hebrew].
Krampf, A. (2010, August). *Central banking in a developmental state: The case of the Bank of Israel in the Post-War period*. Jerusalem Papers in Regulation and Governance, WP 23, Hebrew University, Jerusalem.

Krampf, A. (2014). Between private property rights and national preferences: The early years of the Bank of Israel. *Israel Affairs, 20*, 104–124.
Krampf, A. (2015). *The national origin of market economy: Economic development during the formation of Israeli capitalism*. Jerusalem: Magnes Press.
Lammfromm, A. (2014). *Levi Eshkol: A political biography*. Tel Aviv: Resling [in Hebrew].
Lerner, A. (1944). *The economics of control*. London: Macmillan.
Lerner, A. (1951). *Economics of employment*. New York: McGraw-Hill.
Lerner, A. (1954a, March 30). The inflationary potential of the current CLA agreement. ISA 718/11/Peh, pp. 94–98.
Lerner, A. (1954b). Report on Bank of Israel bill, 27.4.54. ISA 5617-13/Gimmel, pp. 163–188.
Lerner, A. (1954c). Rejoinder to Horowitz, 10.5.54. ISA 5617-13/Gimmel, pp. 2–5.
Lerner, A. (1954d). Stability and economic independence. *Economic Quarterly, 2*, 3–11 [in Hebrew].
Lerner, A. (1955a). Bank of Israel's annual report on money Supply expansion, January 1954 to January 1955, 16.5.55. ISA 5509-15/Gimmel, pp. 166–174.
Lerner, A. (1955b). Export subsidies and unemployed resources, EAS Memo 5.7.55. ISA 5509-15/Gimmel, pp. 116–146.
Lerner, A. (1955c). Inflation: Will it wreck the Israel economy in 1956?- An analysis and an outline of a policy, Memo to Finance Minister Eshkol, 27.11.55. *Lerner Papers*, Library of Congress, Box 13, Folder 2, pp. 16–28.
Lerner, A. (1956a, July 19). The economic rehabilitation of Israel, Summary by A. Gaathon, in *Gaathon Papers*, ISA 1831/2-Peh, pp. 108–119.
Lerner, A. (1956b, January 10). Wage rise will mean disastrous inflation: Prof. Lerner Appeals to public. *Jerusalem Post*.
Lerner, A. (1956c, August). Letter to Israel; *Lerner Papers*, Library of Congress, Box 13, Folder 2, pp. 30–33.
Lerner, A. (1957). The Histadrut and the Israeli economy. *Midstream* (Autumn), 56–86.
Lerner, A. (1962). Review of Milton Friedman's A program for monetary stability (1959). *Journal of the American Statistical Association, 57*, 211–220.
Lerner, A. (1970). *Efficient economics and its applications*. Tel Aviv: Amikam [in Hebrew].
Lerner, A. (1971, July) Recession and inflation in the 70s. *Economic Quarterly 18*, 69–70 [in Hebrew].
Maariv. (1955, August 8, December 29). Newspaper report [in Hebrew].
Maariv. (1956, January 12). Newspaper report [in Hebrew].
Maariv. (1966, June 8). Newspaper report [in Hebrew].
New York Times. (1952, August 14). Newspaper report.
Report of the Public Committee on Indexation of Government Loans. (1955). January 2; Lerner's reservations (appended), January 4, [Lehman Committee]. Jerusalem: Israel.
Rubner, A. (1960). *The economy of Israel: A critical account of the first ten years*. New York: Frederick A. Praeger.
Sharett, M. (1954) [2013]. *Personal diary 1954*, archived at http://www.sharett.org.il/. Accessed 1 February 2017.
Shiffer, Z. (1999). The cost of living adjustment as a tool protecting real wages from inflation surprises. Research Dept., Bank of Israel Discussion Paper [in Hebrew].
Shister, J. (1945). The National War Labor Board: Its significance. *Journal of Political Economy, 53*, 37–56.
State of Israel. (1954). Bank of Israel Law, 5714-1954.
Tishler, I. (1975). Studies worth studying. *Economic Quarterly, 84/85*, 132–135 [in Hebrew].
Workman, A. (2000). Creating the National War Labor Board. *Journal of Policy History, 12*, 233–264.

Chapter 4
Ex-officio Adviser: Kahn in Israel, 1957 and 1962

4.1 Introduction

The famous Cambridge University economist Richard F. Kahn (1905–1989) is renowned for his contributions to Keynes' General Theory—especially his 1931 article on the multiplier and to Joan Robinson's theory of imperfect competition. He is also known (albeit to a lesser degree) for his contributions to economic policy: his UK government service in World War II, his participation in the Radcliffe Report on the UK monetary system (1957–1959), and his role as an adviser to international organizations in the 1950s and 1960s (e.g., UNECE, FAO, OEEC, and UNCTAD). Kahn's role as an adviser to Israel, however, has heretofore not been recognized.

This chapter documents Kahn's activities as an unofficial adviser to the Israeli government in 1957 and 1962, using a combination of published material and archival material from the Kahn papers at King's College, Cambridge (henceforth KCC). The available documentation is rather sparse, in the sense that Kahn did not prepare a formal report or keep a full record of his conversations with Israeli policymakers. Therefore, we use the available documentation to describe Kahn's views on the Israeli economy as fully as possible and make the plausible assumption that Kahn shared these views candidly with his Israeli interlocutors.

Our major findings are as follows: Kahn's advice to the Israeli government was largely consistent with his previously articulated policy views. In 1957, Kahn noted that Israel would be adversely affected by the EEC customs union and predicted correctly that Israel's application for EEC Associate Membership would be rejected. He also proposed a major reform of the cost-of-living allowance (CLA) system, so as to reduce protection against real wage erosion through the CLA and move Israel closer to the Swedish wage setting model, in which the CLA played only a minor role. In 1962, he took a neutral position in the ongoing debate regarding the sustainability of Israel's chronic international imbalances. He also criticized Israeli policymakers for overestimating the potential benefits of an Israel-EEC commercial agreement and argued correctly that the EEC would make reducing Israel's trade deficit more

D. Schiffman et al., *The Role of Economic Advisers in Israel's Economic Policy*,
DOI 10.1007/978-3-319-60682-8_4

difficult, even if the UK did not join. Ultimately, Israeli policymakers disregarded Kahn's advice on both the EEC and CLA issues: They continued their intensive efforts to attain Associate Membership in the EEC, or a PTA at the very least, and failed to adopt Kahn's proposal for reform of the CLA.

As an economic adviser to Israel, Kahn enjoyed limited success at best. He failed in the sense that the government did not follow his advice and probably did not give it serious consideration, but he was probably successful in the more limited sense of helping government officials attain new perspectives on economic issues.

The remainder of this chapter is structured as follows: Sect. 4.2 is a synopsis of Kahn's economic policy views during 1945–1962; Sect. 4.3 sets out Kahn's motivation for visiting Israel and the documentation that is available for each of his visits; Sect. 4.4 describes the structure and challenges of the Israeli economy in 1957; Sects. 4.5 and 4.6 present and evaluate Kahn's views on the Israeli economy in 1957 and 1962, respectively; and Sect. 4.7 concludes.

4.2 A Synopsis of Kahn's Policy Views, 1945–1962

This section briefly describes Kahn's general approach to economics and then summarizes his views on a number of topics that he addressed in Israel: planning, the balance between consumption and investment, monetary policy and control of inflation, international trade and customs unions, and balance of payments (BOP) adjustment.[1]

Kahn was an "applied economist in the old-fashioned sense *par excellence*" who "made it [his] business to know intimately the institutions, the historical sequences and the orders of magnitude of particular situations, and … had a feel for the limits of particular policy recommendations" (Harcourt and Kerr 2009, 220).[2] He was highly skeptical of mainstream economic theory[3] and was vehemently opposed to econometrics (Pesaran and Harcourt 2000).

Kahn was a strong and consistent advocate of planning. In the late 1940s, Kahn, Austin Robinson, and Brian Reddaway (the "Gosplanners") supported government-set targets for sectoral output and employment, in contradistinction to James Meade (a "Thermostatter"), who wished to let the free market determine sectoral activity (Toye 2000). In the 1950s and 1960s, Kahn argued that certain industries should be nationalized (Marcuzzo 1988, 40–3), that the government must ensure the movement of labor from contracting to expanding sectors (Kahn 1952b), that civil servants can allocate credit more efficiently than bankers (Kahn 1952c), and that new towns should limit the number of retail stores within their jurisdictions (Cohen et al. 1964).

[1]In preparing this synopsis, we have utilized the list of Kahn's publications in Pasinetti (1991).

[2]For an assessment of Kahn's contributions in their historical context, see Marcuzzo (2012).

[3]"The economic system is a sticky and patchy affair—very far from the ideal world of perfect mobility and foresight beloved of theoretical economists" (Kahn 1952b).

Kahn was a member of the UK Labour party until the 1980s and took a strong interest in Fabian Socialism (Marcuzzo 1988, 46–7).

Kahn emphasized the need to maintain a balance between consumption and investment, although he never defined the desired balance precisely. He recommended increasing the budget surplus as a remedy for excessive consumption demand; this policy, he argued, would reduce consumption and increase both exports and investment (Kahn 1948, 1956b).

Kahn worried that macroeconomic policy was inherently biased toward overconsumption and underinvestment. In Kahn's macroeconomic framework, the main influence on consumption is fiscal policy, while the main influence on investment is monetary policy. Because contractionary monetary policy is politically easier to implement than contractionary fiscal policy, reducing investment is easier than reducing consumption (Kahn 1958b, 125–6).

Between 1954 and 1958, Kahn changed his approach to monetary theory from liquidity preference to endogenous money. In his evidence before the Radcliffe Committee (Kahn 1958b), he emphasized the interest rate and its effect on credit demand.[4] He was staunchly opposed to monetarism, but did not criticize Milton Friedman by name (Rochon 2001).[5] As a member of the Group of Independent Experts of the OEEC (1959), Kahn was a strong proponent of incomes policies (Fellner et al. 1961).[6] He later recalled that "the control of the behavior of money wages became my major interest" (Marcuzzo 1988, 59).

Kahn's understanding of monetary policy and the inflationary process was as follows:

(a) Inflation results from excessive consumption and investment, excessive costs, and lack of international competitiveness, not excessive money and credit (Kahn 1956b). Monopolistic pricing and special/temporary factors may also play a role (Fellner et al. 1961).
(b) The commonly accepted distinction between "demand inflation" and "cost inflation" is "unhelpful and misleading." Wage growth causes inflation—"in that sense, all price inflations are 'cost inflations' (or wage inflation)"—but the rate of increase in wages and prices depends on the state of demand: "… in that sense there is always some measure of 'demand inflation'" (1958b, 137–48).
(c) While price stability has its advantages (e.g., real exchange rate depreciation), it is not and should not be the main goal of monetary policy. Contractionary policy is ineffective in slowing down nominal wage growth (and by extension, inflation). Any success is only temporary and comes at the exorbitant cost of unacceptably high unemployment. Furthermore, high interest rates reduce investment, so that

[4]For Kahn's retrospective on his role in the Radcliffe Committee, see Marcuzzo (1988, 53–7).

[5]As early as 1951, Friedman rejected the cost-push view of inflation (Nelson 2009), of which Kahn was an adherent. Kahn must have been familiar with Friedman's views; Friedman spent the year 1953–1954 in Cambridge and interacted socially with both Kahn and Joan Robinson. Friedman also debated Robinson concerning flexible exchange rates (Friedman and Friedman 1999, 245–6).

[6]Backhouse and Forder (2013) find Fellner et al.'s (1961) case for incomes policies unconvincing.

the economy generates less capital-embodied technical change and (in turn) slower productivity growth. If restraining AD as an anti-inflationary measure is unavoidable (in the absence of a proper wage policy), fiscal contraction and other measures are preferable to monetary contraction (Kahn 1958b, 137–45).

(d) Price stability can only be achieved via government control of wage setting. Given the lack of a wage policy in the UK, the government should officially renounce the goal of price stability; this step is "economically expedient and politically inevitable" (Kahn 1956b, 1958b, 137–45).

(e) Wage increases have two components: "the vicious spiral," in which wages try to catch up to the cost-of-living (COL), which in turn increases the COL further, and "wage drift," in which labor scarcity leads to actual wages that are above negotiated wages, due to piece rates and employers who bid up wages to recruit workers. Wage drift must be regulated at the national level (Kahn 1958b, 137–45).

(f) One of the leading causes of rising wages is "leapfrogging," also known as the "wage-wage spiral": Workers are concerned about their relative wage position. Therefore, if workers in one sector get a wage increase, workers in other sectors will demand an increase so as to maintain the existing intersectoral wage ratio. Leapfrogging is a procyclical phenomenon. Wages can be frozen if a national agreement can be reached to preserve the current relative wage structure. This requires very strong coordination among different unions and within individual unions. Once agreement has been achieved with respect to relative wages, absolute wages can be kept under control. The absolute wage level should be negotiated in a fully synchronized manner, perhaps on a biennial basis (Kahn 1956b, 1958b, 137–45; Fellner et al. 1961).

(g) With low unemployment, unions will only accept wage moderation if the fiscal system is oriented toward "redistributing income and building up the social services" (Kahn 1956a). The tax burden must be shared equally between labor and capital and between union members and nonmembers. Regulation of monopoly profits (including price controls on essential goods) will probably be necessary (Kahn 1956b). Unions should not be broken up in an attempt to restrain nominal wages (Fellner et al. 1961).

Kahn held a complex view of international trade and customs unions. He favored freer trade in the following senses: He opposed extreme protectionism that bordered on autarky, urged the UK to lead the way toward multilateral trade liberalization (Kahn 1949a) in light of ITO/GATT's failure (Kahn 1952a), and asserted that countries with more competitive domestic markets have higher productivity growth and therefore greater global competitiveness (Kahn 1951).

At the same time, Kahn had sharp differences with the ideological free traders. He believed that a completely free global trading system was unattainable and saw unilateral trade liberalization as irrational as long as other nations maintain trade barriers (Kahn 1947–1948).[7] He also opposed combining unilateral trade

[7] Kahn accepted the Edgeworth-Bickerdike optimum tariff argument: "restrictions on imports, provided that they are not too drastic and provided that they do not cause other countries to do likewise, are bound, on account of the favorable effect on the terms of trade, to benefit a country"

liberalization with devaluation and argued that the nondollar countries should discriminate in trade against the dollar countries (Kahn 1952a).

In February 1957, Kahn took a cautiously optimistic view regarding the EEC customs union and its anticipated effects on non-EEC nations. He stated that if a six-nation Common Market was inevitable, the UK should join it (Kahn 1957a, b).[8] However, Kahn was concerned that the EEC would exacerbate chronic trade imbalances, via two mechanisms: (a) The free-trade ideologues—who were the EEC's strongest advocates—might dominate the rule-setting process. These ideologues failed to see the need for allowing temporary import restrictions as a means of alleviating BOP difficulties (Kahn 1957a). (b) Trade imbalances stemming from long-term competitiveness problems would prove intractable, given the exchange rate rigidity that existed under Bretton Woods (Kahn 1957b). Kahn also expressed concern that trade diversion would harm non-EEC nations, including Israel[9]:

> In so far as the pure diversion effect of free trade in the area preponderates over the real economies of free trade, the balancing of trade will require a movement of the terms of trade adverse to the outside world. And in so far as it is *only* the diversion effect which operates, the benefit to the members of the free trade area is achieved at the expense of other countries.
>
> The possibility of such adverse effects on other countries is a very real one. It is obviously much in the minds of the Canadians, who were looking forward to a rapid growth of their exports of manufactured goods. It may be particularly serious for a country like Malta (if not "integrated") or Israel, which needs a large expansion of exports of miscellaneous manufactured goods in order to achieve a bare equilibrium [emphasis in original]. (Kahn 1957a, 67)

Kahn strongly opposed the use of contractionary monetary policy to achieve BOP balance. He argued that such a policy is counterproductive, for three reasons: (a) It achieves a temporary BOP improvement at tremendous cost: Investment and output decline and unemployment rises. Lower investment implies less capital-embodied technical change and therefore lower productivity growth (Kahn 1952b, 1957b, 1958b, 132–6). (b) Improving the BOP requires a "discriminatory" policy that favors investment in export- and import-competing industries. Monetary contraction is the wrong tool because it is inherently nondiscriminatory—it reduces investment in all industries. (c) Monetary contraction is a "beggar-thy-neighbor" policy: If one country raises interest rates, other countries will do likewise in order

(Kahn 1950a). He also asserted that unilateral liberalization would necessitate higher unemployment in order to prevent the trade deficit from expanding (Kahn 1952a).

[8] In the 1960s and 1970s, UK academic economists were divided concerning the advisability of joining the EEC (King 2009, 103). Later, Kahn changed his position and staunchly opposed UK entry into the EEC (Kahn 1967).

[9] Kahn did not comment on the potential effects of payments unions on Israel. Kahn's proposed alternative to the European Payments Union, the "Discount Scheme," was designed to stimulate imports from within Europe and exports outside of Europe, in order to improve Europe's reserve position in an era of dollar scarcity (Kahn 1949b, 1950b). Obviously, this scheme would have harmed Israel.

to protect their foreign currency reserves. Ultimately, the only effect is a contraction in global output (Kahn 1956b, 1958b, 132–6).

Kahn advocated the following policy to reduce the UK's BOP deficit: Assuming that an "adequate" wage policy is in place and that aggregate demand is not excessive, keep investment constant, increase taxes on consumers, and restrict imports—especially imports from the US and West Germany (Kahn 1956b, 1958b, 134–5).

Kahn supported the sterling devaluation of 1949 and advocated combining devaluation with measures to reduce consumption expenditure in the domestic market (Kahn 1951). However, he regarded devaluation as ineffective unless an effective wage policy was already in place (Kahn 1958b, 132–6).

4.3 Kahn's Visits to Israel: Motivation and Documentation

Richard Kahn visited Israel at least five times: March 1951, June–July 1957, December 1962–January 1963 (henceforth referred to as 1962), April 1967, and January–March 1973. Kahn had three motivations for visiting Israel: personal (family/religious), academic, and business.

Two of Kahn's three (living) sisters, Doris Slutzkin and Beatrice ("Trixie") Lanzkron, resided in Israel.[10] Kahn had been raised as an Orthodox Jew. Although his religious practice lapsed during World War II, he retained a connection to Jewish tradition (Tabor 1989; Pasinetti 1994, 2007, 68) and continued to support Orthodox Jewish causes.[11]

Kahn was a close friend and collaborator of Don Patinkin,[12] the founding father of Israeli economics.[13] Their correspondence is preserved in the Kahn papers (RFK/12/2/19) and in the Patinkin papers at Duke University (Boxes 28 and 65). The Kahn-Patinkin relationship began no later than 1951 (two years after Patinkin's

[10]Doris and Beatrice were Kahn's eldest and second sisters. Beatrice immigrated to Mandatory Palestine before 1939; by 1944, both Doris and Beatrice were already settled in Palestine (*Palestine Post* 1944). Kahn's other siblings were Constance (Connie) Papineau, who was married to a British military officer and resided in both South Africa and the UK; Peggy, a sister who died in the 1930s (Kahn to Denis Smith, 4/4/73, Kahn papers, RFK 18/7); and at least one brother who died in childhood (David Papineau, personal communication).

[11]Kahn was involved in the construction of the Cambridge synagogue (completed 1937) and served as a synagogue trustee from 1936 to 1977 (Tabor 1989). In 1979–1980, he agreed to chair a major event in the history of British Ultra-Orthodox Jewry, the "Centenary of Independent Orthodoxy 1880–1980 and Golden Jubilee of the Jewish Secondary Schools Movement" (RFK 21/4). Furthermore, the notations in his 1962 and 1973 travel diaries (RFK 21/3, 18/7) reflect a traditional but nonpracticing Judaism.

[12]Like Kahn, Patinkin was raised as an Orthodox Jew by European immigrant parents and drifted away from Orthodoxy during World War II (Patinkin 1994, 1995).

[13]Paul Samuelson called Patinkin "an Abraham that all see as the Father of their nation's science … the Adam of Israeli economics and economists" (Leeson 2000).

move from Chicago to Jerusalem), when Kahn presented a paper at Hebrew University (henceforth HU). Kahn and Patinkin subsequently promoted formal cooperation between HU's economics department and KCC.[14] In 1952, Kahn hosted Patinkin on a 1-day visit to Cambridge (Patinkin to Kahn undated,[15] Patinkin Papers, Box 28). In the 1970s, Kahn and Patinkin corresponded extensively on the origins of Keynes' General Theory[16]; Patinkin's desire to continue the discussion in person led to Kahn's 1973 visit (Patinkin to Kahn, 21 September 1972, RFK 18/7). Kahn was also involved in Israel's business arena as a director of the Anglo-Israel Bank (AIB), which was the UK subsidiary of Bank Leumi (Kahn to Nissan Liviatan, 22 September 1972, RFK 18/7).[17]

Let us record the basic facts regarding each of Kahn's visits and describe the available documentation:

(a) 1951—Kahn presented a paper at HU (Patinkin to Walter Weisskopf, 27 March 1951, Patinkin Papers, Box 28).
(b) 1957—Kahn met with Israeli policymakers, bankers, industrialists, and labor leaders and took part in academic and social activities ("Israel Diary 1957," RFK 21/3); Kahn's contacts are listed in his Israel 1957 address book (RFK 19/1/6). Kahn also lectured on economic development at a symposium hosted by HU (Kahn 1958a). In this lecture, Kahn addressed certain aspects of Israeli economic policy; presumably, Kahn shared his views with his (nonacademic) interlocutors.
(c) 1962—Kahn met with Israeli policymakers, a banker, and a labor leader and took part in academic and social activities ("Israel 1962," RFK 21/3). Kahn's contacts are listed in his Israel 1962 address book (RFK 19/1/6). In January 1963, Kahn authored a five-page typescript on Israel's economic outlook, entitled "Note on short visit to Israel in December," 1962 (Kahn 1963; henceforth referred to as "Note 1963"); unfortunately, only three pages—one, two, and five—have survived. The Note of 1963 records Kahn's views on several major policy issues; presumably, Kahn shared these views with his Israeli interlocutors. On one issue (Israel-EEC relations), Kahn recalled the advice that he had given the Israelis in 1957. The purpose and intended audience (if any) of the Note are unknown.
(d) 1967—This visit is documented in the Israel 1967 address book (RFK 18/7). Only family visits are listed; there is no evidence of professional activity.
(e) 1973—This visit was devoted exclusively to academic pursuits. Kahn participated in Patinkin's graduate seminar on Keynesian economics at HU. He also lectured on British economic history at HU and on the international monetary

[14] Kahn's connection with HU predated Patinkin's hiring. In 1938, Kahn (at HU's request) recommended Michal Kalecki and Abba Lerner for a chair in economics. Neither accepted a permanent position, but Lerner served as visiting professor in 1955–1956 (Gross 2005).

[15] The sequence of letters indicates that Patinkin visited Cambridge in 1952.

[16] This correspondence is cited in Patinkin and Leith (1978) and Patinkin (1982).

[17] AIB was founded in 1959 and was later renamed Bank Leumi UK (Halevi et al. 1981, 201).

system after Bretton Woods at Tel Aviv University. The 1973 visit is documented in detail in both the Kahn papers (RFK 4/24, 12/2/113, 18/7) and the Patinkin papers (Box 65).

4.4 Israel's Economy in 1957: A Primer

In order to place Kahn's views in proper context, it is necessary to describe the structure of the Israeli economy in 1957. Israel's main characteristics were developing country status; a large defense burden; massive immigration; a socialist government which controlled organized labor, capital investment, and credit allocation; high taxes; and a massive trade deficit financed by foreign loans and aid. We elaborate below on these and other aspects of the Israeli economy; unless otherwise stated, all figures are taken from Michaely (1975, Appendix A).

Israel's per capita GDP (PCGDP) was 36.6% of PCGDP in the US and 60% of the PCGDP in the 12 leading Western European economies (New Angus Maddison Data Set). Growth in PCGDP and per capita consumption was slowing (Michaely 1975, Appendix A, Tables A-2 and A-3). Over 1956–1966, defense expenditures averaged 10% of GNP. The Sinai Campaign of 1956 caused a one-off doubling of defense expenditures (Gross and Greenberg 1994, 293–4).

The population was just under two million and (since 1953) growing at an increasing rate (Michaely 1975, Appendix A, Table A-1). Over May 1948–December 1957, immigration accounted for 76% of Jewish population growth (Riemer 1960). The massive Jewish immigration reduced the non-Jewish (mainly Arab) population share from 13.6% in 1949 to 10.8% in 1957 (Israel Central Bureau of Statistics). The labor force grew by 6.8% in 1957, the fastest rate since 1952 (Michaely 1975, Appendix A, Table A-1); over 1947–1957, the Jewish labor force grew by a cumulative 160% (Israel Central Bureau of Statistics). Labor force participation (among civilians aged 15+) was 53–54% (Israel Central Bureau of Statistics), which was low by international standards. Unemployment, which had peaked at 11.3% in 1953, declined to 6.9% in 1957 (Pomfret 1976, 142).

The government coalition was led by the socialist Mapai party ("Workers of the Land of Israel," the forerunner of today's Labor Party) under Prime Minister David Ben-Gurion. Mapai was the dominant force in the Histadrut (=General Federation of Labor), which had a membership of over 510,000 in 1955 (Plunkett 1958). The Histadrut owned and managed business enterprises in industry, construction, transportation, retailing, banking, and agriculture; these enterprises accounted for 20% of net domestic product in 1953–1960 (Michaely 1975, 4).

Over 1953–1957, investment accounted for 29–33% of GNP. Over 1953–1955, 51% of investment was undertaken by the public sector; in 1956–1957, 55% of investment was financed by the public sector (Michaely 1975, Appendix A, Tables A-3, A-4 and A-6). The government ensured its control over investment through a regime of financial repression, including a system of directed credit that accounted for one-third of total credit over 1950–1984 (Liviatan 2002). Domestic savings were quite low relative to domestic investment; in each year from 1953 to 1957, domestic savings failed to cover depreciation (as indicated by the negative net savings/NNP ratio shown in Michaely 1975, Appendix A, Table A-3).

During May 1948–December 1957, real wages rose at an annual rate of 7.6%–8.5%; the 1957 wage agreement led to a moderation of real wage growth (Riemer 1960). Real wages were excessive in relation to productivity, which led to excessive capital intensity, lack of competitiveness, and unemployment (Kreinin 1958; Halevi 1957; Lerner 1957; Riemer 1960). Evans (1970) demonstrates the inflationary effects of excessive wage increases. He estimates that over 1952–1965, TFP and labor productivity grew by 3% and 6.5% per year, respectively, while nominal wages grew at 9.3% per year. He concludes that despite rapid labor productivity growth, "wage policy has been severely inflationary near full employment [=4% unemployment, according to Evans' estimate]"; the CLA system was "at least partly" responsible.[18]

Mapai implemented a policy of economic egalitarianism as a means of maintaining social solidarity between new immigrants and veteran Israelis.[19] Wage differentials between professional and nonprofessional employees were deliberately minimized (see Chap. 3 of this book). High incomes were taxed exorbitantly: The top marginal (effective) income tax rate was 81.5% in 1956–1957, up from 70% in 1953–1955 (Radian 1984). In 1949–1951, Mapai imposed rationing and price controls, which, combined with subsidies on essential goods, succeeded in suppressing (official) inflation temporarily (Kreinin 1956); these policies were phased out over 1952–1959.

Over 1953–1960, the public sector accounted for 20% of net domestic product (Michaely 1975, 4). The government allocated 18% of its expenditures to subsidies (Riemer 1960).

Israel's currency was the Lira (=Israeli pound; abbreviated IL). The BOI (founded 1954) was then an arm of the Ministry of Finance. The main monetary policy instrument was the required reserve ratio (which exceeded 50% at times); any change in that ratio required government approval (Liviatan 2002). The exchange rate was pegged and had last been adjusted in August 1954. Over 1955–1961, CPI inflation averaged 5%.[20] The combination of faster inflation than in Western nations[21] and a pegged exchange rate caused a real appreciation of the IL. Israeli politicians attributed inflation solely to cost-push factors (Kleiman 1981).

Israel depended on imports for equipment and many raw materials. In the late 1950s, the cost of imported raw materials as a percentage of the value of Israeli production was 28% overall, 41% in the investment goods sector, and 48% in the

[18]On this issue, see also Halevi (1969).

[19]Simon Kuznets approved of this policy (Kuznets 2012, 95–6).

[20]Kreinin (1958) attributed the 1950s inflation to union wage pressures and low savings.

[21]Over 1955–1961, inflation in the UK, West Germany, and the US averaged 2.8%, 2.0%, and 1.9%, respectively (Sources: the UK and US, http://www.measuringworth.com/inflation/; West Germany: OECD StatExtracts).

export goods sector. From 1955, differential taxes and subsidies on both imports and exports created a system of concealed multiple exchange rates, which applied to 90% of Israel's international trade (Michaely 1975 82–118). On the import side, this system subsidized capital goods while taxing consumption goods (especially luxuries) (Riemer 1962).

Export growth averaged 25% per year over 1950–1957 (see Table 4.1). The major exports in 1957 were citrus fruits (34.5%, or 37.2% including processed citrus products), diamonds (25.2%), non-textile industrial products (13.1%), and textiles (5.7%). The major export destinations were Western Europe (excluding the UK), 43%; the UK, 24%; and the US, 14%. Export growth was limited by excessive real wages, relative price distortions, an unusually large share of services in total employment (for a developing country), and government misallocation of investment (Kreinin 1958).

Israel ran a massive trade deficit—20.5% of GNP in 1957, down from 25.3% in 1956 (Table 4.1). The need to finance the trade deficit made Israel dependent on capital imports,[22] which in 1957 consisted of unilateral transfers (76%) and capital inflows (24%). The sources of capital imports were as follows: Holocaust reparations from the West German government, 38%; transfers from World Jewry, 30%; and US government aid and other, 16% each.[23] A vigorous debate ensued regarding the sustainability of Israel's international imbalances; in Israeli parlance, this was known as the "economic independence" debate (Halevi 1969, 2006; Krampf 2009).

The alarmists included Abba Lerner, BOI and Ministry of Finance economists, and Don Patinkin. Lerner predicted that cessation of foreign aid would make capital imports unsustainable (Chap. 3 of this book). Bruno (1964) related that in late 1957, economists at the BOI and Ministry of Finance predicted that certain sources of capital imports would dry up by 1960–1962[24] and that exports would fall due to greater competition in the global citrus market. In 1959, Patinkin concluded that Israel had made no progress toward economic independence since 1953. For Patinkin, the lack of progress toward economic independence was "the major failure of Israel economic policy in its first decade" (Patinkin 1967, 132).[25] Patinkin recommended curtailing investment (especially by government) and reducing per capita consumption growth by raising taxes, in order to cut the trade deficit in half by 1962 (Patinkin 1967, 136, 139).

[22]Lerner (1957) and Riemer (1960) posited a connection between excessive wages and capital imports.

[23]As Krampf (2009) points out, Michaely (1961) was the first to report data on capital imports, disaggregated by components and sources.

[24]While Bruno (1964) did not specify the categories of capital imports that he expected to decline, others predicted that German reparations would be fully exhausted by 1962 or 1963 (Lerner 1957; Kreinin 1958; Riemer 1960; Patinkin 1967).

[25]A similar view was expressed by Schlomo Riemer, a student of both Patinkin and Kahn: "… the simple, sad truth is that after 14 years of massive, unremitting foreign aid aggregating to upwards of $4,000,000,000 there is not the moral strength and resolve left in Israel society, in the ranks of government and opposition alike, to put the country on its economic feet" (Riemer 1962).

Table 4.1 Exports, imports, trade deficit, and capital imports

Year	Nominal export growth (%)[a]	Nominal import growth (%)[a]	Exports (% of GNP)[b]	Imports (% of GNP)[b]	Trade deficit (% of GNP)[b]	Capital imports (% of GNP)[c]
1950			3.6	25.7	22.1	12.7
1951	45.7	29.9	3.4	21.9	18.5	13.9
1952	28.4	−7.7	5.7	25.5	19.8	19.9
1953	18.6	−7.1	8.9	22.7	13.8	15.1
1954	32.4	2.2	12.7	31.9	19.2	28.8
1955	6.7	14.5	12.2	36.1	23.9	24.9
1956	23.6	25.3	12.6	37.9	25.3	23.1
1957	24.7	4.1	13.6	34.0	20.5	19.4
1958	5.9	2.2	12.4	29.9	17.6	18.8
1959	21.7	5.8	13.1	27.7	14.5	16.5
1960	25.5	15.6	14.7	28.5	13.8	17.7
1961	18.4	23.1	14.5	29.2	14.7	16.8
1962	18.4	11.8	24.1	45.9	21.8	26.0
1963	20.7	5.5	24.1	40.2	16.1	20.6
1964	8.1	21.2	22.5	42.0	19.5	20.2
1965	14.2	3.6	21.5	36.4	14.9	15.4
1966	16.6	3.8	22.8	34.4	11.6	12.4
1967	6.5	10.6	23.3	36.5	13.2	20.9
1968	21.7	24.5	28.2	45.2	17.0	17.5
1969	11.7	20.8	28.0	48.5	20.4	15.4
1970	7.6	21.1	25.5	49.7	24.2	23.6
1971	33.3	16.3	29.1	49.5	20.4	24.9

Source: Michaely (1975, Table 5-1, Appendix A–Tables A-10 and A-14) and authors' calculations
[a]Original series in current US dollars
[b]Original series for exports, imports, and trade deficit are in current US dollars. Original series for GNP is in current IL. Exports, imports, and trade deficit have been converted to current IL using the formal IL/$ exchange rate
[c]Including national institutions (=the Jewish Agency); original series for capital imports in current US dollars. Original series for GNP in current IL. Capital imports have been converted to current IL using the formal IL/$ exchange rate for imports

The anti-alarmists included Daniel Creamer,[26] Michael Michaely, government and Histadrut economists, Simon Kuznets, and Milton Friedman. Creamer et al. (1957) and Michaely (1961) challenged Patinkin's empirical methodology and presented evidence that Israel was indeed progressing toward economic independence. Government and Histadrut economists adopted the Creamer-Michaely view. They also argued that economic independence was not Israel's greatest priority; this argument was motivated at least partially by opposition to Patinkin's policy

[26]After working for the US government and the NBER, Creamer served as the founding director of the Falk Institute in the early 1950s. He subsequently returned to the US and served as a senior economist at the Conference Board and as a member of the Falk Institute's US Advisory Board.

proposals (Krampf 2009). Kuznets viewed capital imports as a necessity, given the heavy burdens of defense and immigrant absorption (Kuznets 2012, 95–97[27]), while Friedman saw capital imports as a partial antidote for the growth-retarding effects of Israeli socialism (Friedman and Friedman 1999, 300).

To sum up, in 1957, Israel faced the following major policy dilemmas: (a) how to absorb immigration without increasing unemployment; (b) how to gradually reduce the trade deficit without harming manufacturing and investment (Bruno 1964) and without sharply reducing per capita consumption growth, which would in turn reduce net immigration; and (c) how to resolve the aforementioned dilemmas without weakening defense. In practice, Israeli policymakers were strongly disinclined to reduce per capita consumption growth or cut the defense budget; they saw such measures as economically inadvisable and politically infeasible (Gross and Greenberg 1994, 293–4).

Before concluding this section, it is instructive to note the similarities between Kahn's views and those of Israel's Labor socialist leadership. Kahn was a member of the UK Labour Party, supported partial nationalization of industry and planning (including directed credit), asserted a cost-push view of inflation, and accepted trade protection under certain conditions. From the ex ante perspective of the Israeli government, Kahn was no radical reformer.

4.5 Kahn's Views on the Israeli Economy, 1957

During his visit of 24 June–9 July 1957, Kahn met with policymakers, government economists, bankers, industrialists, and labor leaders. He also participated in a symposium on "The Challenge of Development," which was held at HU on June 25–26. Kahn's most prominent interlocutors were Foreign Minister Golda Meir; Moshe Bartur, head of the Foreign Ministry Economic Department; Dr. Jacob Arnon, director-general of the Finance Ministry; David Horowitz, the founding governor of the BOI (and a fellow participant in the symposium[28]); Minister of Development Mordechai Bentov; and Minister Without Portfolio Peretz Naphtali. Kahn did not meet with Prime Minister David Ben-Gurion or Finance Minister Levi Eshkol.[29]

Who introduced Kahn to these individuals? Although definitive evidence is lacking, circumstantial evidence points to Patinkin, who maintained strong ties with Bartur, Arnon, Horowitz, and Naphtali.[30]

[27]This passage dates from the late 1950s. Kreinin (1956) expressed a similar view.

[28]Other distinguished participants included Patinkin, Kuznets, and the sociologist Talcott Parsons.

[29]Eshkol was abroad until July 2, having traveled to France and the US to raise funds for immigrant housing.

[30]During 1957–1958, Patinkin worked closely with Bartur as a member of the government's Inter-Ministry Committee on the Common Market and Free Trade Area (Patinkin Papers, Box 69, Krampf 2010b). Arnon, a personal friend of Patinkin's, placed Patinkin's students in positions at the Finance Ministry (Gross 2005). From 1957 to 1968, Patinkin worked with Horowitz as a member of the BOI Advisory Committee (Patinkin 1994), which (despite its name) functioned as a board of directors (Krampf 2010a). Naphtali was instrumental in bringing Patinkin to HU (Patinkin 1995).

Although there is little documentation of Kahn's discussions with Israeli policymakers, we know that Kahn expressed strong views regarding Israel's application for EEC Associate Membership. In April 1957, soon after the signing of the Treaty of Rome (25 March 1957), Minister of Trade and Industry Pinchas Sapir formed the Inter-Ministry Committee on the Common Market and Free Trade, under the direction of Bartur. Patinkin joined the committee soon afterwards (Patinkin Papers, Box 69). Israel approached the EEC about Associate Membership in Summer 1957, before the Treaty of Rome took effect (1 January 1958). Israeli technocrats strongly supported the EEC bid; they wished to exploit the application process in order to impose structural reforms on the Histadrut (Krampf 2010b).[31] Kahn recalled that in 1957, he had predicted "to some of those concerned" that Israel would not attain EEC Associate Membership (Note 1963). Despite Kahn's advice, the Israeli government was not discouraged: The Inter-Ministry Committee (including Patinkin) continued its activities into 1958 (Patinkin Papers, Box 69), and in June 1960, Ben-Gurion requested Associate Membership in a meeting with EEC Commission President Walter Hallstein (Pardo and Peters 2012, 4).

Ultimately, Kahn's pessimism turned out to be justified: Israel was denied Associate Membership in 1962–1963, even after Greece (1962) and Turkey (1963) had attained that status. In rejecting Israel, the Europeans were motivated by economic self-interest and the desire to avoid setting a precedent for other Mediterranean countries (Miller 2004). In 1964, the EEC agreed to a limited commercial agreement. Israel found this agreement unsatisfactory,[32] but its attempt to negotiate a new agreement was thwarted by French opposition. In October 1966, Israel reapplied for Associate Membership. During the Six-Day War of June 1967, the European Commission recommended acceptance, but this was vetoed by France (Pardo and Peters 2012, 73). Israel allowed the 1964 agreement to expire in 1967. After France dropped its opposition to a new agreement in 1969 (on the condition that any Arab country could obtain a PTA on the same terms), Israel-EEC PTA's were finalized in 1970 and 1975 (Pomfret and Toren 1980, 17–18). Only in 2000 was Israel admitted to EU Associate Membership.

At the HU symposium, Kahn gave a paper entitled "The pace of development" (Kahn 1958a), which he later described as "a plea to the governments of underdeveloped countries to utilize their surplus labor drastically to increase their rate of investment, especially in agriculture" (Marcuzzo 1988, 57). In this paper, Kahn addressed several issues that were relevant to Israel: the causes of inflation, the balance between consumption and investment, and wage setting. In the paragraphs that follow, we present Kahn's views on these issues and evaluate them critically.

---

[31]Kreinin (1968) cites import liberalization and exchange rate unification as efficiency-enhancing measures that would fail to pass without external pressure.

[32]The 1964 commercial agreement reduced the common external tariff on some industrial goods that were of importance to Israel, by some 20%. The agreement was non-preferential—i.e., all tariff concessions granted to Israel were also granted to competing countries (Pomfret and Toren 1980, 17).

Kahn opened by stating that he would address problems of development in countries with significant unemployment, including many Asian nations and Israel. He then acknowledged his ignorance of Israeli economic realities:

> … at this point I should make it perfectly clear that my remarks are not directed at Israel. I do so with shame and regret. I do not pretend to have any detailed knowledge of any of the countries to which, in a very general way, my remarks might apply. One does, however, hear quite a lot about them. I wish I could say the same about Israel as far as my part of the world is concerned. While I should hope that there will be some bearing on Israel's problems in what I have to say, I cannot pretend that it is directly prompted by them. (Kahn 1958a, 154–5)

In his treatment of inflation (Kahn 1958a, 176–7), Kahn attacked (unnamed) monetarists but conceded the validity of some of their points. Kahn argued that the word "inflation" is "bewildering and misleading," because it suggests that monetary factors are responsible for inflation and that excess demand for resources is not inflationary unless complemented by monetary factors. In reality, the behavior of prices is determined not by the money supply but by the supply and distribution of consumption goods. The greatest problem with the word "inflation" is that "it distracts attention from the part played by the wage bargain in fostering a progressive upward movement of prices." Nominal wage behavior matters greatly for the price level in Israel, just as it does in advanced economies.

Kahn conceded the following points to the monetarists: (a) Rapid inflation impedes development. (b) "Antisocial methods of holding private wealth"—that is, speculative hoarding of commodities and gold and superfluous real estate investment—lead to misallocation of resources. (c) The prevalence of the above phenomena does depend on monetary policy.

These remarks are partially consistent with Kahn's positions on inflation as articulated elsewhere. The familiar themes are the emphasis on the wage bargain, aggregate demand, and the need to avoid common but misleading terminology and anti-monetarism. What is unusual about these remarks is Kahn's willingness to make concessions to monetarism.

How accurate were Kahn's assertions? The answer depends on the nature of the inflationary process in Israel. Was inflation a cost-push phenomenon (causality runs from prices to money), a demand-pull phenomenon (causality runs from money to prices), or some combination of cost-push and demand-pull? Each of these views had at least one advocate.

Cost-push Evans (1970) attributes inflation to cost-push factors only and denies any role for demand in the inflationary process.[33]

Some combination of cost-push and demand-pull Patinkin (1967, 116–8) concludes that the simple quantity theory explains Israeli inflation well over 1950–1958. In some periods inflation was demand-pull; in others it was cost-push. Halevi (1969)

[33]Evans estimates that wage increases not justified by productivity growth were responsible for 7.8 percentage points of inflation each year; the CLA was at least partially responsible.

concurs, stating that the causes of inflation varied by period (demand-pull, cost-push, or a combination of both). Kleiman and Ophir (1975) find support for the monetarist demand-based view until mid-1961 and support for the cost-push view thereafter.[34] Artstein and Z. Sussman (1977; cited by Bruno and Z. Sussman 1979) find that over 1955–1974, the inflationary process was driven by both cost-push and demand-pull factors.[35]

Demand-pull Michael Michaely (1975, 19–20) leans strongly toward a monetarist demand-based explanation.[36] He identifies the fiscal deficit as a major inflationary force, through its effects on aggregate demand, liquidity, and the money supply. In Michaely's view, cost-push factors played no causative role, but may have influenced the timing of some price increases.

To sum up, Kahn's cost-push view of inflation was consistent with the view held by Israeli politicians. This view was also held by a minority of economists.

With regard to investment, Kahn stated that a suitable compromise must be found between a low rate of interest to promote investment and a high rate of interest to discourage "anti-social methods of holding private wealth." Equating money growth to growth in transactions money demand does not guarantee an appropriate monetary policy. Money growth does influence the target investment rate because there is a need to limit consumption in order to make money balances available for investment. But the rate of investment may be "dangerously high," due to factors that are independent of the monetary and banking system, which provides the financing for investment. "The usual rule for the safe amount of deficit finance" does not assure a correct initial monetary policy, and even if "by some happy chance" initial monetary policy is correct, there is no assurance that it will stay that way (Kahn 1972, 177–8).

Let us assess this statement critically. Kahn assumed a need to limit consumption in order to facilitate higher investment. This assumption was consistent with Kahn's previously published views on the consumption/investment balance but was inconsistent with Israeli reality. Israel was able to increase investment without reducing consumption by allowing the trade deficit and capital imports to increase. Such a policy would have been fiercely opposed by the alarmists in the economic independence debate, but Kahn did not cite their views. By completely ignoring the economic independence issue, Kahn displayed ignorance of Israel's policy constraints (or lack thereof).

---

[34]Kleiman and Ophir use annual and quarterly data for 1955–1965.

[35]Artstein and Z. Sussman find that inflation is explained by the following variables (coefficient sign in parentheses): import prices (+), money growth minus output growth (+), the reciprocal of lagged unemployment (+), Arab workers from the West Bank and Gaza (−, applicable from 1967), the product/labor ratio (+), one minus the rate of indirect tax (−), and a dummy for wage controls (−).

[36]Michaely cites the following empirical regularity: Over 1949–1971, price movements lagged money supply movements by 10–12 months.

As we have seen, Kahn believed that investment in Israel was excessive and that monetary policy was being mismanaged. He hinted that Israeli monetary authorities were keeping the interest rate too low and thus encouraging speculation in the private sector. Here, too, Kahn missed important aspects of Israel's economic reality. Let us accept that investment was excessive and/or misallocated (as argued by Patinkin 1967). Were low interest rates the main culprit? Absolutely not. As shown by Michaely (1975, Appendix A, Table A-6), almost half of investment (and half of residential construction) was undertaken by the government; most investment was financed by the government, which also controlled monetary policy and credit allocation. Thus, excessive and/or misallocated investment was primarily the result of poor government decisions, not the private sector's reactions to low interest rates.

Regarding labor relations, Kahn believed that when labor is organized, its leaders should be able to articulate the extent to which they take into account the overall effects of their wage demands—impeded development and slower employment growth, which implies postponement of the achievement of full employment. Kahn then proceeded to analyze a scenario which he considered especially relevant to Israel. In this scenario, labor leaders are absolutely convinced that the government is attempting to impose an excessive tax burden on "well-established" industrial workers, in order to finance immigrant absorption and general development needs. In order to compensate workers for the tax burden, the labor leadership demands higher (gross) wages. Kahn called on labor leaders to avoid acting in this manner; he viewed excessive wage demands as a "heavy-handed and destructive" approach that would ultimately fail to improve the lot of the workers. Instead, he advocated a "calm, scientific appraisal" of the "implications of a high rate of development" and "severe" taxation of "other classes" in the name of social equity. He also suggested that the government might subsidize "some of the bare essentials of life."

Kahn had the following to say regarding Israel's CLA system: "I need not expand on the futility of tying money wages to a cost of living index, but stabilization of an index based on the prices of a few bare necessities could serve a useful purpose." In a footnote, he elaborated as follows: "It is worth noting that the last round of Swedish wage negotiations, which will result in very modest increases over the ensuing two years, has led to agreement that an escalator clause, which becomes effective if the cost of living rises by more than a certain critical amount, will not operate if the rise in the cost of living is attributable to special taxes imposed for anti-inflationary purposes."[37]

[37]Kahn was referring to the Swedish wage agreement of February 1957, whose key provisions were the following: Hourly wages would increase by 2% or 10 öre per hour (whichever was greater) in 1957 and by 3.5% in 1958; piece rates would rise by 2% in 1958. Workers could reopen the agreement to demand a CLA if the CPI (1949=100) increased from 143 to 150 over March–November 1957, unless the increase was caused by new taxes on consumption (Sen Gupta 1958). This represented an increase of 7.4% at an annualized rate, which was substantially higher than the 4.6% year-over-year inflation rate recorded in February 1957 (up from 3.6% in December 1956). Actual inflation in Sweden for March–November 1957 was 3.6% (annualized), so this provision was never triggered (Swedish inflation data is taken from OECD StatExtracts).

Kahn realized that striving for wage restraint in Israel could be an uphill battle: "I am touching here on the tricky field of social psychology, and of the possible influences of education and propaganda in communities with which I am entirely unacquainted." Nevertheless, he expressed cautious optimism about the prospects for reform: "I am not convinced that nothing could be achieved if the issues were presented on a straightforward and common sense sort of basis."

Briefly stated, Kahn proposed to link wages to the prices of staple goods rather than to the CPI and to significantly restrict the operation of the CLA. By adopting these measures, Israel would move toward a Swedish-style wage system—that is, a wage system in which the CLA plays a minor role in protecting against real wage erosion. This would facilitate wage moderation by minimizing Kahn's "vicious spiral"—the mechanism that linked the CLA to higher inflation.[38]

Kahn's proposal amounted to a radical reform of the Israeli wage system. The Israeli CLA system was vastly different from its Swedish counterpart and was so strongly entrenched that reform was virtually impossible.

The CLA was an integral component of the Israeli wage setting system. Officially, the CLA granted workers 100% compensation for increases in the CPI (Liviatan 1982; Prager 1986); the actual rate of protection averaged 91% over 1957–1973, never falling below 90%. A minor reform was adopted in July 1957; among its provisions was the exclusion of the fruits and vegetables component of the CPI.[39] In Sweden, on the other hand, indexation was not a central component of the wage setting system; rather, non-CLA instruments were the primary means of protecting real wages from erosion (Braun 1976).

Israel's CLA enjoyed broad-based political support, due to the popular view that the CLA was an essential instrument of real wage protection (Liviatan 1982; Prager 1986). Before the adoption of a major CLA reform in 1975, proposals for reform of the CLA and/or the wage system were repeatedly rejected. For example: (a) In 1954, Schlomo Riemer (a future student of Kahn's at KCC) advocated replacing the CPI with "a cost-of-subsistence index based on an iron ration composed of biological necessities only" (Riemer 1960); this was exactly what Kahn proposed in 1957. (b) Abba Lerner advocated replacing the CLA with a Wage Authority, which would set wages based on productivity and the degree of competition (Chap. 3 of this book). (c) In 1966, a joint Histadrut-Manufacturers' Association committee proposed several reforms to the CLA, including the exclusion of price increases due to changes in import prices or effective exchange rates (Committee of Experts 1966).

Because Israeli policymakers were so strongly disinclined toward major CLA reform, it is unlikely that Kahn's proposal was taken seriously; even if it was taken seriously, it was certainly never implemented. As we shall see, when Kahn returned in 1962, he condemned the CLA as "a destabilizing force on money costs and prices" but did not reiterate his proposal for CLA reform, perhaps because he came to understand that it was a political nonstarter.

---

[38]While in Israel, Kahn did not articulate a fully developed conception of wage policy.

[39]From 1968 to 1975, the housing component was also excluded.

4.6 Kahn's Views on the Israeli Economy, 1962

Kahn visited Israel again from 21 December 1962 to 6 January 1963. He described his visit as follows: "My visit was a private one. I did, however, meet some of the University economists and saw something of the people in the Bank of Israel, the Bank Leumi, and the Economic Planning Authority" (Note 1963).

In order to place Kahn's ideas in proper context, let us update our description of the Israeli economy through 1962. Kahn arrived 10 months after the adoption of the second new economic policy (henceforth SNEP, February 1962). Why was the SNEP adopted? What were its major components?

In early 1962, the Israeli economy was at full employment. Foreign currency reserves were high and increasing. Although inflation was rising (Michaely 1975, Appendix A, Table A-17), it was not seen as potentially destabilizing. Nevertheless, the government was not content with the status quo; it feared that a BOP crisis would develop as a result of a sharp fall in capital imports (especially German reparations) and an expansion of the trade deficit. To forestall this doomsday scenario, the government adopted the SNEP.[40] The SNEP consisted of the following major components:

(a) Devaluation—The IL was devalued by 67% against the US dollar, from IL 1.80/$ to IL 3/$.
(b) Partial trade liberalization—in a gradual process, many tariffs were reduced and most export subsidies were abolished, so as to reduce the variance of effective exchange rates and move toward a unified exchange rate. Import quotas were converted to tariffs. Most of the liberalization occurred over 1963–1965; by 1965, liberalized goods accounted for 35% of manufacturing value (excluding diamonds).

The average net devaluation (taking into account the changes to tariffs and export subsidies) was approximately 30–37% for imports and 13% for exports. The devaluation was accompanied by strongly expansionary monetary and fiscal policies; thus, the initial real exchange rate depreciation was completely dissipated by mid-1965.[41] The SNEP failed in two respects: (a) it failed to reduce the trade deficit, and (b) it failed to achieve a unified exchange rate—higher inflation forced the government to reintroduce multiple exchange rates (Michaely 1975, 58–75, 121, 123–33, 144–5, Bruno and Z. Sussman 1979).

Over 1956–1963, Israel became more integrated with the EEC (Tables 4.2 and 4.3).[42] The alarmist prediction that capital imports would dry up in 1962 or 1963

[40]Patinkin endorsed the SNEP in a letter to BOI Governor Horowitz (Patinkin 1962).

[41]The nominal exchange rate was frozen until November 1967, when the IL was devalued by 16.7%.

[42]Exports to the EEC expanded sixfold, while the EEC's share in Israeli exports rose from 17.4% to 30% (Kreinin 1968 and Table 4.2). In 1961, the EEC and the UK (which was outside the EEC until 1973) accounted for 27.5% and 14.2% of Israeli exports, respectively (Table 4.3); the combined share of the EEC and European Free Trade Area (EFTA) countries (including the UK) was over 50% (Riemer 1962).

Table 4.2 Israel's exports by destination in selected years (% share)

Destination	1949	1959	1972
UK	53.7	18.9	9.7
US	15.5	15.4	19.7
W. Germany	0.1	9.9	9.0
Switzerland	2.2	5.4	5.4
Belgium	0.2	5.2	4.1
Turkey	0.2	5.0	0.2
Netherlands	6.9	4.4	5.7
Yugoslavia	0.3	3.0	0.7
Hong Kong	0.0	2.8	5.3
Italy	0.2	2.5	2.7
France	0.6	2.3	4.8
Sweden	6.2	2.2	1.1
Finland	0.8	1.7	0.7
Denmark	1.1	1.3	0.6
Canada	0.2	1.3	1.7
Norway	1.0	1.3	0.4
Cyprus	0.2	1.2	0.6
Romania	1.0	1.1	0.9
Greece	0.0	1.0	1.6
Japan	0.0	0.9	6.2
Other	9.6	13.2	19.9
EEC countries[a]	8.0	24.3	26.3

Source: Pomfret (1976, 59)
[a]Excludes Luxembourg

turned out to be incorrect. Although German reparations to the Israeli government ended in 1963, restitution payments to households continued (Michaely 1975, Appendix A, Table A-14). In 1964–1966, capital imports as a percentage of GNP declined from 20.2% to 12.4% due to recession, but in 1967 (the year of the Six-Day War), capital imports surged to 20.9% of GNP. Thereafter, capital imports remained high, averaging 20.5% of GNP over 1967–1971 (Table 4.1).

Kahn's views in 1962 are documented in his Note of 1963. Here, we reproduce selected passages from the Note, with analysis and commentary as appropriate. For the sake of brevity, we refrain from commenting on passages that are broadly consistent with Kahn's general policy views, as elaborated in Sect. 4.2.

Kahn had the following to say regarding Israel's GNP growth:

> About one-half of [GNP] growth is attributable to increasing productivity per person employed. The other half is to be associated with the increasing labor force. This has been growing somewhat faster than the population.

Patinkin had estimated in 1959 that 30–42% of GNP growth could be attributed to productivity growth, although he admitted that this might be an underestimate (Patinkin 1967, 73–75):

Table 4.3 Share of EEC Six countries and the UK in Israeli goods exports (%), 1959–1961

	1959			1960			1961		
	Agriculture	Industry[a]	All goods	Agriculture	Industry[a]	All goods	Agriculture	Industry[a]	All goods
EEC Six	37.9	15.1	23.8	41.6	21.4	28.8	39.9	22.2	27.5
UK	34.9	13.6	18.4	32.5	12.3	16.4	30.5	10.7	14.2
EEC Six + UK	72.8	28.7	42.2	74.1	33.7	45.2	70.4	32.9	41.7

Source: Sitton and Ravid (1964, Table 7)
[a]Excludes diamonds

> The increase in the national product has in effect been largely devoted to increasing consumption. Of the addition to the national product over the period 1955 to 1961, 90 per cent is represented by the increase in private and public consumption. Private consumption per head has been rising at the rate of 5 per cent a year (indeed at a somewhat higher rate in 1961 and 1962) ... certainly the word "austerity" which was appropriate only two or three years ago is no longer applicable, taking the population in the broad.

The estimate of 90% was not Kahn's own, but was taken from a government report (Economic Planning Authority 1962) which Kahn cites elsewhere in the Note:

> ... The rapid rise in the standard of living, achieved in spite of the rapid growth of population, is to be associated with the somewhat militant attitude over wages adopted by the Histadrut (the single trade union which covers almost the whole economy and, apart from acting as a trade union, is an important participant in many industrial enterprises). Wages costs and prices have continued to rise rapidly. In 1959 and again in 1960 the rise in the cost of living had slackened to only 2 1/2 per cent a year, but in 1961 it rose by 9 per cent, the sharpest increase since the early fifties.

Clearly, Kahn was not convinced of the Histadrut's commitment to wage moderation, despite claims to that effect by its Secretary-General Aharon Becker (Becker 1960), whom Kahn had met in 1957.[43]

Turning to the SNEP and its effects on wages and labor relations, Kahn wrote as follows:

> On the 9th February, 1962, the Israeli pound was devalued. A uniform effective rate of $3 to the IL was substituted for the rate of $1.80 which, originally introduced in May, 1953, as one of three different rates, had become somewhat nominal ...
>
> All wages and most lending and borrowing ... are now linked to the cost of living index ... The linking to the cost of living, especially of wages, serves as a destabilizing force on money costs and prices.
>
> An attempt at a "wage freeze" is at present being made by the Government, with some co-operation from the Histadrut, but increases on account of the recent rise in the cost of living will still take place. Acceptance of the idea of a "wage freeze" has been secured, insofar as it has been secured (and it must be borne in mind that the central authorities of the Histadrut do not exercise a dictatorship over their industrial branches), at the expense of a commitment by the Government to refrain from imposing additional taxes for the time being.
>
> Since the devaluation of February, 1962, the rise in the cost of living has been remarkably small, the reason partly being the elimination of various surcharges on imports which had been imposed on account of the artificial character of the official exchange rate. Some further rise in the cost of living cannot be avoided even if basic money wages (as opposed to cost of living supplements) are, for the moment, kept fairly stable, but some attempt is being made by direct intervention with suppliers by the Government to prevent further price increases.

In 1957, Kahn had urged the Histadrut to avoid increasing its wage demands in response to tax increases. In 1962, he seemed to lament the government's promise

[43]Becker (1960) stated that the Histadrut "is opposed to wage increases that lack a foundation of increased productivity, since this will inevitably produce inflationary pressure and lower the real wages of the worker." This is broadly consistent with Kahn's views. But as Evans (1970) demonstrates, "wage increases that lack a foundation of increased productivity" were rampant during 1952–1965.

not to increase taxes in return for what he saw as a dubious wage freeze. Presumably, Kahn did not want the government to forswear contractionary fiscal policy, because (as discussed in Sect. 4.2) he saw fiscal contraction as the main tool for reducing consumption when necessary, and as a more palatable anti-inflation policy than monetary contraction, in a country without a wage policy (such as Israel).

Regarding the BOP problem, Kahn articulated the following view:

> The physical achievement of Israel in the economic sphere is remarkable, especially when taken in relation to the heavy burden of defense and of the housing and equipment of immigrants. Whether too much of the improvement [in Real GNP-authors] has gone into raising the standard of living and not enough into securing an even faster growth of productivity and an improvement in the Balance of Payments, depends on one's attitude to the Balance of Payments.

Kahn took a rather vague, noncommittal position on the economic independence issue. Apparently, Kahn had come to understand the arguments on both sides of the debate (of which he had been unaware in 1957), but found neither side completely convincing.

As discussed above, in 1957, Kahn had a negative view of Israel's aspirations to EEC Associate Membership. In 1962, he offered the following assessment:

> Having, in more or less definite terms, been refused Associate Membership of the Common Market (in accordance with the prediction which I made to some of those concerned five and a half years ago), there now seems to be unjustified optimism about a possible comprehensive commercial agreement with the Common Market. The draft Four Year Development Plan [which was not approved by the government but served as "a basis of discussion"[44]] seems to be based on the view that the existence of the Common Market will assist Israel in reducing her surplus of imports over exports. My own view is that it will make it more difficult even if the United Kingdom does not become a member.

At first glance, this passage is puzzling. In order to interpret it accurately, we must examine the draft Four-Year Development Plan (Economic Planning Authority 1962) and the pattern of Israel's international trade ca. 1962.

The authors of the Plan viewed the achievement of economic independence as "a central goal," given their expectation that certain categories of capital imports (e.g., German reparations) would soon be exhausted. They envisioned a gradual reduction

[44]The draft Four-Year Development Plan (Economic Planning Authority 1962) was a very ambitious document, which called for rapid export-led growth, price stability, a higher savings rate, and slower growth in per capita private and public consumption. Although the Plan was written in Hebrew, Kahn was sufficiently familiar with it to cite it in his Note. For example, the following sentence from the Note (cited above) was based on the Plan: "Of the addition to the national product over the period 1955 to 1961, 90 per cent is represented by the increase in private and public consumption." Regarding the Plan's fate, Kahn wrote: "While I was still in Israel I was told that the draft plan had already been substantially softened and that the planned brake on further improvement in the standard of living had to a considerable extent been released. It is relevant that the original plan would almost certainly have required heavy additional taxation if it was to be fulfilled" (Note 1963). According to Halevi (1969), the Plan was shelved because Finance Minister Pinchas Sapir (who took office in June 1963) was "less committed to the concept of overall national planning."

of the trade deficit and capital imports, to be achieved via annual growth of 20% in exports, 9% in imports, and −9.5% in the trade deficit. The attainability of this goal depended critically upon several assumptions, including the following:

> The plan assumes that an agreement will be attained with the European Common Market, under which its members will refrain from imposing quantitative restrictions or tariff restrictions on Israel's exports to the Common Market and the countries associated with it. The realization of this assumption is an important condition for the attainment of the goals of the plan for rapid economic growth and the improvement of the Balance of Payments, in light of the great weight that European countries have in the current composition of Israel's exports, and especially in the increased exports in the future.
>
> ... such an agreement will require an improvement in the competitiveness of the Israeli economy ... it ... will require the adjustment of the local market to a gradual removal of import restrictions.

The Plan acknowledged the prevailing uncertainty regarding the parameters of a future Israel-EEC agreement. Nevertheless, its assumption of full liberalization of Israeli exports to the EEC was extremely overoptimistic and was most probably what Kahn had in mind when he criticized "the view that the *existence of the Common Market* will assist Israel in reducing her surplus of imports over exports" (emphasis ours).

In 1957, Kahn had recognized that the EEC customs union would be harmful to Israel (Kahn 1957a). He sympathized with Israel's need to expand exports (Kahn 1957a) but thought that its bid for Associate Membership was doomed to fail (Note 1963). In 1962, he added that the EEC customs union would harm Israel even if the UK did not join (Note 1963), but did not provide any reasoning to justify this conclusion. While we can never know Kahn's reasoning with certainty, we can justify his conclusion using Sitton and Ravid's (1964) detailed study of Israel-EEC trade, which was completed in August 1962, shortly before Kahn's arrival (Table 4.4).

Sitton and Ravid (1964) pointed out that without Associate Membership or a commercial agreement, a significant percentage of Israeli exports would be adversely affected by the EEC's Common External Tariff (CET), which was expected to take effect in 1969. Using 1961 data from Sitton and Ravid, we calculate that the affected goods accounted for 7.2% of total Israeli exports if the UK were to remain outside the EEC and 13.2% of total Israeli exports if the UK were to join the EEC (Table 4.5).

To see why the CET was so harmful to Israel's exports, consider orange exports to the EEC Six and the UK, which accounted for 5.5% of Israel's total exports in 1961.[45] Table 4.6 shows the anticipated effect of the CET on orange exports. In 1961, the UK tariff on oranges was 10%, regardless of origin. Tariffs in Germany and the Benelux countries were 13% and 15% (respectively) on Israeli oranges and 7% and 9% (respectively) on EEC (e.g., Italian) oranges. The anticipated CET on

[45]The 5.5% share was broken down as follows: EEC Six 2.3% and UK 3.2%. This calculation is based on data from Tables 4.3 and 4.4, plus the fact that oranges accounted for 81.2% and 86.7% of Israel's citrus exports to the EEC Six and the UK, respectively.

Table 4.4 Composition of Israel's exports to EEC Six and the UK, 1961 ($1000)

	EEC Six	UK	EEC Six + UK
Agriculture	24,879	19,362	44,241
Citrus	11,919	16,169	28,088
Eggs	8755	1323	10,078
Bananas	779	67	846
Wheat	929	0	929
Industry and mining	21,345	12,024	33,369
Of which: Citrus products	1842	3525	5367
Diamonds	17,786	3688	21,474
Total	64,010	35,074	99,084
Agriculture share (%)	38.9	55.2	44.6
Citrus share (%)	18.6	46.1	28.3
Industry and mining share (%)	33.3	34.3	33.7
Diamonds share (%)	27.8	10.5	21.7
Citrus and citrus products share (%)	21.5	56.1	33.8

Source: Sitton and Ravid (1964, Table 3) and authors' calculations
Note: In 1961, Israel's total exports were $425 million—goods, $238 million; services, $187 million (Michaely 1975, Appendix A, Table A-10)

Table 4.5 Israeli exports (1961) expected to be subject to the CET (1969),[a] EEC Six, and the UK[b] ($1000)

	EEC Six	UK[b]	EEC Six + UK[b]
Goods exports subject to the CET[c]	30,657	25,393	56,050
Total goods exports	64,010	35,074	99,084
Share of goods exports subject to the CET	47.9%	72.4%	56.6%
Share of Israeli exports (to all destinations, goods and services) subject to the CET in 1969 if the UK did not join the EEC: 7.2%			
Share of Israeli exports (to all destinations, goods and services) subject to the CET in 1969 if the UK joined the EEC: 13.2%			

Sources: Sitton and Ravid (1964, Table 6), Michaely (1975, Appendix A, Table A-10), and authors' calculations
[a]In practice, the CET took effect on 1 July 1968
[b]Based on the assumption that the UK would join the EEC. In practice, the UK did not join until 1973
[c]These goods comprised certain categories of agricultural and industrial products. Services and diamonds were not subject to the CET

oranges was 20%. Thus, by 1969, the UK would have to gradually raise its tariff on non-EEC oranges to 20%, while phasing out its tariff on EEC and North African oranges. Germany and the Benelux countries would have to do likewise, but the impact would be smaller than in the UK case, for two reasons: (a) The UK market absorbed 50% of Israeli citrus exports vs. 27% for the EEC Six and (b) the expected tariff increase was smaller in Germany/Benelux than in the UK.

Table 4.6 Tariffs on Israeli and EEC oranges by destination, 1961 and 1969[a]

Destination	Tariff on Israeli oranges, 1969 (%)	Tariff on EEC oranges, 1961 (%)	Tariff on Israeli oranges, 1969 (%)[a]	Tariff on EEC oranges, 1969 (%)[a]
UK	10	10	20	0
W. Germany	13	7	20	0
Benelux countries	15	9	20	0

Source: Sitton and Ravid (1964)
[a]Expected tariff under the CET, which ultimately took effect on 1 July 1968

To sum up, Kahn provided a cogent analysis of the EEC customs union. He understood that the EEC would harm Israeli exports and make it more difficult to reduce the trade deficit. He asserted without evidence that the harm to Israeli exports would be substantially greater if the UK were to join. This assertion can be substantiated by an analysis of the anticipated effects of the CET (which was supposed to take effect in 1969), which shows that the CET was expected to adversely affect a large percentage of Israeli exports to both the EEC Six and the UK (Israel's leading export destination at the time).[46] At the same time, Kahn correctly predicted Israel's failure to significantly expand its access to EEC markets, whether by means of EEC Associate Membership or by means of a PTA. Despite Kahn's pessimism, the government refused to be discouraged and continued its intensive efforts on the EEC front.

4.7 Conclusion

This chapter has documented a heretofore unknown aspect of Richard Kahn's intellectual biography—his role as an unofficial adviser to the Israel government in 1957 and 1962. In this role, Kahn took strong positions on two issues: the need for CLA reform as a means to promote wage moderation and the need for a realistic assessment of the prospects for Israel-EEC trade. At the same time, he professed neutrality regarding one of the leading issues of the day—the sustainability of Israel's international imbalances.

In 1957, Kahn proposed to reform Israel's CLA by linking wages to the prices of staple goods rather than to the CPI, so as to reduce the degree of protection from real wage erosion due to the CLA. He also proposed to increase subsidies on staple goods, in order to increase Israel's reliance on non-CLA instruments to protect real wages. Through these reforms, Kahn wished to move Israel closer to the Swedish wage setting system, in which the CLA was limited in scope and played only a

[46]The CET was a cause for concern in Israeli government circles throughout the 1960s. Kreinin (1968) estimated that the CET would reduce Israeli exports by 6% and pointed out that general uncertainty regarding EEC trade policy was depressing investment in Israel.

minor role in protecting real wages. Kahn's proposals were never implemented, which is unsurprising in light of the failure of other experts (both foreign and Israeli) to bring about significant CLA reforms.

In the realm of Israel-EEC trade relations, Kahn sought to dampen the excessive optimism of Israeli policymakers regarding the potential for trade with the EEC. While Kahn understood Israel's need to expand exports to Europe, he predicted in 1957 that the EEC would reject Israel's application for Associate Membership. In 1962, he criticized Israeli authorities for assuming that the EEC would grant full trade liberalization, which would help Israel to reduce its massive trade deficit and dependence on capital imports. He asserted without evidence that the EEC would harm Israeli trade—even more so if the UK (Israel's leading export destination at the time) were to join the EEC. This assertion can be justified based on an analysis of the anticipated effects of the CET (which was supposed to take effect in 1969), which shows that the CET was expected to adversely affect a large percentage of Israeli exports to both the EEC Six and the UK. Despite Kahn's (justified) pessimism, Israeli policymakers were not discouraged and continued their aggressive push for EEC Associate Membership or, at the very least, a PTA that would significantly expand Israel's access to EEC markets.

How successful was Kahn as an economic adviser to Israel? It is difficult to answer this question conclusively because there is no universally accepted criterion for evaluating the success of foreign economic advisers. We suggest three possible criteria for success (arranged in order from the strictest to the least strict): (a) implementation of the adviser's recommendations (Edwards 2005; Seers 1962), (b) serious consideration of the adviser's views but no implementation (Bronfenbrenner 1963), and (c) a contribution to helping government officials attain greater clarity on economic issues, but without serious consideration or implementation (Seers 1962). While Kahn's recommendations were never implemented, and most probably did not receive serious consideration, he almost certainly helped his interlocutors to improve their understanding of economic issues. It is only in this limited sense that Kahn can be considered successful as an economic adviser to Israel.

References

Artstein, Y., & Sussman, Z. (1977). *Wage and price controls and the effectiveness of devaluations: The Israeli experience*. Unpublished Working Paper, Bank of Israel.

Backhouse, E., & Forder, J. (2013). Rationalizing incomes policy in Britain, 1948–1979. *History of Economic Thought and Policy, 1*, 17–35.

Becker, A. (1960). The work of the General Federation of Labour in Israel. *International Labor Review, 81*, 436–455.

Bonne, A. (Ed.). (1958). *The challenge of development*. Papers of a Symposium Held in Jerusalem. Eliezer Kaplan School of Economics and Social Science, Hebrew University, Jerusalem.

Braun, A. (1976). Indexation of wages and salaries in developed economies. *IMF Staff Papers, 23*, 226–271.

Bronfenbrenner, M. (1963). Balm for the visiting economist. *Journal of Political Economy, 7*, 293–297.

Bruno, M. (1964). The use of national accounting frameworks for economic policy and development forecasting: A survey of Israel's research experience 1958–61. *Review of Income and Wealth, 10*, 1–22.

Bruno, M., & Sussman, Z. (1979). Exchange rate flexibility, inflation and structural change: Israel under alternative regimes. *Journal of Development Economics, 6*, 483–514.

Cohen, R., et al. (1964). Statement submitted by R. Cohen, R. Kahn, W. Reddaway and J. Robinson to the Committee on Resale Price Maintenance. *Bulletin of the Oxford University Institute of Economics and Statistics, 26*, 113–121.

Committee of Experts to Examine the CLA. (1966). *Report*. Tel Aviv: Histadrut (Labor Federation) and Industrialists' Association [in Hebrew].

Creamer, D., et al. (1957). *Israel's national income, 1950–1954*. Falk Project for Economic Research and Central Bureau of Statistics Special Series, n. 57, Jerusalem.

Economic Planning Authority, State of Israel. (1962). *A proposal for establishing goals and principles for a development plan for the four years 1963/64–1966/67* (Draft). Jerusalem [in Hebrew].

Edwards, S. (2005). *Establishing credibility: The role of foreign advisors* (NBER Working Paper 11429).

Evans, M. (1970). An econometric model of the Israeli economy, 1952–1965. *Econometrica, 38*, 624–660.

Fellner, W., et al. (1961). *The problem of rising prices*. Paris: Organization for European Economic Cooperation.

Friedman, M., & Friedman, R. (1999). *Two lucky people*. Chicago: University of Chicago Press.

Gross, N. (2005). The social sciences at the Hebrew University until 1948/9: Plans and beginnings. In H. Lavsky (Ed.), *The history of the Hebrew University of Jerusalem: A period of consolidation and growth*. (Vol. 2). Jerusalem: Magnes Press [in Hebrew].

Gross, N., & Greenberg, Y. (1994). *Bank Hapoalim: The first fifty years*. Tel Aviv: Am Oved [in Hebrew]

Halevi, N. (1957). The Israeli Labor Movement. *Annals of the American Academy of Political and Social Science, 310* (1), 172–181.

Halevi, N. (1969). Economic policy discussion and research in Israel. *American Economic Review, 59*, 74–118.

Halevi, N. (2006). The development in Israel of the concept of economic independence. *Israel Economic Review, 4*, 7–11 [in Hebrew].

Halevi, N., et al. (1981). *Banker to an emerging nation: The history of Bank Leumi Le-Yisrael*. Jerusalem: Shikmona Publishing Company.

Harcourt, G., & Kerr, P. (2009). *Joan Robinson*. Basingstoke: Palgrave Macmillan.

Kahn, R. *Kahn Papers*. King's College Archive Centre, Cambridge University.

Kahn, R. (1947–1948). Tariffs and the terms of trade. *Review of Economic Studies, 15*, 14–19.

Kahn, R. (1948, May 6). The 1948 budget: An economist's criticisms. *The Listener*, pp. 738–739.

Kahn, R. (1949a, February 3). Our economic complacency. *The Listener*, pp. 166–167, 181.

Kahn, R. (1949b). A possible intra-European payments scheme. *Economica, 16*, 293–304.

Kahn, R. (1950a). *The dollar shortage and devaluation*. Reprinted in Kahn (1972), pp. 35–59.

Kahn, R. (1950b). The European payments union. *Economica, 17*, 306–316.

Kahn, R. (1951). Home and export trade. *Economic Journal, 61*, 276–289.

Kahn, R. (1952a). International regulation of trade and exchanges. In *Banking and foreign trade* (5th International Banking Summer School, Oxford). London: Institute of Bankers, Europa Publications.

Kahn, R. (1952b). *Monetary policy and the balance of payments*. Reprinted in Kahn (1972), pp. 60–71.

Kahn, R. (1952c). Comments II. *Bulletin of the Oxford University Institute of Economics and Statistics, 14*, 147–153.

Kahn, R. (1956a). *Full employment and British economic policy, Nihon Keizei Shimbun*. Reprinted in Kahn (1972), pp. 97–102.
Kahn, R. (1956b, May 3 and 10). Lord Keynes and contemporary economic problems. *The Listener*. Reprinted in Kahn (1972), pp. 103–123.
Kahn, R. (1957a). The free trade proposals a symposium: A positive contribution? *Bulletin of the Oxford University Institute of Economics and Statistics, 19* (1), 63–68. Reprinted in Worswick (1960), pp. 61–66.
Kahn, R. (1957b, February 28). Doubts about the free trade area. *The Listener*, pp. 331–333.
Kahn, R. (1958a). *The pace of development*, in Bonne (1958), pp. 163–198. Reprinted in Kahn (1972), pp. 153–191.
Kahn, R. (1958b). *Memorandum of evidence submitted to the Radcliffe Committee*. Reprinted in Kahn (1972), pp. 124–152.
Kahn, R. (1963). Note on Short Visit to Israel in December, 1962. *Kahn Papers*, King's College, Cambridge University, 21/3/1.
Kahn, R. (1967). *The European Economic Community*. Speech before the House of Lords, House of Lords Historic Hansard, HL Deb 08 May 1967, Vol. 282, cc1197-300.
Kahn, R. (1972). *Selected essays on employment and growth*. Cambridge: Cambridge University Press.
King, J. (2009). *Nicholas Kaldor*. Basingstoke: Palgrave Macmillan.
Kleiman, E. (1981). Israel: Economists in a new state. *History of Political Economy, 13*, 548–579.
Kleiman, E., & Ophir, T. (1975). The effects of changes in the quantity of money on prices in Israel, 1955–1965. *Bank of Israel Review, 42*, 14–37 [in Hebrew].
Krampf, A. (2009). The coining of the expression "economic independence" in the Israeli economic discourse. *Iyunim Betkumat Yisrael, 19*, 1–34 [in Hebrew].
Krampf, A. (2010a). *Central banking in a developmental state: The case of the Bank of Israel in the postwar period*. Working Paper No. 23. Jerusalem Papers in Regulation and Governance, Hebrew University.
Krampf, A. (2010b). Economic planning of the free market in Israel during the first decade: The influence of Don Patinkin on Israeli policy discourse. *Science in Context, 23*, 507–534.
Kreinin, M. (1956). Controlled inflation in Israel, 1949–54. *Journal of Political Economy, 64*, 111–127.
Kreinin, M. (1958). Israel's export problem and its policy implications. *Southern Economic Journal, 25*, 202–212.
Kreinin, M. (1968). Israel and the European Economic Community. *Quarterly Journal of Economics, 82*, 297–312.
Kuznets, S. (2012). Jewish economies: Development and migration in America and beyond. In S. Lo & E. G. Weyl (Eds.), *The economic life of American Jewry* (Vol. 1). New Brunswick, NJ: Transaction Publishers.
Leeson, R. (2000). Patinkin, Johnson, and the shadow of Friedman. *History of Political Economy, 32*(4), 733–763.
Lerner, A. (1957). The Histadrut and the Israel economy. *Midstream, 3*(Autumn), 74–80.
Liviatan, O. (1982). *The development of the CLA and a test of the frequency of wage adjustments to prices*. Bank of Israel Research Department Discussion Paper, 9–82 [in Hebrew].
Liviatan, N. (2002). Remarks on the monetary history of Israel against the background of world trends. *Economic Quarterly, 49*(1), 9–29 [in Hebrew].
Marcuzzo, C. (1988). *Richard F. Kahn: A disciple of Keynes*. Working Paper, Department of Political Economy, University of Modena.
Marcuzzo, C. (2012). The "elusive figure who hides in the preface of Cambridge books": An appraisal of Richard Kahn's contributions. In C. Gehrke et al. (Eds.), *Classical economics versus modern theories: Essays in honour of Heinz D. Kurz* (Vol. 2, pp. 185–206). Oxford: Routledge.
Michaely, M. (1961). Capital imports to Israel: Sources, magnitude and significance. *Economic Quarterly, 31*, 217–242 [in Hebrew].

Michaely, M. (1975). *Foreign trade regimes and economic development: Israel*. New York: National Bureau of Economic Research.

Miller, R. (2004). The PLO factor in Euro-Israeli relations, 1964–1992. *Israel Affairs, 10*, 123–155.

Nelson, E. (2009). Milton Friedman and U.K. economic policy: 1938–1979. *Federal Reserve Bank of St. Louis Review, 91*(5 (Part 2)), 465–506.

Palestine Post. (1944, September 25). Obituary for Augustus Kahn.

Pardo, S., & Peters, J. (2012). *Israel and the European Union: A documentary history*. Lanham, MD: Lexington Books.

Patinkin, D. *Patinkin papers*. David M. Rubenstein Rare Book and Manuscript Library, Duke University.

Patinkin, D. (1962, March 21). Professor Patinkin's letter to the Governor of the Bank of Israel. *Herut* (Newspaper) [in Hebrew].

Patinkin, D. (1967). *The Israel economy: The first decade*. Jerusalem: Maurice Falk Institute for Economic Research in Israel.

Patinkin, D. (1982). *Anticipations of the general theory? And other essays on Keynes*. Chicago: University of Chicago Press.

Patinkin, D. (1994). From Chicago to Jerusalem. *Economic Quarterly, 41*(2), 165–195 [in Hebrew].

Patinkin, D. (1995). The training of an economist. *Banca Nazionale del Lavoro Quarterly Review, 48*, 359–395.

Patinkin, D., & Leith, J. (Eds.). (1978). *Keynes, Cambridge, and the general theory: The process of criticism and discussion connected with the development of the general theory*. London: Macmillan.

Pasinetti, L. (1991). Richard Ferdinand Kahn, 1905–1989. *Proceedings of the British Academy, 76*, 432–443.

Pasinetti, L. (1994). Richard Kahn. 10 August 1905-6 June 1989. *Cambridge Journal of Economics, 18*, 3–6.

Pasinetti, L. (2007). *Keynes and the Cambridge Keynesians*. Cambridge: Cambridge University Press.

Pesaran, M., & Harcourt, G. (2000). Life and work of John Richard Nicholas Stone 1913–1991. *Economic Journal, 110*, 146–165.

Plunkett, M. (1958). The Histadrut: The General Federation of Jewish Labor in Israel. *Industrial and Labor Relations Review, 11*, 155–182.

Pomfret, R. (1976). *Trade policies and industrialization in a small country: The case of Israel*. Tubingen: J.C.B. Mohr.

Pomfret, R., & Toren, B. (1980). *Israel and the European common market: An appraisal of the 1975 Free Trade Agreement*. Tubingen: J.C.B. Mohr.

Prager, J. (1986). Wage indexation and the Israeli Labor Market: The institutional imperative. *International Journal of Middle East Studies, 18*, 259–273.

Radian, A. (1984). The dynamics of policy formation: Income tax rates in Israel, 1948–1975. *Environment and Planning C: Government and Policy, 2*, 271–284.

Riemer, S. (1960). Israel: Ten years of economic dependence. *Oxford Economic Papers, 12*, 141–169.

Riemer, S. (1962). The devaluation of the Israel Pound. *Kyklos, 15*, 657–670.

Rochon, L. (2001). Cambridge's contribution to endogenous money: Robinson and Kahn on credit and money. *Review of Political Economy, 13*, 287–307.

Ronen, Y. (Ed.). (1964). *The economy of Israel: Theory and practice*. Tel Aviv: Dvir Publishing [in Hebrew].

Seers, D. (1962). Why visiting economists fail. *Journal of Political Economy, 70*, 325–338.

Sen Gupta, A. (1958). Appendix II: Survey of wage-price links in various countries. *IMF Staff Papers, 6*, 343–368.

Sitton, S., & Ravid, A. (1964). Israel and the European common market. In Y. Ronen (Ed.), *The economy of Israel: Theory and practice*. Tel Aviv: Dvir Publishing [in Hebrew].

Tabor, D. (1989). *Funeral for Richard Ferdinand Kahn*, Monday 12th June 1989 (9th Sivan 5749), typescript, archived at Cambridge Traditional Jewish Congregation, Cambridge, UK.

Toye, R. (2000). Gosplanners versus thermostatters: Whitehall planning debates and their political consequences, 1945–49. *Contemporary British History, 14*, 81–106.

Worswick, G. (Ed.). (1960). *The free trade proposals*. Oxford: Basil Blackwell.

Chapter 5
Politicization of Policy Prescriptions: Friedman and Israeli Economic Reform, 1977

5.1 Introduction

In May 1977, a political sea change took place in Israel, when the center-right Likud Party replaced the Labor Party that had ruled (in various incarnations) since 1948. The government in formation, led by Likud leader Menachem Begin, invited Milton Friedman, the 1976 Nobel Laureate in Economics, to serve as an unofficial economic policy adviser. Friedman visited Israel during 3–8 July 1977 and proposed a broad package of free market reforms. On 28 October 1977, the government announced an "economic revolution": It liberalized exchange controls, reduced export subsidies and import tariffs, and essentially floated the currency. Unfortunately, inflation accelerated and the trade balance deteriorated (see Figs. 5.1 and 5.2), forcing the government to largely reverse the "revolution" by mid-1979. Friedman's ideological opponents, both in Israel and abroad, held him responsible for Israel's disastrous economic performance; Friedman and his supporters denied responsibility.

Although Friedman's advisory role in Israel was highly publicized at the time, it has received little attention from academic economists. Other than Friedman himself (Friedman and Friedman 1999, 463–464), the only academic economists who mentioned this episode were Nadav Halevi and Yakir Plessner. Halevi (1979) viewed Friedman's visit as a true signal of a change in policy, while Plessner (1994, 220), on the other hand, argued that the Begin government used Friedman's visit to falsely signal a change in policy.

Their accounts, however, are too brief and general to answer the fundamental questions: What was Friedman's actual role in shaping the "economic revolution" of October 1977? For that matter, to what extent was he responsible for Israel's economic debacle of 1978–1979?

D. Schiffman et al., *The Role of Economic Advisers in Israel's Economic Policy*,
DOI 10.1007/978-3-319-60682-8_5

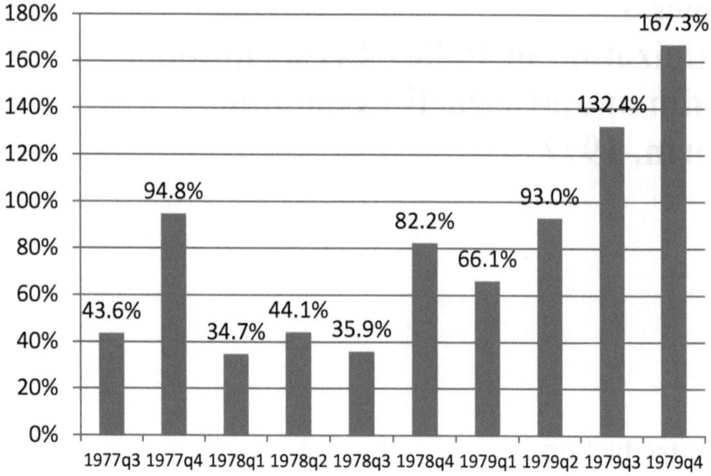

Fig. 5.1 Quarterly CPI Inflation (Annualized), 1977q3–1979q4

In this chapter, we provide, for the first time, an account of Friedman's involvement with Israel in 1977—his views on the Israeli economy, his activities in Israel, and his influence on government policy.[1] Our account is based on a wide range of primary sources in English and Hebrew: Friedman's personal papers, audio recordings, and publications; archive footage from US and Israeli television; and US and Israeli newspapers. We find that contrary to conventional wisdom, the "economic revolution" of October 1977 did not originate with Friedman. Rather, it was driven by two independent factors: Begin and Erlich's long-standing policy commitments and IMF conditionality. While Friedman was not to blame for Israel's economic debacle (as charged by J.K. Galbraith and other critics), he underemphasized or failed to anticipate the fatal flaws of the "economic revolution."

The remainder of this chapter is organized as follows: Sect. 5.2 surveys the state of the Israeli economy in mid-1977; Sects. 5.3–5.5 document Friedman's views, activities, and influence in Israel, both before and during his July 1977 visit; Sect. 5.6 discusses the "economic revolution" of October 1977; Sect. 5.7 documents the IMF's role in the "economic revolution"; Sect. 5.8 (Conclusion) explains the failure of the "economic revolution"; and Sect. 5.9 (Afterword) documents the evolution of Friedman's retrospective views regarding the 1977 visit and its aftermath.

[1]This chapter contributes to a small but growing literature on the activities and influence of eminent economists in foreign countries: Friedman in Australia (Courvisanos and Millmow 2006), Robinson in Australia (Millmow 2009), Hayek in Chile (Caldwell and Montes 2014), Friedman in Chile (Montes 2016), and Kahn in Israel (Schiffman 2014).

5.2 The Israeli Economy in Mid-1977: A Primer

In this section, we present a primer on the state of the Israeli economy in mid-1977.

Per Capita GDP When Likud came to power in May 1977, it inherited an economy whose per capita GDP in 1976 was 59% of US per capita GDP and 79% of per capita GDP in the twelve leading Western European economies (Maddison Project Database 2013).

Growth and Unemployment Israel was already a few years into its "Lost Decade" (1974–1984)—a decade of "low growth, high inflation and financial crises amid policy seesawing" (Barkai and Liviatan 2007, 10). Due to the Yom Kippur War and the 1973 energy shock, both real GDP growth and per capita GDP growth slowed dramatically, from 11.9% and 8.9% (respectively) in 1972 to 1.4% and −0.3% in 1976 (Kleiman 1986). Productivity growth fell from 4.3% during 1961–1972 to 0.1% during 1973–1981 (Metzer 1986). Nevertheless, official (male) unemployment remained low, rising to just 3.1% in 1976 (Ben-Porath 1986).

Inflation The first oil shock, which followed the October 1973 Yom Kippur War, marked a major transition in the inflationary process. The period 1970–October 1973 was characterized by demand-pull inflation, at an average rate of 14%, vs. 5.5% in the industrialized nations. The first oil shock, which increased Israel's fuel costs by 277% from 1973 to 1974 (Halevi 1986), precipitated a cost-push inflation (to which higher defense expenditures and higher commodity prices also contributed); inflation rose to an average of 36% over October 1973–May 1977, vs. 11% in the industrialized nations (Barkai 2002). However, inflation was slowing when Likud came to power, from a 46% annual rate in the second half of 1976 to a 19% annual rate during January–May 1977.

Labor Relations The economy was dominated by the government and the Histadrut-General Federation of Labor. The government was "the country's executive arm, its largest employer, initiator of laws dealing with labor relations, and both negotiator and partner in labor disputes" (Tzabag 1995). The Histadrut was "the second-largest employer in the country, representative of the workers, and [after May 1977—authors] the only executive arm of the now oppositional Labor Party" (Tzabag 1995).

Fiscal Policy The "Lost Decade" was a period of "fiscal dominance." That is, macroeconomic policy was conducted according to fiscal targets, without a nominal target (Barkai and Liviatan 2007, 4, 10). Government expenditure, the budget deficit, and the public debt expanded dramatically between 1972 and 1976; almost all of the expenditure increase was attributable to defense, transfer payments, and subsidies (Table 5.1). Due to a severe deterioration in the BOP (reflected in the dramatic deterioration in Israel's net asset position in 1974–1975; see Table 5.3), the first Rabin government (1974–1977) was forced to implement a sharp fiscal contraction, which reduced the budget deficit from 21% of GDP in 1975 to 9.9% of GDP in 1976; this was almost entirely achieved by means of higher tax revenues

Table 5.1 Fiscal indicators, 1970–1980 (% of GDP)

	Expenditures	Of which: net domestic defense consumption	Of which: direct defense imports	Of which: transfer payments + general subsidies + credit subsidies	Receipts	Of which: tax receipts	Deficit (−)	Of which: domestically financed	Net public debt
1970	58.9	13.7	11.4	14.6	46.7	36.2	−12.2	−1.7	
1971	59.0	14.3	8.8	16.6	50.1	40.4	−8.9	−1.1	
1972	58.9	12.1	8.2	17.2	48.1	37.9	−10.8	−4.0	
1973	73.7	14.6	17.0	21.0	60.1	38.3	−13.6	−10.5	
1974	74.9	17.4	12.4	24.2	56.2	41.6	−18.7	−12.8	92.1
1975	80.1	16.2	16.2	26.8	59.1	40.9	−21.0	−14.3	109.4
1976	79.6	14.7	14.0	29.0	69.7	47.7	−9.9	−7.4	122.8
1977	76.1	13.8	9.0	30.2	61.6	45.4	−14.4	−11.3	124.2
1978	77.6	13.1	12.7	26.7	60.5	43.1	−17.1	−10.7	135.8
1979	75.5	13.5	7.5	27.6	65.3	45.5	−10.3	−10.9	131.4
1980	75.9	13.6	9.6	28.3	61.1	42.7	−14.8	−11.9	131.7

Source: Bank of Israel (Net Public Debt is from Sargent and Zeira (2011), who cite the Bank of Israel Research Department as their source)

Table 5.2 Summary balance of payments (% of GDP)

	Exports	Imports	Trade balance	Net unilateral transfers	Net long-term capital inflow	Net short-term capital inflow
1970	24.3	46.2	−21.9	11.3	11.8	−0.2
1971	31.4	51.8	−20.4	13.2	10.6	−4.5
1972	29.3	43.7	−14.4	14.0	9.7	−9.8
1973	29.5	56.4	−26.9	23.0	9.9	−5.7
1974	27.2	51.7	−24.5	13.2	4.4	9.6
1975	27.9	56.9	−29.1	13.4	7.8	4.7
1976	31.2	53.0	−21.8	15.7	8.8	0.4
1977	37.7	54.0	−16.3	14.2	7.1	−3.8
1978	47.4	69.7	−22.3	16.1	8.0	−2.8
1979	44.1	64.1	−20.1	15.3	6.6	3.0
1980	47.2	65.4	−18.2	14.3	5.8	1.0

Source: Authors' calculations, using Table 1 of Halevi (1986) and GDP in US dollars from IMF World Economic Outlook Database (September 2000)

(Table 5.1). The fiscal contraction, combined with devaluations under the crawling peg (to be described below), narrowed the trade deficit from 29.1% of GDP in 1975 to 16.3% of GDP in 1977 (Table 5.2). However, the Rabin government backed away from this policy in the first half of 1977; fiscal and monetary expansion led to increased private consumption and (as expected) a deterioration in the trade balance (Gafny 1977).

Monetary Policy The Bank of Israel (henceforth BOI) was completely subservient to the government and consequently lacked control over the nominal instruments of monetary policy. The BOI was forced to partially monetize the fiscal deficit; over 1974–1976, BOI credit to the government averaged 3% of GDP. The BOI was also charged with administering the government's directed credit (DC) program, which accounted for 35% of bank credit in mid-1977 (down from 47% in 1976) (Barkai 2002) and financed 39% of gross industrial investment in 1973–1975 (Meyshar 1986). DC was heavily subsidized: During 1976–1977, the real interest rate on DC was −13% or lower (Barkai 2002). The implicit inflation subsidy on government loans was 4% of GDP in 1975 (and rising), while seigniorage revenues were 2–2.5% of GDP. Thus, the net inflation tax was negative (Barkai and Liviatan 2007, 183).

Exchange Rate Regime Israel's currency unit was the Israeli pound (Hebrew: Lira; henceforth IL). After devaluing the IL by 43% (from IL 4.20/$ to IL 6/$) in November 1974, the government decided in June 1975 to replace the adjustable peg regime with a US dollar crawling peg, with a maximum monthly devaluation of 2%.[2] Under the adjustable peg (1948–1975), infrequent large formal devaluations

[2]See Bruno and Z. Sussman (1979) and http://www.boi.org.il/en/Markets/ForeignCurrencyMarket/Pages/shearim48-77.aspx.

had been supplemented by frequent use of "devaluation substitutes"—changes in taxes and subsidies on imports, exports, and other international transactions. The acceleration of inflation in 1974–1975 necessitated more frequent formal devaluations, thus making the adjustable peg untenable (Halevi 1986). It is important to bear in mind that even after the adjustable peg was abolished, taxes on international transactions remained in place; these taxes created a system of multiple exchange rates. From June 1975 to June 1976, the currency was devalued by close to 2% per month, with the exception of a special 10% devaluation in September 1975 (which was intended to counteract the dollar's appreciation against European currencies). In July 1976, the government switched from a US dollar crawling peg to an export-weighted basket crawling peg; in practice, the rate of monthly devaluation remained close to 2%. The crawling peg regime signaled the government's willingness to accept 30–40% annual inflation (Barkai and Liviatan 2007, 157).[3]

Current Account Over 1974–1977, the export/GDP ratio grew steadily from 27.2% to 37.7%, while the import/GDP ratio rose from 51.7% to 54%. The trade deficit/GDP ratio was a massive 21.8% in 1976, but the current account deficit/GDP ratio was considerably smaller due to net unilateral transfers of 15.7% of GDP (Table 5.2); these unilateral transfers consisted largely of US foreign aid (which accounted for roughly half of long-term unilateral transfers; see Halevi 1986) and contributions by US Jewry. Over 1974–1977, foreign currency liabilities (both gross and net) expanded rapidly, and the share of short-term liabilities increased (Table 5.3). This shift was driven by greater foreign borrowing by Israeli banks and a decline in foreign currency reserves (Halevi 1986).

Investment and Saving Gross investment was 30% of GDP before 1975 and then declined to 24.7% in 1978–1982 (vs. an average of 22% in countries similar to Israel). The capital/output ratio rose in the mid-1970s, which implies overinvestment. The government-controlled financial sector misallocated investment in housing and public services. Private saving as a percentage of GDP was at a reasonable level, falling from 35.3% in 1973–1977 to 30.5% in 1978–1982 (Meyshar 1986).

Key Reforms The Rabin government introduced an employers' tax of 4% on 30 March 1975. In July 1975, it announced a comprehensive income tax reform, based on the recommendations of the Ben-Shahar Committee. Marginal tax rates on middle and high incomes were reduced and compulsory loans abolished; the tax base was broadened to include payments to workers categorized as expenses and benefits; personal exemptions were abolished, and child allowances were integrated into a new, unified system of credits and allowances; and credits, allowances, and

[3]Friedman reacted as follows: "I am for a free market in the IL … But if a devaluation [is unavoidable], a crawling devaluation is preferable to a large, one-time devaluation." (Transcript of Israel Radio Interview [Hebrew], November 26, 1976; in Talking Points [for 1977 general election], Likud Publicity Dept., Begin Papers Folder OP-016.

Table 5.3 External assets and liabilities (% of GDP, unless otherwise noted)

	Assets	Liabilities	Of which: short-term liabilities	Of which: long-term liabilities	Short-term liabilities as a % of total liabilities	Net liabilities	Bank of Israel foreign currency reserves	Net assets = actual foreign currency reserves = assets-short-term liabilities
1970	14.7	57.3	10.6	46.8	18.4	42.6	6.1	4.2
1971	26.5	79.6	26.1	53.6	32.7	53.1	9.2	0.5
1972	37.4	74.1	24.8	49.2	33.5	36.7	14.7	12.6
1973	40.6	72.5	24.3	48.2	33.5	31.9	18.5	16.3
1974	24.4	63.9	21.5	42.3	33.7	39.4	8.2	2.9
1975	26.8	76.7	27.0	49.7	35.2	49.9	7.9	−0.2
1976	28.9	83.2	26.5	56.7	31.9	54.3	8.2	2.4
1977	34.3	93.5	31.1	62.4	33.3	59.2	9.3	3.2
1978	51.6	117.6	44.2	73.4	37.6	66.0	16.0	7.4
1979	46.6	107.5	44.4	63.1	41.3	60.9	15.3	2.2
1980	49.3	106.8	46.4	60.4	43.4	57.5	13.7	2.9

Source: Authors' calculations, using Table 5 of Halevi (1986) and GDP in US dollars from IMF World Economic Outlook Database (September 2000)

tax brackets were indexed to the CPI (Ben-Porath and Bruno 1977; see also Yitzhaki 1986).

Concurrently, the government implemented a cost-of-living allowance [CLA] reform, based on the recommendations of the Sussman Committee. The indexation rate was reduced from 100% to 70%; CLA payments were made at 6-month intervals (instead of ad hoc payments), provided that prices had increased by at least 5% since the last payment (instead of 3%); the CPI was used as the basis for the CLA (instead of the CPI excluding housing); and the partial tax exemption of CLA payments was canceled (Shiffer 2004). Despite the reform, real wage protection via the CLA remained incomplete. Nevertheless, real wages could (and did subsequently) rise, as increases in other wage components overcompensated for the CLA-related real wage erosion (Kleiman 1986; Shiffer 2004). Real wages rose by 2% in 1976 after falling by 2.8% and 2.1% in 1974 and 1975, respectively (Kleiman 1986).

The government also introduced an 8% VAT on 1 July 1976, based on the recommendations of the 1972 Asher Committee. The government was motivated by the need for a quick and easy source of additional tax revenue and by the rapid rise of the VAT in Western Europe.[4]

5.3 Israel Turns to Friedman (May 1977)

In early 1977, Milton Friedman agreed to accept an honorary doctorate from the Hebrew University, to be conferred in Jerusalem the following July.[5] The parliamentary election of 17 May 1977 brought about a seismic change in the political landscape (known as the "political revolution" in Israeli discourse[6]): Menachem Begin and his Likud Party came to power, ending a 29-year period of uninterrupted Labor Party rule. It was well known that Begin planned to appoint his close friend, MK Simha Erlich, as finance minister. Erlich was second to Begin on the Likud Knesset slate and headed the free market Liberal faction, which was traditionally supported by businessmen and independent farmers.[7] He had played a key role in

[4]During 1967–1973, twelve Western European nations adopted the VAT (tabulated from Ebrill et. al 2001, 9–12).

[5]Hebrew University announced the honorary degree at the end of March. It was Don Patinkin who suggested conferring this honor upon Friedman (Friedman and Friedman 1999, 463). Patinkin also helped draft the University's letter of invitation and defended Friedman from leftist faculty who sought to rescind the invitation because of Friedman's March 1975 visit to Chile (Patinkin Papers, Box 38).

[6]The word "revolution" should not be taken literally; it is our best attempt to translate the Hebrew word *Mahapach*, which has no precise English translation.

[7]Following the 1977 election, Likud had 45 members of Knesset (MKs), which were divided among its various factions as follows: Begin's Herut, 20; Erlich's Liberals, 15; La'am, 8; Ariel Sharon's Shlomzion (which ran independently but merged with Likud after the election), 2.

drafting Likud's economic platform (Likud Party 1977), which had promised disinflation, faster growth, reduction of the BOP deficit, privatization, and extensive free market reforms. Immediately after the election, Liberal MK Gideon Patt,[8] who would soon be appointed minister of housing, suggested that Erlich invite Friedman to advise the government that was about to be formed. With Erlich's approval, Patt telephoned Friedman and invited him on Erlich's behalf (Friedman to Stanley Goldstein, Milton Friedman Papers [henceforth MFP] 197/1). Friedman accepted and extended his stay in Israel in order to hold consultations with government officials (Friedman and Friedman 1999, 463).[9]

On May 22, Erlich, during his first post-election press conference, announced that Friedman would advise the new government. Erlich's protégé MK Yehezkel Flomin (who would soon be appointed deputy finance minister) explained Likud's choice of Friedman to the US Embassy's political officer, who cabled Washington as follows: "Aware that Friedman's philosophy represents extreme laissez faire, Flomin said he was chosen so as to invest the Likud's idea for liberalizing Israel's economy with the prestige of Friedman's name. 'We had to pick someone who represents a 180 degree turn-about from Israel's present course in the hope that we will eventually end up somewhere in between'" (US State Department 1977a).

At this press conference, Erlich also presented an economic plan, which was mostly consistent with Likud's economic platform (Likud Party 1977). It consisted of the following measures:

- Reduce inflation by almost half.
- Cut $531 million from the $15 billion budget proposal for Fiscal Year 1977–1978 (a 3.5% cut) by cutting defense spending and subsidies to industry and reducing the number of government ministries from 18 to 14.
- Introduce compulsory arbitration of labor disputes in essential services.
- Cut 6000–10,000 government jobs but increase National Insurance transfer payments.
- Gradually reduce subsidies on basic foods.
- Privatize government companies.
- Continue the policy of devaluing the Israeli pound while introducing compensation for foreign investors.
- Abolish the travel tax of almost $100 per passenger.
- Rent out rather than sell government-constructed apartments.
- Offer amnesty to tax evaders (tax evasion cost the government an estimated $1 billion per year).

(Associated Press 1977a)

Meanwhile, Friedman prepared for his advisory role by consulting with two Israeli economists—Michael Bruno of the Hebrew University and Reuven Brenner, a University of Chicago postdoc who had worked at the BOI during 1974–1975.

---

[8]Patt had met Friedman in 1969 (Blitzer 1977a).

[9]During the 1970s, Friedman visited the following countries (besides Israel): Yugoslavia (1973), Italy (1973–academic activities only), Australia (1975; see Millmow and Courvisanos 2006), South Africa (1976), Rhodesia (1976), Chile (1975), and the UK (1970, 1974, 1978; see Nelson 2009). His first meeting with Margaret Thatcher took place during the 1978 UK visit.

Brenner offered the following historical perspective: "Remembering Abba Lerner's experience in Israel [as adviser to the government in 1953–1956; see Chap. 3 of this book—authors] (in different reports I have read, his name always appeared in a footnote objecting to the plan accepted by the other members of the particular committee. And how right he was!), I wish you better luck" (Reuven Brenner to Friedman, May 26, 1977, MFP 84/4).

How did Friedman view the role that he was about to play in Israel? The following statements are highly instructive [authors' emphasis]:

> I will make a contribution. I would be delighted to if I could. But you know, *people ask for advice from people who they know will give them the advice they want to hear.* Well, there's no shortage of good economists in Israel … They know what to do … [The Likud] party … proclaims its belief in private enterprise. It proclaims its desire to reduce the size of government and to give greater opportunities to individuals. *Their objectives are excellent. I hope they achieve them. I'm not wholly confident that they will. In fact, I have many doubts about whether they will succeed …* (Friedman 1977b)

> … *I believe that I can be most useful simply by providing some respectability and prestige to their economic program.* Moreover … *I am not very optimistic about very favorable results* since by this time the various forms of governmental subsidization have gone so far that *it is hard for me to see where there is any kind of constituency for a true free-market policy for Israel.*
> (Friedman to Micha Gisser, 10 June 1977, MFP 197/1)

In short, Friedman saw Likud as strongly and sincerely committed to free market policies. However, he doubted Likud's ability to overcome the opposition of vested interests and actually implement his recommendations.

5.4 The Unemployment Controversy (May–June 1977)

With the official unemployment rate at 3.5–4%, many observers, including Erlich, saw significant hidden unemployment, especially in the public sector. In March 1977, with the general election campaign in full swing, Erlich advocated a deliberate increase of up to one percentage point in the unemployment rate and promised that if elected, Likud would perform "a painful surgery," followed by a lengthy recovery which the public would accept "with love" (*Davar*, 13 March 1977). In late April, Erlich went so far as to say that a 0.5–1 percentage point increase in unemployment was a precondition for healing the economy. By increasing unemployment, the government would generate improved worker discipline and overcome its labor relations problems. Erlich added that he was unafraid to advocate an unpopular policy just two-and-a-half weeks before the election (*Davar*, 2 May 1977).

On May 15, two days before the general election, Israel Television hosted a debate between Begin and his Labor opponent, Peres. Begin promised not to solve the inflation problem by causing unemployment, to which Peres retorted that Begin's declaration was inconsistent with the views of Erlich, who had declared that unemployment was a necessary evil for curing the economy's illnesses (*Davar*, 16 May 1977).

Immediately following its historic upset victory in the general election of May 17, the Likud faced a new political challenge: The Histadrut leadership election of June 21. Its nominee for secretary-general was MK David Levy (of Begin's Herut faction), whose economic ideology was far to the left of Erlich's. The incumbent MK Yerucham Meshel (Labor) ran a spirited campaign; after being humiliated in the general election, Labor could not afford to lose control of the Histadrut. On May 24, Erlich, now the presumptive finance minister, made a 180-degree turn: He promised on national television to reduce the number of unemployed, thus aligning himself with Begin (*Davar*, 25 May 1977).

That same day, the Israeli newspapers *Davar* and *Yediot Aharonot* published lengthy interviews with Friedman (Barnea 1977; Kiviti 1977), who had the following to say regarding unemployment and the labor market (authors' translation):

> Q: What is your view regarding unemployment?
> A: In my view, there must be a free labor market and a certain amount of unemployment must influence people in the transition from one job to another. When there is no unemployment, that is a waste, because there isn't sufficient flexibility in transitioning from job to job. There is no mobility.
> Q: But in Israel the government cannot fire workers …
> A: That is very bad. In many countries you cannot fire [government employees]. Israel is not unique in that [respect]. But these are very bad laws and they cause more damage than benefit.
> Q: But in Israel, [unemployment] is a sacred cow …
> A: Perhaps [unemployment] is a sacred cow, but sometimes you get buried by what the cows produce.
> (Barnea 1977)

> Q: Can the inflation rate, which is now 40% per year, be reduced?
> A: Of course. There are many precedents. Japan, which suffered from hyperinflation after the War, did [disinflation] in a dramatic way, by means of monetary reform. The question is not whether it is possible to reduce inflation but whether Israel can afford not to do so … The experience of other nations proves without any doubt that high inflation in and of itself causes unemployment. Israel's [feasible] choice is reduced inflation, with adjusted unemployment during the transition period. There is no possibility of stopping inflation without unemployment. In both Germany and Japan inflation was reduced without a significant impact on unemployment.
> (Kiviti 1977)

In the *Davar* interview, Friedman recommended a deliberate and permanent increase in Israel's rate of unemployment (the word "permanent" is implicit), on the grounds that greater unemployment promotes greater labor mobility and thus greater efficiency.[10] While Friedman's main point was clear, he left his readers with two unanswered questions, which could only be answered by professional economists: (a) What is the link between labor mobility and efficiency? (b) Friedman implicitly assumes that the efficiency gains associated with higher

[10]Friedman made the same point in the *Jerusalem Post* (Blitzer 1977a).

unemployment outweigh the socioeconomic costs. What is the basis for this assumption?

In the *Yediot Aharonot* interview, Friedman urged Israeli policymakers to accept higher short-run unemployment as an unavoidable consequence of disinflation. Here too, Friedman left his readers with two unanswered questions, which could be answered only by professional economists: (a) It is unclear why "high inflation in and of itself causes unemployment," unless the reader is familiar with Friedman's Nobel Lecture (Friedman 1976), which offers a hypothesis to explain the (then) recently observed positive correlation between inflation and unemployment. (b) The last two sentences appear to be contradictory. The ostensible contradiction must be resolved in accordance with Friedman's Expectations-Augmented Phillips Curve: In the short run, disinflation is inevitably associated with higher unemployment (unless the disinflation is 100% credible), but there is no such tradeoff in the long run, as demonstrated by the German and Japanese cases.

To sum up, Friedman simultaneously offered two different justifications for increased unemployment, one of which supported a permanent—albeit small—rise in unemployment. However, he presented both justifications in a manner that was largely incomprehensible to the general Israeli public. This lack of clarity was uncharacteristic of Friedman, who was renowned for his extraordinary ability to popularize economic ideas (Burgin 2013).

Friedman's remarks caused a firestorm of controversy. As the *Jewish Telegraphic Agency* reported on May 25 (1977c),

> Meir Tzaban of the left-wing Sheli movement immediately called for a meeting of the Histadrut Executive to discuss Friedman's recommendations on unemployment. The left-wing group also noted that Friedman was an adviser to the Chilean junta [in March 1975] … Histadrut leaders also stressed that they would not allow Friedman's views on unemployment to be applied in Israel. This brought a statement today from David Levy, Likud's candidate for Histadrut Secretary-General, that a Likud-led Histadrut will not allow increased unemployment and will not allow the government to abolish the cost-of-living allowances or to abolish subsidies to essential commodities.

Levy also declared that Friedman "can advise on some issues but he will not make Likud policy" (Torgerson 1977).

The Labor campaign exploited Friedman's remarks to the maximum. In an election advertisement (*Jerusalem Post* 1977a), Labor accused Likud of wanting "to capture control—in order to transform the Histadrut into an instrument of the capitalists. An instrument to carry out the programs of my Lords Simha Erlich and Milton Friedman: unemployment, reduction of essential services, lowering of the worker's standard of living." Meshel attacked Erlich for inviting Friedman and made the exaggerated claim that Erlich "wants to cure the economy by means of mass unemployment," especially among Histadrut members (*Davar*, 17 June 1977). Former Prime Minister Meir charged that "Erlich's first [public] message is unemployment. He wants to bring Milton Friedman, who is a Nobel Laureate, but has the most reactionary economic outlook, which has been rejected in the US and other countries" (*Davar*, 15 June 1977). Labor MK Yitzhak Navon argued that Friedman's plan to disinflate by causing unemployment would harm large families, immigrants and demobilized soldiers (*Davar*, 9 June 1977). Labor spokespeople also cited Friedman's pariah status within the international labor movement, due to his visit to Chile (*Davar*, 6 June 1977).

The Labor broadside forced Begin and Erlich to publicly repudiate Friedman's ideas on unemployment. At a Likud campaign rally on June 19, Begin denied any intention to cause unemployment and promised a new minimum wage law and a negotiated wage and price freeze. On June 21, the day of the Histadrut election, Erlich took office as finance minister. At the traditional transfer of power ceremony, outgoing Finance Minister Rabinowitz (Labor) "urged his successor to continue the effort to reduce inflation and foreign payments deficits but to reject the advice of American economist Milton Friedman which would lead to unemployment. In reply, Erlich promised to strive for full employment, adding that he does not believe in revolutions: Any new economic program would be implemented in stages" (US State Department 1977b). To underscore his point, he exclaimed: "Heaven forbid that a Jew should remain unemployed" (*Jerusalem Post* 1977b).[11]

Immediately after Labor's landslide victory (Labor 57%, Likud 28%), Meshel told the US ambassador to Israel that "the threats of reducing employment and of using Milton Friedman as a government adviser had frightened many workers who otherwise might have voted for the Likud" (US State Department 1977d). However, Flomin (2014) argues that Friedman's remarks had no impact on the election's outcome because Levy never had a realistic chance of winning.

Following the Histadrut election, Begin and Erlich continued to publicly oppose unemployment. On June 29, Erlich told the Manufacturers' Association that Likud disavowed the use of planned unemployment to reduce inflation and sought full employment in the long run. However, the economy needed "a surgery" to eliminate hidden unemployment in public services and labor shortages in industry. Regarding Friedman, Erlich said that there is nothing wrong with hearing the views of a brilliant economist, especially when there is no obligation to implement all of his advice (*Jewish Telegraphic Agency* 1977c; *Davar*, 30 June 1977).

The usually media-savvy Friedman had unwittingly injected himself into the Histadrut election campaign (of which he was unaware; Begin and Erlich obviously neglected to inform him). Friedman apparently realized his mistake; as soon

[11]However, in an English language interview published just 4 days before the Histadrut election, Erlich took a more positive view of planned unemployment and of Friedman. On unemployment: "It's either [controlled unemployment] or economic collapse … We have to get out of the rut, and it's not going to be a painless process. I don't come as an angel down from heaven, bringing balm to all. The economic body in Israel is sick. Surgery is needed, and that will hurt. The pain is part of the cure. For the next two or three years life will not be easy." On Friedman: "We had never thought of engaging him as an adviser. The administration already has an adviser, the Governor of the Bank of Israel…[However,] we plan to set up an economic advisory board, made up of serious-minded individuals. We shall mull over the country's problems at our meetings, and shall invite guests with special knowledge or challenging ideas to come and talk with us … Dr. Friedman has agreed to devote a fortnight each year to consultations with us. He is arriving for a first visit on July 4 [Erlich established an advisory board in August 1977, but Friedman had no connection with it—authors]." Erlich also dismissed the Chile-related attacks on Friedman (Krivine 1977).

as he arrived in Israel, he attempted to quell the controversy by softening his remarks.

Upon landing in Tel Aviv on July 3, Friedman was met by journalists at the airport. After stating that he knew nothing of the controversy that his visit had generated, he proceeded to address the inflation-unemployment tradeoff, as he had done in the May 24 *Yediot Aharonot* interview. He asserted that inflation can be reduced [in the short run] by cutting government spending and ending the printing of new money. The economy will then enter a transition period, which is generally characterized by higher unemployment. He concluded: "I do not recommend or encourage unemployment. It is a phenomenon that sometimes appears when stopping inflation is attempted …" (*Davar*, July 4).[12] Thus, Friedman attempted to quell the controversy by softening (but not abandoning) the Phillips Curve justification for higher unemployment.[13]

To sum up, Friedman's remarks on unemployment in Israel were a tactical blunder. Fairly or unfairly, they were widely interpreted as a call for permanently higher unemployment. This was politically unpalatable and an easy target for attack, given the strong local aversion to unemployment (which resulted from the traumatic 1965–1967 recession; see Fischer 1984). Friedman's remarks embarrassed Begin and Erlich at a politically sensitive time, to the extent that they were forced to distance themselves from Friedman's ideas. Thus, Friedman's potential influence was diminished even before he set foot in Israel.

5.5 Friedman's Visit to Israel (July 1977)

As expected, Begin appointed Erlich as finance minister and deputy prime minister. While Erlich lacked formal education and ministerial experience, he was a highly regarded political organizer. Erlich's protégé MK Flomin, an accountant and tax attorney, was appointed deputy finance minister. For the most part, Erlich retained the Finance Ministry officials who had served in the previous Labor government. Thus, Erlich ensured that his Ministry would continue to be staffed by qualified professionals, who were in short supply among Likud members. On the other hand, Erlich risked having his policies sabotaged by subordinates who were not personally loyal to him and did not share his economic ideology (Flomin 2014).

[12]On July 6, Friedman told Israel Television: "Unemployment is not a cure for inflation. But inflation is not a cure for unemployment." He also stated that curing an economy afflicted by inflation is similar to curing an alcoholic: A short-term rise in unemployment is the inevitable result of disinflation, just as the cure for alcoholism entails unavoidable short-term pain (Friedman 1977e).

[13]On this occasion, Friedman did not revisit the labor mobility justification for higher unemployment. But as we shall see, in his subsequent public statements, he unequivocally advocated reforms that would increase both labor mobility and unemployment.

Friedman came to Israel for six days (3–8 July 1977). On July 4, he delivered the keynote address at the Hebrew University's honorary degree ceremony, on the topic of capitalism, freedom, Jewish economic history, and the State of Israel. He concluded as follows:

> The true hope of Israel—and of freedom everywhere—is the enterprise, initiative, ingenuity, drive, and courage of the individual citizens, cooperating voluntarily with one another, producing that miracle of progress in every sphere that comes only from the achievements of the individual. The threat from your neighbors unfortunately mandates a large military effort on Israel. That effort must be coordinated and administered by government. You cannot escape having a sizable socialist sector. But that sector can remain, as it has been, relatively efficient, only so long as it is supported by a free people and a strong, productive, private economy.
> (Friedman 1977d)

The following day, Friedman made a seminar presentation at the Hebrew University economics department on "Floating Exchange Rates for Israel" (Friedman 1977c).[14] He argued that Israel should float the currency and abolish capital controls, for the following reasons:

a. Since the breakdown of the Bretton Woods system in 1973, Israel, like many other countries, is in the midst of a gradual but inevitable transition toward flexible exchange rates.
b. "Today's form of foreign exchange control was perfected in 1934, by Hjalmar Schacht, the German central banker, for the explicit purpose of despoiling the Jews of Germany."
c. The current system of capital controls is counterproductive: Israelis have a strong incentive to keep assets abroad, and illegal foreign bank accounts are rampant.
d. A new regime of flexible exchange rates and no capital controls will make possible "the abolition of the multiple exchange rates and the arbitrary subsidies and restrictions that are spread throughout your economy, and that waste your substantial capital."
e. Israel does not have a BOP problem, due to its close relationships with Diaspora Jewry and the US government.
f. Israel has the potential to replace Beirut as an international financial center.
g. Some fear that under the new regime, the outbreak of war will lead to capital flight and deterioration in the terms of trade. This fear is unwarranted.
h. Once Israel floats the currency and eliminates capital controls, "The exchange rate would settle down very rapidly … Any fears that somehow or other there would be a terrific attempted flow of capital out immediately are false … I would not be surprised if freeing exchange transactions would produce an inflow of capital." Currency speculation by private actors is stabilizing, but foreign exchange intervention by central banks is destabilizing.

[14]The seminar was advertised in the newspapers and open to the public.

On the policy front, Friedman met with Prime Minister Begin, Finance Minister Erlich, and other senior officials (including Housing Minister Patt), BOI Governor Gafny, the Knesset Finance Committee (State of Israel, Knesset Finance Committee 1977), and the leadership of major economic associations (industry, banking, agriculture, and the Histadrut[15]). He also gave an interview to Israel Television (Friedman 1977e).

In his various appearances, Friedman proposed "a wholesale transition to a relatively free and private market and a major reduction in the power and control of the government" (Friedman 1985a). Friedman's proposal included the following measures:

- Achieve zero inflation over 3–4 years. Implement a monetary growth rule based on 5% annual growth in potential output. Reduce money growth and the inflation tax ("a very bad tax") by cutting government spending. The government "should spend less money, it should print less money and it should interfere less in the economy."
- Float the Israeli pound and abolish exchange controls immediately (gradualism would lead to undesirable speculation).[16] Phase out import restrictions and export subsidies over 2–3 years (to give economic actors time to adjust to the new reality), and rely exclusively on the exchange rate for BOP adjustment. Thus, Israel will join the US and Hong Kong as the only countries with full exchange rate flexibility and no capital controls.
- Make an "extensive revision" of banking regulation—eliminate directed credit, simplify bank requirements, and allow free competition. Banking sector reform, together with currency liberalization and floating, can transform Israel into an international financial center.
- Abolish reduced income tax rates for export sector employees, subsidized development loans, and subsidized DC. Where subsidies are necessary, give them openly. Reform aid to development areas by replacing nonindexed loans with grants.
- Phase out renter protection laws.
- Eliminate hidden unemployment, reform housing regulations that impede labor mobility, and abolish legal restrictions on firing workers. Introduce a negative income tax. Reforms to the social welfare, housing, and employment systems should be made gradually, but "gradually" does not mean "standing still."
- Privatize government enterprises, except for defense industries, where government ownership may be unavoidable.
- Sell or lease state lands at market prices; index leases to the CPI.

[15]Meshel apparently did not participate.

[16]When Friedman was introduced to the Finance Ministry's Supervisor of Foreign Currency, he said with a laugh: "The first thing that you need to do is to fire this man" (Flomin 1978). This anecdote is consistent with Friedman's remarks at the Hebrew University seminar the day before: "The final requirement, establishing confidence in the continuance of freedom, is the hardest. There would be only one effective way to do that: eliminate and disband the agencies now charged with enforcing controls and manipulating exchange rates. In principle, that is the right thing to do—but you won't do it. And I recognize that I would be spitting in the wind to suggest that you should" (Friedman 1977a).

(Friedman 1977a, July 5; Friedman 1977e, July 6; State of Israel, Knesset Finance Committee (1977), *Davar*, July 7–8; Friedman to E. Magnus Oppenheim, 29 July 1977, MFP 197/1).[17]

On July 6, Friedman presented his economic philosophy and policy ideas to Erlich, Flomin, and other Finance Ministry officials. They all listened, but Erlich and Flomin did not reveal to Friedman that they were actively planning a reform (Friedman 1987a, b; Flomin 2014). Flomin (2014) elaborates:

> He [Friedman] wasn't informed about what we were going to do. He had no idea whatsoever … we wanted to see whether according to his philosophy we are doing something which [is] absolutely wrong … He wasn't given any indication that whatever we talked with him, we were checking ourselves not in theory but in real practice: Are we going on the right path or should we do some amendments … take some diversions, whatever? … We solicited advice indirectly, without revealing the main purpose. But we did it just to have a second opinion … We wanted to see if we are not making nonsense … you can do A which self-contradicts B; … we lacked the confidence that what we were doing was the right thing to do—not ideologically but from the technical aspect.

Why did Erlich and Flomin keep Friedman in the dark? Flomin (2014) explains that he and Erlich needed to maintain absolute secrecy, for fear of leaks and sabotage by their Labor-affiliated subordinates. For the same reason, Erlich and Flomin did not consult with any other economists: "… we didn't consult anyone deliberately, purposely … we didn't consult with anybody except—by accident—with Professor Friedman. If he were not here [already] then there would [have been] nothing … for sure. We took advantage of his visit."

The fear of leaks was not unwarranted. On the day after the meeting, *Davar* newspaper published a hostile report, based entirely on anonymous leaks (free translation):

> Professor Milton Friedman succeeded yesterday in embarrassing the leadership of the Finance Ministry. He repeated his advice to Israel, the main elements of which are: abolish currency controls, float the IL, abolish export subsidies and remove import restrictions.
>
> Senior Finance Ministry officials said that perhaps Friedman is correct in theory, but the economic mechanisms in Israel do not operate solely according to his theory. Friedman argued with the officials; he characterized them as conservative by nature and fearful of taking the risks that are necessary in order to implement his ideas. He acknowledged that

[17]Friedman had already advocated some of these measures during previous visits. In 1969, Friedman advocated currency liberalization and floating, abolishing tariffs, and making all subsidies transparent (Har Gil 1969). In 1972, Friedman advised Israel and other developing nations as follows: First-best policy—close the central bank and unify the currency with "a large, relatively stable developed country with which [the domestic country] has close economic relations." In Israel's case, this meant dollarization. Second-best policy—float the currency and adopt a monetary growth rule. Friedman recognized that his second-best policy "has far greater political feasibility in the present climate of opinion" (Friedman 1973, 59). He reiterated these points in the Israeli context during his Hebrew University seminar of 5 July 1977. Friedman's remark concerning the political infeasibility of currency unification proved to be prescient: In 1983, the government was forced to abandon its dollarization plan after it leaked to the media and encountered overwhelming opposition (Gross 2008, 110–111).

risk-taking is more difficult in Israel than it is elsewhere, but stated that these risks were a help, not an obstacle to the Israeli economy.

Other officials stated after the meeting that it is embarrassing to hear that a person who is in Israel for several days purports to solve all of Israel's economic problems, while Israeli officialdom has been "breaking its head" for years in an unsuccessful attempt to solve these problems. Friedman stuffs his ideas into the heads of the Finance Ministry leadership, without being sufficiently familiar with Israeli economic developments and problems. Some officials said that he gave the impression of being a frequent flyer who gives identical advice in every country; when he speaks, it is doubtful whether he knows which country he is advising![18]

Nevertheless, senior officials had gotten the impression that Friedman had succeeded in convincing Erlich and his closest aides.

(*Davar*, 7 July 1977)

Later that day, Friedman gave a half-hour long interview on Israel Television.[19] He described Erlich as "a very sympathetic, able and talented man. We had a very fruitful conversation." He continued: "The real question is, whether Mr. Erlich will be able to persuade the government as a whole, and the people as a whole, to go along with the right policies. The impression I have is that Mr. Erlich has a very real understanding of what needs to be done." When asked "What did you say to Mr. Erlich?", Friedman replied: "I won't answer the question in that form, but if you ask me about particular problems in the Israeli economy, I'll be glad to give answers" (Friedman 1977e).

On July 7, Erlich held a press conference. He declared that the government did not commit to following Friedman's prescriptions. Although some of his prescriptions are good for Israel, others are incompatible with Israel's economic structure. Erlich had submitted some of Friedman's policy prescriptions for evaluation (he did not say to whom), and the government would consider each prescription on its merits and decide whether or not to accept it (*Davar*, July 8).

Early on the morning of July 8, Begin met with Friedman for 90 minutes (US State Department 1977c); Friedman later described this meeting as "very long and friendly" (Friedman and Friedman 1999, 463). He recalled: "I was very much impressed by Begin, but I was also impressed with the fact that economics was a subject in which he had zero interest" (Friedman 1987a, b).[20] After meeting with

[18]Friedman did not deny this. He argued that Israel's economic problems were the same as in other countries such as the UK and Italy (Barnea 1977; Kiviti 1977). Apparently anticipating criticism on this point, he argued as follows: "When the doctor establishes that a child has rubella, he does not need to know the father's name in order to prescribe medicine. In principle, the problem is identical, only the details are different. Israel suffers from a very common disease" (Kiviti 1977). Meltzer (2011) sums up Friedman's modus operandi as an adviser to foreign countries: "In each of these countries, and many others, he gave the same general advice, modified in most countries by the institutional arrangements."

[19]Because the interview was broadcast in English without Hebrew subtitles, Friedman was unable to make his case directly to the Israeli public. However, *Davar* published a brief summary in Hebrew.

[20]Friedman likened Begin to Winston Churchill, who was "clearly a great man, but every time he touched an economic issue, he came down on the wrong side, from 1908 until he left office."

Begin, Friedman concluded his visit and returned to the US. He told the Associated Press (1977b) that his ideas "were well-received by the Likud Party" but he had "no great optimism they will be put into effect."

On July 17, Erlich announced his first policy measure: The government would cut $143 million in defense spending (approximately 1% of 1976 GDP), cut food and fuel subsidies by 25%, and devalue the IL by 2%.[21] The timing was no coincidence: Begin was to meet US President Jimmy Carter in Washington on July 19–20 and was expected to request $2.3 billion in US aid for Fiscal Year 1978 (a 30.5% increase from Fiscal Year 1977-authors) (Broder 1977). The Carter Administration was reportedly pressuring Israel to implement a fiscal adjustment or face a cut in US foreign aid (Ofner 1977); as Erlich told the Knesset, the Israeli people must demonstrate to President Carter and the American people that they were "making demands on themselves" (*Jewish Telegraphic Agency* 1977c). Friedman told Israel Radio: "These were not my suggestions, but they are a step in the right direction" (Ofner 1977).

On August 13, *The New York Times* published a story based on an interview with Flomin, entitled "Israel is moving to make pound convert freely" (*The New York Times* 1977). The *Times* wrote:

> Various liberalization measures were introduced by the Treasury this past week, marking the opening of a step-by-step program to make Israeli pounds as freely convertible as American dollars within five years … the Government … started a full study to estimate the effect of decontrol on the economy … such a study would take time and it was decided, meanwhile, to introduce reforms according to a list of priorities. The first measure introduced this week permits Israelis to keep part of their foreign-currency incomes in special accounts from which they will be permitted to draw dollars for travel without paying the 15 percent surtax …

Flomin also expressed confidence in Friedman's prediction that the IL would appreciate following floating.

On August 22, Friedman wrote the following in his *Newsweek* column:

> Prime Minister Begin and his government have proclaimed their intention to cut government down to size and to give greater scope to the free market. Much as I approve of these objectives, their attainment will not be easy. Too many groups have a vested interest in government subsidies, including many of the strongest supporters of the Likud. In a discussion that I had in Israel with a group of private businessmen, private farmers and private bankers, the business leaders expressed support for eliminating government subsidies—provided the process started with agriculture. The leaders of agriculture expressed support for eliminating government subsidies—provided the process started with business. Ditto the bankers. It will be a triumph of leadership and idealism if Prime Minister Begin and his government can untangle the snarl they inherited from the 29-year rule of their socialist opponents. Their success is vital both for Israel and for free men everywhere. I wish them well.
>
> (Friedman 1977f).

[21]Erlich stated that these measures were conceived and prepared in complete secrecy. Apparently, Erlich's July 7 statement that subsidy cuts would be considered in 2 months was a smokescreen.

5.6 "The Economic Revolution" of 28 October 1977

On Friday, 28 October 1977, Begin called a special, secret cabinet meeting.[22] In his opening statement (Begin 1977), he exhorted the ministers to approve "a most fundamental reform"—the elimination of currency controls, which had been instituted by the British Mandatory Government in 1939. Begin blamed currency controls for creating black markets and turning many citizens into "criminals."[23] But the worst aspect of currency controls was, in Begin's view, their association with a lack of economic freedom: "Currency controls are the symbol of a nation that lacks a free economy. As long as there are foreign currency controls, an economy cannot be free." A vote to abolish currency controls would transform Israel into "a free state according to the model of Switzerland or the US." While there might be an immediate outflow of foreign currency, "we hope that the situation will stabilize as time goes on, and the State will, in the main, benefit from the reform because it will be able to, first and foremost, attract foreign investment from abroad, especially from among American Jewry." Foreign investors would be attracted by the newfound ease of repatriating profits and dividends in their own currencies, without the need to apply for licenses and deal with government bureaucracy. Toward the end of his remarks, Begin acknowledged "the aides to the Minister of Finance, the Deputy Finance Minister and his advisers, who worked a lot to prepare this reform." Begin did not mention Friedman's name.

After almost 4 hours, the cabinet approved the following twelve-point reform package (State of Israel The Knesset 1977; Flomin 1978):

Macroeconomic and international trade measures:[24]

---

[22]The ministers were not informed of the agenda in advance (Begin 1977). The reform that would become known as "The Economic Revolution" was prepared in extreme secrecy. Of the approximately 200 individuals involved, only five had the full picture: Erlich, Flomin, Finance Ministry Director-General Amiram Sivan, Industry and Trade Minister Igal Horowitz, and Gafny (Flomin 2014). These officials communicated via handwritten notes (*Davar*, Oct. 30; Arye Naor, personal communication) and met in Erlich's hotel suite (Flomin 1978). But Begin revealed the secret to an American audience, just before his first meeting with Carter. As the *Christian Science Monitor* reported on July 19 (Ofner 1977): "In New York Prime Minister Begin announced that Israel would soon take a further step toward implementing Professor Friedman's ideas—a far-reaching relaxation in foreign currency controls." Apparently, Begin's desire to impress the Americans with his commitment to reform overcame the need for secrecy; perhaps he intended to publicize in advance what he was planning to tell Carter at the White House. (It is unclear when Begin and Erlich first informed the Carter Administration of their plans; we do know that Erlich informed US Treasury Secretary Michael Blumenthal on October 26, 2 days before the reform was announced). Luckily for Begin and Erlich, the *Christian Science Monitor* story was not picked up by the Israeli media.

[23]As Flomin said (*The New York Times* 1977), many Israelis were unable to comply with the currency laws, including former Prime Minister Rabin, who had been forced to step down as Labor's candidate for prime minister in March 1977 because he and his wife had held an illegal US dollar bank account in Washington. Under the currency laws, Rabin should have closed the account in 1973, when he concluded his term as Israel's ambassador to the US (*Jewish Telegraphic Agency* 1977b).

[24]The categorization of the various measures is our own.

1. Eliminate foreign currency controls, thus making the IL fully convertible.
2. Unify the exchange rate (the difference between the official rate and the maximum effective rate had been as high as 30%), devalue the IL by 47% (from IL 10.35/$ to IL 15.20/$), and then float it.[25] The BOI will be authorized (but not required) to intervene in the foreign exchange market; it will do so whenever necessary to prevent unusual, random exchange rate movements.
3. "Restrict the flow of means of payment to the public" (=contractionary monetary policy) while ensuring credit availability for export activities.
4. Change tax policy as follows: Abolish the defense tax (*Hetel Bitachon*) of 15% on imported goods, the service import tax of 15% on foreign currency allocations, and the travel tax, reduce purchase tax and import tariff rates, cancel the temporary import surcharge (*Hetel Yivu*) of 15% (thus, the rate of effective devaluation for imports is 25%), and increase VAT from 8% to 12%, the financial institutions tax from 6% to 9%, and the nonprofits tax from 3% to 5%. To prevent unjustified profits as a result of the devaluation, levy an inventory tax (*Hetel Mlai*) on inventories of imported goods held by businesses. Reduce or abolish purchase taxes on many goods (mainly raw materials, intermediate goods, and basic consumer goods) at a budgetary cost of IL 2 million.
5. Abolish "export incentives" (=rebates of indirect taxes to exporters; synonymous with "export subsidies") and export promotion funds.

Supplementary measures:

6. Cut subsidies on staple foods and set the maximum food subsidy at 20%; as a result, staple foods prices will increase by 15% on average. Allow administered food prices to increase in line with the devaluation.
7. Increase bus fares by 15% on average; allow a corresponding increase in passenger rail fares, domestic airfares, taxi fares, trucking rates, and rail freight rates.
8. Increase user fees for communications, seaports, and airports in line with the devaluation.
9. Increase electricity rates across the board by IL 0.11 per KW/h.
10. Increase water rates in line with the increase in supply costs;
11. The government and government-supported institutions will absorb these higher costs within their current budgets.
12. Welfare recipients will receive a onetime compensation of 12%.

Erlich immediately announced the reforms at a televised press conference (for a brief video excerpt, see Israel Television 1977a). He made the following additional points (*Jewish Telegraphic Agency* 1977d):

[25]As Friedman (1977f) would later state, "reports in the media that the Israeli pound has depreciated by 30–50 per cent … are extremely misleading." Taking the changes in subsidies and tariffs into account, the effective rates of devaluation were 20.4% for exports (goods 6.3%, services 43.9%) and 17.1% for imports (goods 9.4%, services 47.0%) (Tov 1988).

- Israel had sufficient foreign currency reserves to stabilize the exchange rate if necessary.[26]
- For some time, the IMF had been pushing Israel to abolish export incentives and thus unify the effective exchange rate.[27]
- As a result of the reform, foreign investment and production of import substitutes will increase, and Israelis who hold (heretofore) illegal foreign currency accounts abroad will repatriate an estimated $3 billion.
- The cost-of-living is expected to increase by 10% through the end of 1977. Families with children and welfare recipients will be compensated by 12%.
- The government knows that it is taking a major risk—a risk that is necessary in order to fix Israel's economy. The adjustment process will necessarily entail uncertainties and difficulties.

Erlich omitted from his announcement a reform measure that would prove to be of critical importance: Concurrent with the elimination of foreign currency controls, the public would be permitted to hold foreign currency-linked bank accounts, known as PATAM (or Isradollars) (Michaely 1983).[28]

When Friedman heard about the liberalization, he was "much surprised." He waxed ecstatic: "This is one of the greatest things that has happened to Israel since it was founded. It's really a step—a fundamental change—in the attitude of Israel from a paternalistic, collectivist, socialist view to a view of human freedom. It's a major step towards broadening the personal freedom of the Israeli citizen … [I have been] recommending this kind of program for many years [but I did not] think that [the government] would find it politically feasible to put it into effect. I give [the government] great credit for having the courage and wisdom to do it"[29,30] (*Jerusalem Post* and *Davar*, October 30).

[26]In the weeks before October 28, the BOI was so concerned about a possible flight from the IL to the US dollar that it arranged $600 million in standby credit from the IMF and the BIS (*Davar*, October 30; see also Gross 2007, 108–110 and Flomin 1978). The BOI's deputy governors also consulted with the Bank of England, the National Bank of Austria, and the IMF regarding the practicalities of floating (Flomin 1978, 2014; *Davar*, October 31). Immediately after October 28, the BOI declared that it would intervene in the foreign exchange market if necessary, so as to maintain long-term economic stability, minimize risks to exporters, and prevent speculative profits (*Davar*, October 31).

[27]Three days later, Erlich told the Knesset that abolishing export subsidies had "removed the threat of sanctions that various countries are threatening to impose on Israeli exports" (State of Israel, The Knesset 1977).

[28]Previously, the foreign currency-linked accounts known as TAMAM and PAZAK had been legal only for recipients of Holocaust restitution payments and were not highly liquid.

[29]Similarly, Friedman had attributed excessive significance to a September 1976 speech by UK Prime Minister Callaghan, in which Callaghan seemed to adopt major elements of Friedman's macroeconomic framework (Nelson 2009).

[30]Friedman was silent regarding the VAT increase, despite his strong general opposition to VAT (Friedman 1972). Not only that, he never recommended that Israel reduce or eliminate its VAT. But just 2 years later, Friedman would brand UK Prime Minister Thatcher's VAT increase a "retrograde step" (Friedman 1979). This ostensible inconsistency can be resolved as follows:

Friedman predicted a huge success: "On the whole, I would expect that the major effect would be to reduce inflationary pressures because it would permit the economy to be more efficient … The effect is to give the Bank of Israel far greater independence with respect to the internal monetary situation …" He rejected the notion that Israel would move to a dollar standard: "I believe that at least after maybe a month or two, after people get used to the idea, the effect will be to give the Israeli people greater confidence in the pound because up until now if you held dollars, you would not turn them into pounds unless you couldn't help yourself."[31] He urged the government to refrain from intervening in the foreign exchange market or asking foreign central banks and/or the IMF to do so. With a fully flexible exchange rate, "you will have an honest system in which there is a single exchange rate and it will be possible to say what is the value of the Israeli pound."

Friedman also expressed optimism regarding Israel's long-run prospects. Because the reform signaled the government's seriousness about freeing the economy, he said, Israel would surely become a more attractive location for foreign investment and might develop into a larger international financial center (*Jerusalem Post* and *Davar*, 30 October 1977).

But once again, Begin and Erlich distanced themselves from Friedman's ideas. Begin told Israel Television: "There is no connection between the [economic] plan and Friedman" (Begin, Israel Television 1977b). When opposition MK's accused Erlich of following Friedman's advice and falsely denying it, he replied: "We were unable to accept Professor Friedman's proposals, because they are unsuitable for the structure of the Israeli economy" (State of Israel, The Knesset 1977).

Nevertheless, Friedman continued to sing Begin's praises:

> Israel's radical economic measures—abolition of foreign-exchange controls, freeing of the pound, elimination of export incentives and import levies, reduction of subsidies on basic commodities—reflect the same combination of boldness, vision and courage that marked the Six Day War and the Entebbe rescue [of July 4, 1976—authors]. And they may well be no less important for Israel's future …
>
> If Israel's dash to freedom is maintained, I predict that it will produce the same kind of economic miracle that Germany's similar dash produced in 1948 … It may also convert Israel into a major financial center, a partial replacement for Beirut and … attract both capital and immigrants from the advanced Western countries.
>
> (Friedman 1977g)

(a) Friedman (1972) was willing to tolerate a VAT increase if it was associated with reduction or elimination of taxes that are even more distortionary than VAT. Erlich's reform package appears to have met this condition; (b) Israel's fiscal deficit/GDP ratio was approximately 15%, vs. 4% in the UK (UK data from Keep 2015). Because Friedman saw Israel's fiscal deficit as inflationary, he may have viewed the VAT increase as a necessary evil.

[31]This prediction turned out to be correct. Initially, the public converted foreign currency into IL, in response to the large devaluation. But this phase lasted just 2 weeks (Bank of Israel 1977).

5.7 The IMF's Role in the "Economic Revolution"

Unbeknownst to Friedman, Erlich had inherited from the previous government a record debt to the IMF, coupled with a formal commitment to follow its advice. As we shall demonstrate, it was the IMF, not Friedman, which was the driving force behind major components of the October 28 reform.

In the wake of the first oil shock, Israel's net financial position with the IMF deteriorated dramatically, from 25% of quota (=no transactions with the IMF) to an historical low of −219% in November 1976 (computed by the authors using data from the International Financial Statistics database, using the method of Boughton 2005). In July 1978, Israel's debt to the IMF was SDR 248.25 million (=$312.76 million) (IMF Archive Catalog, EBS/78/465, Table 5.1), equal to 2.2% of 1978 GDP. During the 1972–1978 period, Israel ranked ninth among non-oil developing nations in amount borrowed under IMF standby arrangements (De Vries 1985, 432).

In September–October 1976, Erlich's predecessor, Rabinowitz, negotiated a standby credit of SDR 29.25 million (=$33.77 million), for 1 year, ending 19 October 1977. In a letter to IMF Managing Director H. Johannes Witteveen, Rabinowitz pledged to implement the following "stabilization program" (Rabinowitz to Witteveen, 17 September 1976, EBS 76/442 Supplement 1, 21 October 1976) [our comments appear in brackets]:

a. Implement "tight monetary and fiscal policies and substantial exchange rate action … to hold down domestic demand so that import growth can be reduced and productive resources can be directed to the export sector." [This condition was a standard feature of IMF standbys; see Connors 1979].
b. Maintain the crawling peg [of which the IMF approved, as we shall see].
c. Disinflate to 25% in 1977, in part by "containing the increase in [its] expenditures and limiting recourse to [borrowing from] the Bank of Israel."
d. Abolish purchase taxes that remained in effect after the tax reform of July 1975.
e. "… Remove the surcharge on exchange purchases for foreign travel and for certain other invisible payments [in Erlich's terminology, the Service Import Tax] and the increase in the travel tax as soon as circumstances permit. While these measures remain in effect, Israel will consult with the Fund regarding their retention and in any event will review them with the Fund not later than June 30, 1977." [Not long afterwards, the IMF and GATT demanded that Israel abolish these measures as soon as possible.] Refrain from introducing "multiple currency practices" and new or intensified "restrictions on payments and transfers for current international transactions or … restrictions on imports for balance of payments purposes without prior consultation with the Fund."
f. "… Minimize the use of short-term commercial credits."
g. "… Consult with the Fund and agree on ceilings for net domestic assets of the banking system and on Bank of Israel credit to the Government … before requesting any purchases under the stand-by arrangement subsequent to June 30, 1977." [This was also a standard condition for IMF standbys.]
h. Hold regular consultations with the IMF at the initiative of either side.

But political exigencies intervened. On 22 December 1976, Rabin dissolved the government and called new elections for 17 May 1977. In March 1977, Rabin's caretaker government, having failed to pass a regular budget, passed an interim budget for the 4 months April–July 1977; the IMF criticized the interim budget as over-expansionary (SM/77/109). Political uncertainty thus begat economic uncertainty. The IMF's Article XIV mission, which visited that same month, "reportedly expressed alarm over the state of Israel's economy" (*Jewish Telegraphic Agency* 1977a). Under these circumstances, Rabinowitz was unable to reach agreement with the IMF by the March 31 deadline regarding the ceilings for end-June and end-September 1977. This led to the suspension of SDR 17 Million (=$19.71 million) in undrawn standby credit (SM/77/109, 12 May 1977; EBM/77/80, 2 June 1977; EBM/77/151, 2 November 1977).[32] It was agreed that the ceilings would be negotiated with the new government (SM/77/109). In the meantime, Rabin's caretaker government made sure to coordinate all modifications to export incentives with the IMF.[33]

On June 3, the IMF Executive Board (EB) discussed Israel's Article XIV consultation. The EB decision consisted of two clauses:

1. "The Fund considers it important that policies to shift resources from domestic uses to the foreign sector be intensified in order to lay the ground for sustainable growth of the economy."
2. The EB extended until 30 June 1978 the permission that it had granted in 1976 to maintain certain "exchange measures." Furthermore, it undertook to "review the surcharges on payments for imports of goods and certain invisibles, and the travel tax on the occasion of the next Article XIV consultation and, in any event, not later than June 30, 1978." (SM/77/109 supplement 2). The EB was sending a clear message: Israel could significantly strengthen its case for restoring the standby if it abolished the 15% import surcharge, the service import tax, and the travel tax.

On June 26 (a week before Friedman's arrival), Erlich met in Jerusalem with H. Onno Ruding, the new IMF executive director (ED) responsible for Israel.[34] Ruding called for export-driven growth and decreased consumption along with stable investment. He praised the crawling peg and the recent export-led decline in the BOP deficit, but criticized the current wage policy and increased consumption. Erlich made a generic statement, to the effect that the IMF's advice was consistent with the new government's policy plans (*Davar*, 27 June 1977).

In July, the IMF approved Israel's request to reschedule the repayments of a 1974 standby agreement in the amount of SDR 32.5 million (=$38.07 million in

[32]Israel did not borrow from the IMF in 1977.

[33]Export incentives were increased in April 1977 (*Davar*, April 17) and indexed to a currency basket instead of the US dollar in May 1977 (*Davar*, May 4).

[34]This was a routine meeting, not a special meeting that was motivated by IMF concerns about the state of the Israeli economy (H. Onno Ruding, personal communication).

July 1977); the new payment schedule called for “five quarterly installments equivalent to SDR 6.5 million each beginning not later than March 31, 1978” (EBM/77/114). Apparently, Israel was having difficulty servicing its short-term external debt.

At the IMF/World Bank annual meetings in Washington (September 26–30), Erlich asked Witteveen to restore the suspended standby credit; it was agreed that an IMF mission would arrive in January to evaluate Israel’s request. After returning to Jerusalem, Erlich told *Davar* newspaper that he had not committed himself to abolishing export subsidies as demanded by the IMF and that he had “proven” to Witteveen that “the export subsidies are given in order to compensate for price increases and the reduction in the value of the IL, and that the exporter does not get wealthy from them” (*Davar*, October 14). But contrary to Erlich’s claims, Witteveen was apparently unconvinced; the IMF ratcheted up the pressure and conditioned the restoration of standby credits on abolishing export subsidies (*Davar*, October 24). This was consistent with Witteveen’s general message to member countries facing BOP difficulties: Eschew competitive devaluations, trade protection and capital controls, and rely on the IMF’s (expanded) financing mechanisms (see De Vries 1986, 136–148).

While still in Washington, Erlich and his staff held a formal consultation with Ruding and L. A. Whittome, director of the IMF’s European Department. The Israelis presented Ruding and Whittome with a preliminary version of the reform package that would be announced on 28 October and received their blessing (Flomin 1978; however, Ruding does not recall any such consultation). The IMF approved a special standby facility of $200–300 million, to be used for foreign exchange market intervention if necessary (Gafny in *Davar*, October 30; Flomin 1978).

When the reform was announced on 28 October, BOI Governor Gafny immediately notified the IMF in writing. Gafny’s version of the reform differed from Erlich’s in one respect: Instead of Erlich’s vague commitment to “restrict the flow of means of payment to the public,” Gafny pledged that “the BOI will freeze domestic credit for an initial period of three months with the exception of directed credit from the BOI.” Gafny concluded, “We trust that this program of liberalization of exchange measures and of constraints on domestic demand will gain Fund approval and support” (EBS/77/396).

As Gafny predicted, the IMF granted its approval. The IMF EB issued the following decision (the text was written by Ruding; EBM/77/151):

> The Fund notes the new exchange rate arrangements communicated by Israel as indicated in EBS/77/396 (10/28/77) and welcomes the comprehensive liberalization of the exchange system and the significant reduction in restrictions.

Ultimately, Israel and the IMF never reached agreement to restore the suspended SDR 17 million, and the 1976 standby expired on 19 October 1977. However, in September 1978, Israel requested and received SDR 72.4 million (=$92.75 million) from the IMF’s Compensatory Financing Facility (CFF—for countries experiencing adverse export fluctuations). In his presentation to the EB, Ruding cited the "important and far-reaching reform" of 28 October as a reason to approve Israel's request (EBM/78/136).

Having completed our account of the IMF's role, we now assess the influence of Friedman and the IMF (and GATT) on the reform measures of 28 October:

1–2. Eliminate foreign currency controls, thus making the IL fully convertible. Unify the exchange rate, devalue the IL by 47%, and then float it: Both Begin and the Liberals had publicly advocated currency liberalization and floating since the 1950s (regarding the Liberals, see Kleiman 1981); obviously, they did not need Friedman to convert them to the cause. Although Likud's economic platform (Likud Party 1977) deferred currency liberalization and floating to the 1980s,[35] Begin decided not to wait. On 22 or 23 June, just 2 or 3 days after the formation of the government, he asked Erlich to move forward (Begin, Israel Television 1977b; *Davar*, 30 October 1977). By the time Friedman arrived in Israel (3 July 1977), Erlich and his staff were already preparing the reform. Furthermore, Friedman never recommended devaluation. We therefore conclude that Begin and Erlich were speaking truthfully when they denied having taken Friedman's advice. The IMF played no role in the decision to float; until 28 October, it endorsed the crawling peg (1977 Article XIV report, issued May 12, SM/77/109).

3. Contractionary monetary policy while ensuring credit availability for export activities: This measure was devised by Erlich and Gafny. It contradicted Friedman's recommendations in several respects: There was no explicit goal for fiscal deficit reduction, no commitment to achieve zero inflation over 3–4 years, and no monetary growth rule. Furthermore, Gafny's credit freeze excluded DC, which Friedman wanted to abolish. Policymakers failed to implement the IMF's recommendation concerning fiscal policy: "The policies of restraint pursued in 1975 and 1976 should be continued and, if possible, intensified … [The government should] ensure that fiscal policy for the year as a whole is, as a minimum, no more expansionary than in 1976/77" (SM/77/109).

4. Tax policy changes: abolish the defense tax of 15% on imported goods, the service import tax of 15% on foreign currency allocations, and the travel tax, reduce purchase tax and import tariff rates, cancel the temporary 15% import surcharge, and increase VAT from 8% to 12%, the financial institution tax from 6% to 9%, and the nonprofit tax from 3% to 5%. Levy an inventory tax (*Hetel Mlai*) on inventories of imported goods held by businesses. Reduce or abolish purchase taxes on many goods (mainly raw materials, intermediate goods, and basic consumer goods). The IMF and GATT demanded the abolition of the import surcharge, the service import tax, and the travel tax; the IMF EB notified Israel that it would review these policies by 30 June 1978 (1977 Article XIV report, SM/77/109; GATT BOP/R/90). Friedman did not mention these taxes. The Likud platform had pledged to abolish the travel tax on the grounds that it was

[35] This was the result of a compromise within the Likud economic platform committee, whose members were divided concerning the near-term practicability of currency liberalization and floating (Likud Party 1977; Flomin 1978).

"inconsistent with individual rights as accepted in democratic regimes, which include freedom of movement," and Erlich had repeated that pledge on May 22. The VAT increase was obviously Erlich's idea; neither Friedman nor the IMF advocated it. As noted above, Friedman strongly opposed VAT, unless it was the least of all evils (Friedman 1972). None of the other tax policy changes were advocated by Friedman or by the IMF.

5. Abolish export incentives (=rebates of indirect taxes to exporters) and export promotion funds: Erlich stated explicitly that the IMF had urged him to abolish export subsidies. Reportedly, Witteveen had told Erlich that the IMF would condition resumption of the suspended standby on the abolition of export subsidies (*Davar*, 14 and 24 October 1977). Furthermore, the decision to abolish export subsidies while retaining most tariffs, thus favoring the production of import substitutes (as stated by Erlich on 28 October),[36] was consistent with the Likud platform's explicit call for import substitution (and its silence on tariffs). It contradicted Friedman's recommendation to phase out export subsidies and import restrictions over 2–3 years. While the IMF advocated gradual import liberalization, it did not address import substitution in its 1977 Article XIV report (SM/77/109).

7–12. Supplementary measures. All supplementary measures were initiated by Erlich. None were recommended by Friedman or by the IMF (although the IMF issued a general call to cut subsidies).

In summary, the reform of 28 October consisted of measures that were initiated by Erlich or undertaken as a result of IMF (or IMF/GATT) pressure. Some measures strongly contradicted Friedman's recommendations. Others were consistent with Friedman's recommendations, but only coincidentally. Friedman's lack of influence is not at all surprising. As documented above, during the policy planning stage (22 or 23 June–28 October 1977), the government held (at most) token consultations with Friedman (July 1977), followed by genuine consultations with the IMF (September 1977).

5.8 Conclusion: The Failure of the 1977 Economic Revolution

After an ostensibly auspicious beginning, the Begin government abandoned its overall agenda of economic reform and made due with stopgap measures.[37] Inflation accelerated from 66% in 1979Q1 to 167% in 1979Q4 (Fig. 5.1). Real wages rose (Kleiman 1986), DC was expanded (Barkai and Liviatan 2007, 162), and privatization targets were not met (Shlomo Eckstein et al. 1993, 242). The trade deficit ballooned (Table 5.2); this was accompanied by an increase in foreign debt,

[36]BOI economist Richard Ablin (1978) argued that this was a serious mistake.

[37]According to Bruno (1986), the government squandered the opportunity to implement structural reforms in 1977–1979, between the first and second oil shocks (e.g., unlike Finland).

with short-term foreign debt growing faster than long-term foreign debt (Table 5.3). These developments left the Israeli economy ill-equipped to deal with the second oil shock, which hit in the first half of 1979 (Halevi 1986). The acceleration of inflation, combined with short-term capital inflows and currency appreciation, led to the institution of a managed float and the reimposition of capital controls, so that by mid-1979, little was left of the liberalization (Michaely 2007, 79–80; see Appendix for details).[38]

The only positive development during Erlich's term was an increase in per capita GDP growth (Kleiman 1986, Table 15.1). Erlich lost the confidence of his Likud colleagues, including Flomin,[39] and was forced to resign as finance minister on 7 November 1979.

What caused the economic debacle of 1977–1979? We begin with Friedman's own retrospective view. Friedman argued that the reform of October 28 "served a useful purpose" but was insufficient by itself to solve Israel's problems. The experiences of the UK and New Zealand in the 1980s demonstrate that "when liberalization has been accompanied by a broader range of measures, it has always been a great success" (Friedman 1987a, b). He attributed the government's failure to implement his agenda to Begin's disinterest and lack of training in economics, the power of special interests, and the new government's failure to take advantage of its "honeymoon"—a 6–9-month window of opportunity for implementing significant reforms (Friedman and Friedman 1999, 464).

While Friedman's description is partially correct, the reality was much more complex. The reform of October 28 had four fatal flaws, all of which Friedman underemphasized or failed to anticipate: lack of fiscal discipline (underemphasized), currency substitution, rapid growth of foreign borrowing, and incorrect sequencing of economic reforms (failed to anticipate all three).[40] While some Israeli economists strongly protested the government's fiscal irresponsibility, they also failed to anticipate the other three flaws.

Lack of Fiscal Discipline As the "economic revolution" was in its planning stages, Gafny urged the government to eliminate the budget deficit in the second half of 1977 (*Davar*, 15 July 1977 and 16 October 1977). Since the deficit for the first half of 1977 was roughly 10% of GDP, Gafny's recommendation implied a

[38]As Michaely (2007, 79) puts it, this episode "was, in effect, the only significant setback to the continuous fifty-year process of liberalization of current account or capital account transactions."

[39]Erlich resigned as deputy finance minister on 30 July 1979 and publicly called for Erlich's dismissal. Flomin had privately urged Erlich to resign together with him, but Erlich had refused (Flomin 2010).

[40]Other factors may have contributed to the debacle. Bruno (1986) and Michaely (2007, 79) argue that the devaluation of October 28 was excessive; O. Sussman (1992) disagrees. Frenkel (1984) emphasizes that the acceleration of inflation was caused by the interaction of the devaluation and subsidy cuts with the CLA system. Sylvia Piterman points out that Erlich was guilty of poor planning but also suffered from bad luck—the implementation of his reforms coincided with the second oil shock (Gross 2007, 115).

deficit of roughly 5% of GDP for the full year 1977.[41] Erlich went even further: He told Gafny privately that he would push for a zero deficit for the full year 1977 (Amodi 2005).[42] But when government ministers balked, Begin gave in (Amodi 2005; Gross 2007, 109); with the peace process with Egypt moving into full gear (beginning with Sadat's visit to Israel on November 20), Begin could ill-afford reforms that would undermine the stability of his coalition (Flomin 2010, 2014).[43]

In mid-December 1977, the cabinet approved a budget plan with a projected deficit of 10% of GDP (Amodi 2005). Gafny, who was present at the cabinet meeting, criticized the government publicly and was immediately reprimanded by Begin (Amodi 2005; Gross 2007, 109). Ultimately, the government failed to keep the deficit at 10%; the deficit widened from 9.9% in 1976 to 14.4% in 1977 and 17.1% in 1978, before narrowing to 10.3% in 1979 (Table 5.1).

Where did Friedman stand on fiscal policy? During his visit in early July, Friedman called upon the government to cut the inflation tax by cutting expenditures. After his return to the US, he praised the defense and subsidy cuts of July 17. But in November–December 1977, at the critical point in Israel's budget process, Friedman was surprisingly silent: He praised the government effusively for the October 28 reform and urged further reforms in the most general terms ("If Israel's dash to freedom is maintained …" (Friedman 1977f)).[44] Unlike Gafny, Friedman did not warn that the reform would fail without a major fiscal adjustment.

Currency Substitution In November 1977, the government, seeking to limit demand for US dollars in the wake of the October 28 liberalization (Barkai and Liviatan 2007, 177), made available to the wider public an asset known as PATAM. The PATAM was a dollar-denominated demand deposit (or short-term time deposit) in an Israeli bank, with a 100% required reserve ratio in foreign currency. According to Bufman and Leiderman (1993), PATAM accounts "provided partial hedging against inflation, and against devaluations, as did government indexed bonds." The expansion of access to PATAM caused a massive currency substitution: Between 1975 and 1980, M1/GDP fell from 13% to 5% and M1/M4 fell from 28% to 12% (Liviatan and Piterman 1986; M4 includes PATAM and tradable foreign currency-indexed bonds). PATAM's share in M2 increased from 40% in

---

[41]Gafny consistently demanded deficit reduction without tax increases, both before and after the elections (*Davar*, various issues). The following economists also advocated deficit reduction (among others): former BOI Governor David Horowitz, chair of the BOI advisory council (*Davar*, 22 July 1977), and the academic economists Michael Bruno, Haim Barkai (both staunch Laborites), Eitan Berglas (who was about to be appointed by Erlich as budget director) (*Davar*, 15 December 1977), and Michael Michaely (Hanoch et al. 1977).

[42]Gafny publicized Erlich's commitment on more than one occasion (Gross 2007, 109). Apparently, Gafny saw publicity as a commitment device—with publicity, it would be more difficult for Erlich to renege.

[43]Alternatively, it is arguable that significant deficit reduction was unachievable as long as defense expenditures remained above 20% of GDP.

[44]Only in August 1978, after the failure of the 28 October 1977 reform had become painfully obvious, did Friedman reiterate the need to "reduce government spending" (Friedman 1978).

October 1977 to 71% in November 1979, while the share of foreign currency denominated deposits in total bank deposits increased from 70% to 84% (Michaely 1983). The contraction in the domestic money supply reduced the base of the inflation tax; thus, a higher rate of inflation was required in order to keep inflation tax revenue constant.[45]

Despite his seminal contributions to the inflation tax literature (Cagan 1956;[46] Friedman 1971), Friedman failed to foresee the massive currency substitution and its inflationary effects. He made the following erroneous prediction: "The major effect would be to reduce inflationary pressures … the effect is to give the BOI far greater independence with respect to the internal monetary situation" (Blitzer 1977b).

Did Israeli economists anticipate currency substitution? No. While Nadav Halevi and Ephraim Kleiman predicted that the October 28 reform would be inflationary, they did not discuss currency substitution as a possible mechanism (Hanoch et al. 1977).

Rapid Growth of Foreign Borrowing The October 28 reform led to a rapid expansion in domestic credit. The BOI tightened domestic credit by mid-1978, which led to large-scale borrowing abroad through Israeli banks. Throughout 1978, the expected effective interest rate on foreign exchange credit (taking into account devaluation expectations) was lower than the interest rate on domestic currency credit. Toward the end of 1978, borrowers anticipated (correctly) that the BOI would soon impose controls on foreign currency credit. This caused foreign exchange credit to expand by 324% in 1978Q4, while domestic currency credit declined by 30%.

In January 1979, new foreign borrowing was temporarily prohibited and then permitted subject to a fine. In March 1979, the BOI announced that it would intervene to maintain the PPP of the IL (see Appendix). These measures were only temporarily successful. The growth of foreign currency credit slowed to 80% in 1979Q1 (vs. 79% for domestic currency borrowing), but accelerated to 205% and 211% in 1979Q2 and 1979Q3, respectively. Why was the BOI unable to control foreign currency credit growth? The BOI was simply unprepared for the complex task of monetary control with a free foreign currency market. Israeli policymakers had always been concerned about destabilizing capital outflows,[47] but they had never considered the opposite possibility of destabilizing capital inflows (Michaely 1983).[48]

[45]For theoretical and empirical analyses of this episode, see Zilberfarb (1991), O. Sussman (1992), Bufman and Leiderman (1993), Melnick and Yashiv (1996), and Sargent and Zeira (2011).

[46]This paper was based on Cagan's Ph.D. dissertation, which Friedman supervised. Cagan wrote in the acknowledgments: "I owe a great debt to Milton Friedman for his helpful suggestions at every stage of the work."

[47]This is why the BOI arranged $600 million in standby credit from the IMF and the BIS.

[48]For further details on the boom in foreign borrowing and the BOI's regulatory response, see Zilberfarb (1991).

For his part, Friedman (1977a) had a highly favorable view of the capital inflows that would result from floating and capital account liberalization.[49] He failed to predict that capital inflows would cause a loss of monetary control; on the contrary (as quoted above), Friedman was certain that the BOI would only attain greater independence and control.

Israeli economists also failed to predict destabilizing capital inflows. At the Hebrew University Symposium on the October 28 reform, two speakers, Ephraim Kleiman and Deputy BOI Governor Zvi Sussman, addressed speculative capital flows. Both were concerned about capital outflows, although Kleiman briefly mentioned the destabilizing effects on foreign countries of bi-directional Petrodollar flows (Hanoch et al. 1977).

Incorrect Sequencing of Reforms According to the literature on sequencing, floating and capital account liberalization should not be attempted until inflation, fiscal deficits, BOP deficits, and external debt have been brought under control (McKinnon and Mathieson 1981; McKinnon 1982; Edwards 1984). Because the 1977 liberalization blatantly violated this prescription, it was doomed to failure from the very beginning (McKinnon and Mathieson 1981; McKinnon 1982; Frenkel 1984; Ben Bassat 2002; Michaely 2007, 79, 89).

Friedman failed to see the need for correct sequencing of reforms. This is clearly demonstrated by the following two examples: (a) During his July 1977 visit, Friedman recommended immediate floating and capital account liberalization, along with a gradual 3–4-year disinflation. But according to the sequencing literature, he should have recommended delaying the float and capital account liberalization until the disinflation had been completed—that is, until mid-1980 at the earliest. (b) Friedman was silent on fiscal policy after the reform of 28 October 1977, despite the lack of progress on deficit reduction. But according to the sequencing literature, he should have warned (as Gafny did) that the reform would fail without significant fiscal adjustment.

Should Friedman be blamed for ignoring the sequencing literature? Yes, to some degree. Although the sequencing literature was in its infancy in 1977, two key insights that were directly applicable to Israel had already been published:

---

[49] "So far as the big sums of money are concerned, I would not be surprised if freeing exchange transactions would produce an inflow of capital. If you really abolished overnight your foreign exchange controls, if overnight you allowed the exchange rate to go free, and if you could establish confidence that the policy would be maintained, the package would surely attract capital not repel it ... But even if you don't establish full confidence that the policy will be retained, many people might be induced to bring capital into this country from the outset. And over a period of time, the promotion of international financial transactions would almost surely produce an inflow of capital into the country not an outflow. So I would not be at all surprised to see the true exchange rate of the Israeli pound appreciate rather than depreciate, if you were to follow such policies. Again, I don't mean to predict that it will happen, because as I say prediction is very unreliable in this area" (Friedman 1977c).

a. Trade liberalization should not be accompanied by capital account liberalization. Countries that attempt to do so usually fail to complete the trade liberalization (McKinnon 1973).
b. Capital account liberalization is likely to be inflationary because it reduces the demand for domestic currency, thus eroding the base of the inflation tax. Therefore, "The elimination of capital market restrictions may be one of the goals of a counter-inflationary policy, but it is not one of the tools to accomplish that end" (Nichols 1974).[50]

On the other hand, Israeli economists were also unfamiliar with the sequencing literature at the time. At the Hebrew University's symposium on the October 28 reform, Ephraim Kleiman argued that the capital account should have been liberalized in stages, not all at once, but did not base his argument on the sequencing literature (Hanoch et al. 1977).

We now return to our original question: Was Friedman to blame for the Israeli economic debacle of 1977–1979? Our answer is no. And this for four reasons: (a) The government did not inform him of the planned "economic revolution," much less consult him regarding its details; (b) Begin (and Erlich's predecessors) had advocated floating and currency liberalization since the 1950s; (c) the decision to abolish export subsidies was motivated by IMF conditionality, not Friedman's advice; (d) certain measures, such as the VAT increase, directly contradicted Friedman's advice. Nevertheless, Friedman deserves some measure of blame for failing to advocate fiscal adjustment in the aftermath of the October 28 reform, failing to foresee the pernicious effects of currency substitution and foreign borrowing, and failing to see the need for correct sequencing of reforms.

Did the abandonment of most of Friedman's agenda make his advice a complete failure? Certainly not. Friedman was ahead of his time, in the sense that much of his agenda was implemented by subsequent Israeli governments:

- The stabilization program of July 1985 reduced annual inflation from 445% in 1984 to 185% in 1985 to 20% in 1986 (by 1999, annual inflation had fallen to 1.3%). The key to the stabilization was a massive fiscal adjustment which reduced the budget deficit from 15.3% of GDP in 1984 to zero in 1985. The fiscal adjustment included drastic cuts in consumer subsidies; subsidies to factors of production were abolished in 1987 (Zvi Eckstein and Ramot-Nyska 2008).
- Over 1988–2002, Israel implemented full capital account liberalization and made its currency fully convertible (Michaely 2007, 80–82); the currency was floated in 1997 (a clean float was maintained until 2008).
- DC was phased out, from 65% of bank credit in 1985 to 5% in 1998 (Ben Bassat 2002, 14).[51]
- A negative income tax was introduced in 2008.

---

[50]Friedman almost certainly saw Nichols' paper; it appeared immediately before Friedman's own paper in the March–April 1974 issue of the *Journal of Political Economy*.

[51]In this context, DC includes earmarked deposits, which the BOI defines as "deposits for which the depositor determines to which borrower or group of borrowers the amount of the deposits

5.9 Afterword-Friedman's Retrospectives

Despite his initial enthusiasm, Friedman's association with the Begin government ended on a sour note. A mutual distancing occurred; Friedman reported that there were "no formal contacts" between himself and the government after July 1977 (Friedman 1978). From 1978 until 1999, Friedman made every effort to dissociate himself from the Begin government and its policies; in so doing, he offered divergent accounts of his interactions with Erlich.

In an August 1978 letter to the *Times of London*, John Kenneth Galbraith (1978a) blamed Friedman for Israel's poor economic performance.[52] Friedman (1978) strongly denied responsibility:

> I am not now and never have been "economic adviser" to Prime Minister Begin …
>
> My friends tell me that floating the Israeli pound and the associated reduction in exchange controls are the only government policy actions that correspond to my advice—and these measures seem to have been highly successful. For the rest, my impression is that there has been little if any change in economic policy in Israel in the direction that I have urged,[53] not alone for Israel but for the US and the UK as well.
>
> It would be just as wrong for me to attribute the failure of the Carter measures to stem inflation in the United States to the Administration's use of Galbraith's rhetoric as it is for him to attribute Israeli inflation to Mr. Begin's expression of regard for my views.

In January 1979, Galbraith told the *Jerusalem Post*: "The situation just begs saying that you deserve your 50% inflation for taking Milton's advice. But he claims that his advice wasn't taken, so it would be somewhat unfair to lay that sin at his door" (Goell 1979).

In July 1979, Friedman wrote to Dr. Asher Halperin (director-general of the Association of Banks in Israel) to express his disappointment with Israel's economic policies. Friedman's letter to Halperin was published in the Israeli media, with Friedman's authorization. Friedman wrote as follows (Elitzur 1979; translated from Hebrew):

> I am very dispirited concerning what is happening in Israel … I have not visited Israel since my brief visit in July 1977, except for a lunch in San Francisco with Arnon Gafny, when he passed through there approximately one year ago … The government did not adopt any of the measures that I recommended when I was there in July 1977, except currency liberalization. It was without a doubt a desirable and positive step, but by itself, it is absolutely

will be granted as loans" (http://www.boi.org.il/en/BankingSupervision/Data/Pages/DefinitionsAndExplanatoryCurrent.aspx).

[52]On the Friedman-Galbraith relationship, see Burgin (2013).

[53]Friedman would reiterate this point in 1987 (Friedman 1987). Galbraith published a rejoinder (Galbraith 1978b). The Friedman-Galbraith debate over Israel continued into 1979 and was featured prominently in the Israeli press.

Table 5.4 Fiscal indicators, 1980 and 1990 (% of GDP)

	Defense expenditures	Civilian expenditures	Total expenditures	Total receipts	Deficit
1980	22.3	51.7	74.0	62.0	12.0
1990	13.0	44.5	57.5	52.7	4.8
Change, 1980–1990	−9.3	−7.2	−16.5	−9.3	−7.2

Source: Bank of Israel, new SNA data

> insufficient to solve the problems that Israel confronts … Apparently government expenditures will continue to rise, government subsidization of private industries continues, and the money supply continues to grow rapidly.
>
> It is a tragedy for Israel and the free world that the government did not act quickly to reduce the statist nature of the Israeli economy, and even … went further [in a statist direction] than the previous government.
>
> The peace treaty with Egypt … is undoubtedly a step of tremendous importance … But if this step is accompanied by a continuing deterioration of the economy, a continuing movement towards superinflation [sic], then the long-term outlook is indeed very depressing.[54]

Galbraith penned the following reply, which was also published in the Israeli media (Galbraith 1979, translated from Hebrew):

> I accept, of course, that the Likud did not act according to Friedman's prescription, just as I accept his emphasis that he had no communication with members of the government, except the lunch with Mr. Arnon Gafny. But I am not sure that this explanation casts my friend [Friedman] in a favorable light; the one thing that harms the reputation of an economist more than giving incorrect advice is to give advice that must be rejected because it is found to be impractical. And in my opinion, that was exactly the fate of Prof. Friedman as an adviser to the current government of Israel … The recommendations of Prof. Friedman are not technically wrong; he and his followers, including those in Israel, are certainly qualified in a pure technical sense. The problem is that what they recommend is socially and culturally irrelevant and therefore politically impossible.

In 1985, an Israeli critic charged that Friedman had "managed to trap Simcha Erlich into undertaking that economic move under the ruins of which we are trying to dig ourselves today." In a *Jerusalem Post* op-ed, Friedman responded: "This statement is an exceedingly misleading half-truth. True enough, the advice was given and perhaps even heard; but it clearly did not 'trap' anyone, let alone Simcha Erlich, into undertaking anything." Referring to his meeting with Erlich, Friedman wrote: "… As I recall it, that was a particularly unrewarding session, since I speak no Hebrew and Mr. Erlich no English, so the conversation was carried on through

[54]Like many economists, Friedman did not foresee that the Camp David Accords would make possible a large, permanent defense cut. Between 1980 and 1990, total government expenditures as a percentage of GDP declined by 16.5 percentage points; the defense cut accounted for 56.4% of that decline (Table 5.4).

The large expenditure cut made it possible to combine tax cuts with deficit reduction; as is well known, deficit reduction was the key to the success of the 1985 stabilization.

an interpreter, and I ended with no very clear view of Erlich's position" (Friedman 1985a, also published in Hebrew—Friedman 1985b).[55,56]

In a 1987 interview with Daniel Doron and Steven Plaut (Friedman 1987), Friedman acknowledged for the first time that Erlich did not inform him of the government's planned "economic revolution." This time, he did not mention the existence of a language barrier between himself and Erlich.

By 1999, when Milton and Rose Friedman published their autobiographical memoir *Two Lucky People*, the Israeli inflation dragon had finally been slain, and the public controversies over Friedman's activities in Israel (and Chile) had died down. Friedman no longer saw the need to downplay his advisory role in Israel. As he and Rose recalled, "The 1977 trip was in many ways *the most memorable of our trips to Israel*, partly because of its coinciding with Menachem Begin's election victory ... [Begin's victory] only briefly preceded my visit and led to our extending our stay in order to *consult with the new government*" (Friedman and Friedman 1999, 463; authors' emphasis).

Appendix: Chronology of Major Events, 1977–1979

1977	
March	IMF mission visits Israel and is reportedly "alarmed" by the state of the economy. Finance Ministry and BOI officials promise action after the May 17 elections.
March 31	Rabin's caretaker government loses access to IMF standby credit, due to its inability to negotiate ceilings on bank credit and BOI credits to the government, as previously agreed with the IMF.
May 17	Menachem Begin's Likud Party defeats the Labor Alignment in the general elections (the "political revolution"). Labor (in its various incarnations) had been the ruling party since Israel's founding in 1948.
May 22	Finance Minister-designate Simha Erlich announces that Milton Friedman will advise the soon-to-be-formed Begin government.
May 24	Friedman causes a firestorm by calling for an increase in unemployment during the Histadrut election campaign.

(continued)

[55]Erlich died in 1983; there is no record of his recollections of the meeting.

[56]The latter claim is problematic for three reasons: (a) Flomin, who was present at the Friedman-Erlich meeting, identifies the translator as Finance Ministry spokesman David Ben-Haim. Although Ben-Haim's English was "average," it was adequate for the task; no ideas were lost in translation (Yehezkel Flomin, personal communication); (b) it strongly contradicts Friedman's contemporaneous account on Israel Television (Friedman 1977e) (however, this contradiction may be resolved by hypothesizing that Friedman was speaking diplomatically in 1977 but candidly in 1985); (c) it does not appear in any of Friedman's pre-1985 communications, public or private, including those that excoriated the Begin government.

June 20	The Begin government is sworn in with a narrow Knesset majority of 62-58. The coalition parties are Likud (45 Members of Knesset), National Religious Party (12), Agudat Yisrael (4), and Moshe Dayan's one-person faction (1).
June 21	The Begin government takes office. In the Histadrut election, Secretary-General MK Yeruham Meshel (Labor Alignment) (57%) is reelected, defeating MK David Levy (Likud) (28%).
June 22 or 23	Begin asks Erlich to move forward on currency liberalization and floating.
June 26	Erlich meets with IMF Executive Director H. Onno Ruding in Jerusalem.
July 3	Friedman lands in Israel.
July 4	Friedman receives an honorary Ph.D. from Hebrew University in the presence of Israel's President, Prof. Ephraim Katzir. Speaking on behalf of the other honorary Ph.D. recipients, he delivers an address on capitalism, freedom, Jewish history, and the State of Israel.
July 5	Friedman lectures on "Floating Exchange Rates for Israel" at the Hebrew University economics department. At the Finance Ministry, he meets with Finance Minister Simha Erlich, Deputy Finance Minister Yehezkel Flomin, and Director-General Amiram Sivan. He meets separately with senior Finance Ministry staff.
July 6	Friedman is interviewed on Israel Television.
July 7	Friedman meets with the Knesset Finance Committee.
July 3–8 (exact date unknown)	Friedman meets the leaders of the major economic associations—the Manufacturers' Association, the Histadrut, and banking and agricultural associations.
July 8	Friedman meets with Prime Minister Begin in the early morning and then departs from Israel.
July 17	Erlich announces a cut in defense spending, cuts in food and fuel subsidies, and a devaluation of 2%. Friedman expresses his support.
July 19–21	Begin meets President Carter and other US officials in Washington.
September 26–30	Erlich attends the IMF annual meetings in Washington and holds discussions with IMF Managing Director H. Johannes Witteveen, World Bank President Robert McNamara, and US Treasury Secretary Michael Blumenthal. According to one account, Erlich consults formally with IMF officials Ruding and Whittome and receives their blessing for his planned reform.
October 17	At a top secret meeting held in Erlich's Jerusalem hotel suite, Erlich, BOI Governor Arnon Gafny, and their staffs hammer out the details of the impending reform and choose October 28 as the date for implementation.
October 23	At a second meeting in Erlich's hotel suite, the reform is finalized, and a green light is given for implementation.
October 24	The 15-seat Democratic Movement for Change (Hebrew: Dash), a centrist party led by Yigael Yadin, joins the government, broadening the government's Knesset majority to 77-43 (Dash would leave the government after less than one year, then disintegrate). Begin informs Yadin of the impending reform.
October 24–26	US Treasury Secretary Michael Blumenthal visits Israel. On October 26, Erlich informs Blumenthal of the impending reform.

(continued)

October 28	Erlich announces an "economic revolution." The main elements are as follows (for a complete list, see the main text): Almost all exchange controls are abolished, export subsidies and import tariffs are reduced, and the IL is devalued by 47% and floated. The VAT rate is increased from 8% to 12%. Gafny notifies the IMF in writing.
October 31	Friedman lauds the government for its "courage and wisdom." Begin and Erlich deny taking Friedman's advice. Erlich makes a statement to the Knesset on behalf of the government. After a stormy debate, the Knesset votes 53-32 (with two abstentions) to enter his statement into the Knesset record.
November 20	Egyptian President Anwar Sadat addresses the Knesset, which leads to the signing of the Camp David Accords on 17 September 1978. In the Israeli economic discourse, the peace process with Egypt was often cited as a significant factor in the expansion of the budget deficit.
Mid-December	Several leading academic economists join the BOI in calling for a major fiscal consolidation. Erlich goes even further and tells Gafny that he is committed to eliminating the budget deficit. But Begin caves in to pressure from his coalition partners, and the government adopts a deficit target of 10% of GDP. Gafny publicly criticizes the government and is reprimanded by Begin.
1978	
August 15	Friedman publicly denies J.K. Galbraith's accusation that he is responsible for high inflation in Israel. He stands by his original advice and maintains that it was only partially implemented.
1979	
Early January	Short-term foreign borrowing is temporarily prohibited.
February	The BOI prohibits short- and medium-term foreign borrowing for 60 days. Soon afterwards, it extends the prohibition to all foreign borrowing.
Early March	The BOI announces that it will intervene (if necessary) to maintain the PPP of the IL.
April	Foreign borrowing is permitted, subject to a penalty: Israeli banks must pay a 12% surcharge and also deposit with the BOI the amount of 30% of the foreign credit, at a (penalty) interest rate of −17%. Thus, the capital account liberalization of 28 October 1977 is partially reversed.
Mid-1979	By now, the capital account liberalization of 28 October 1977 has largely been reversed. The only remaining provisions are partial freedom of capital movements (subject to a penalty and to foreign exchange intervention) and the $3000 foreign exchange allowance for Israelis traveling abroad.
July 18	Erlich informs Begin (in writing) that he is considering resigning as finance minister. Begin strongly dissuades Erlich.
October 16	Erlich asks Begin (in writing) to accept his resignation. Erlich explains that he cannot continue, due to his failure to develop a cooperative working relationship with many of his ministerial colleagues.
November 7	Erlich resigns as finance minister, but remains in the cabinet as deputy prime minister.

References

Ablin, R. (1978). Note on the Latest N.E.P- 1977. *Economic Quarterly, 96/97*, 126–132.

Amodi, D. (2005, January 23). The Bank of Israel is 50 years old: A class picture, *Forbes Israel* [in Hebrew]. Accessed February 1, 2017, from http://www.nrg.co.il/online/16/ART/858/597.html

Associated Press. (1977a, May 23). Israel to Friedman: Economy needs you. *Chicago Tribune*.

Associated Press. (1977b, July 17). End currency controls, Friedman tells Israel. *New York Times*.

Bank of Israel. (1977, May). *Annual report 1977*. Jerusalem.

Barkai, H. (2002). A central bank in chains. In *Five decades of Israel's economy: A Festschrift for M. Zanbar's 75th anniversary*. Rishon Lezion: College of Management.

Barkai, H., & Liviatan, N. (2007). *The Bank of Israel* (Vol. 1: A monetary history). Oxford: Oxford University Press.

Barnea, N. (1977, May 24). Milton Friedman: Israel must strive for a certain amount of unemployment and allowing for worker layoffs. *Davar*, pp. 1–2.

Begin, Menachem. *Begin Papers*. Begin Heritage Center Archives.

Begin, M. (1977). Remarks in a Cabinet Meeting, October 28, 1977: The economic policy. In A. Naor and A. Lammfromm (Eds.), *Menachem begin, the sixth Prime Minister: Selected documents (1913–1992)* (p. 320). Jerusalem: Israel State Archives, 2014 [in Hebrew].

Ben Bassat, A. (2002). The obstacle course to a market economy in Israel. In A. Ben Bassat (Ed.), *The Israeli economy, 1985–1998: From government intervention to market economics*. Cambridge, MA: MIT Press.

Ben-Porath, Y. (1986). The Israeli economy: Maturing through crises. In Y. Ben-Porath (Ed.), *The Israeli economy: Maturing through crises*. Cambridge, MA: Harvard University Press.

Ben-Porath, Y., & Bruno, M. (1977). The political economy of a tax reform: Israel 1975. *Journal of Public Economics, 7*, 285–307.

Blitzer, W. (1977a, May 24). Workers in Israel will have to be fired. *Jerusalem Post*.

Blitzer, W. (1977b, October 30). Milton Friedman tells *Post*: New measures will cut inflationary pressures. *Jerusalem Post*.

Boughton, J. (2005). *Does the world need a universal financial institution?* IMF Working Paper, WP/05/116.

Broder, J. (1977, July 19). Israel acts to spur economy before asking step-up in aid. *Chicago Tribune*.

Bruno, M. (1986). External shocks and domestic response: Macroeconomic performance, 1965–1982. In Y. Ben-Porath (Ed.), *The Israeli economy: Maturing through crises*. Cambridge, MA: Harvard University Press.

Bruno, M., & Sussman, Z. (1979). Exchange-rate flexibility, inflation and structural change: Israel under alternative regimes. *Journal of Development Economics, 6*, 483–514.

Bufman, G., & Leiderman, L. (1993). Currency substitution under nonexpected utility: Some empirical evidence. *Journal of Money, Credit and Banking, 25*, 320–335.

Burgin, A. (2013). Age of certainty: Galbraith, Friedman, and the public life of economic ideas. *History of Political Economy, 45* (Suppl. 1), 191–219.

Cagan, P. (1956). The monetary dynamics of hyperinflation. In M. Friedman (Ed.), *Studies in the quantity theory of money* (pp. 25–117). Chicago: University of Chicago Press.

Caldwell, B., & Montes, L. (2014). Friedrich Hayek and his visits to Chile. *Review of Austrian Economics, 28*, 261–309.

Connors, T. (1979). The apparent effects of recent IMF stabilization programs. International Finance Discussion Paper 135, Board of Governors of the Federal Reserve System.

Courvisanos, J., & Millmow, A. (2006). How Milton Friedman came to Australia: A case study of class based political business cycles. *Journal of Australian Political Economy, 57*, 112–136.

Davar (1977, May 25, July 5–8).

De Vries, M. (1985). *The International Monetary Fund, 1972–1978: Cooperation on trial* (Vol. 1). Washington, DC: International Monetary Fund.

De Vries, M. (1986). *The IMF in a changing world 1945–85*. Washington, DC: International Monetary Fund.

Ebrill, L., et al. (2001). *The modern VAT*. Washington, DC: International Monetary Fund.

Eckstein, S., et al. (1993). Privatization in Israel: Constraints and impacts. In V. Ramanadham (Ed.), *Constraints and impacts of privatization*. London: Routledge.

Eckstein, Z., & Ramot-Nyska, T. (2008). Twenty years of financial liberalization in Israel: 1987–2007. In *Financial globalization and emerging market capital flows*, Paper 44, Monetary and Economic Department, Bank for International Settlements.

Edwards, S. (1984). *The order of liberalization of the external sector in developing countries*. Princeton Essays in International Finance #156. Princeton: International Finance Section, Princeton University.

Elitzur, Y. (1979, July 8). The economist Milton Friedman is disappointed: "A tragedy in Israel". *Maariv*.

Fischer, S. (1984). The economy of Israel. *Carnegie-Rochester Series on Public Policy: Monetary and Fiscal Policies and Their Application, 20*, 7–52.

Flomin, Y. (1978, November). The economic revolution: How the decision was taken. *Nihul* [in Hebrew].

Flomin, Y. (2010). *Oral history*. Menachem Begin Heritage Center Archives, November 3.

Flomin, Y. (2014, March 10). Personal Interview.

Frenkel, J. (1984). Comments on the economy of Israel. *Carnegie-Rochester Conference Series on Public Policy, 20*, 57–68.

Friedman, M. (1971). Government revenue from inflation. *Journal of Political Economy, 79*, 846–856.

Friedman, M. (1972). *Current monetary conditions, value added tax, subscribers' questions*. Economics Cassette Series #93, February 23, Instructional Dynamics Inc. Accessed February 1, 2017, from http://hoohila.stanford.edu/friedman/ecs.php

Friedman, M. (1973). *Money and economic development: The Horowitz lectures of 1972*. New York: Praeger.

Friedman, M. (1976, December 13). *Inflation and unemployment*. Nobel memorial lecture. [reprinted as Friedman, M. (1977). Nobel lecture: Inflation and unemployment. *Journal of Political Economy 85*, 451–472].

Friedman, M. (1977a). Floating exchange rates for Israel. *Economic Quarterly, 95*, 309–320 [in Hebrew]. English version: Robert Leeson and Charles G. Palm (Eds.), *Collected works of Milton Friedman*. Hoover Institution, Stanford University. Accessed May 5, 2017, from http://miltonfriedman.hoover.org/collections. Record Number 2016c21.1095.

Friedman, M. (1977b, May 31). Interview with R. Hefner, The Open Mind Program, PBS Television (US). Accessed February 1, 2017, from http://www.thirteen.org/openmind/public-affairs/a-nobel-laureate-on-the-american-economy/

Friedman, M. (1977c). *General economic conditions, Alaska, Israel*. Economics Cassette Series #214, May 1977 #2, Instructional Dynamics Inc. Accessed February 1, 2017, from http://hoohila.stanford.edu/friedman/ecs.php

Friedman, M. (1977d, July 4). Commencement talk, delivered at Hebrew University of Jerusalem. In Robert Leeson and Charles G. Palm (Eds.), *Collected works of Milton Friedman*. Hoover Institution, Stanford University. Accessed February 1, 2017, from http://miltonfriedman.hoover.org/collections. Record Number 2016c21.1094.

Friedman, M. (1977e, July 6). Interview with A. Kushnir, Moked Program. *Israel Television*.

Friedman, M. (1977f, August 22). Israel's other war. *Newsweek*.

Friedman, M. (1977g, November 14). Entebbe Again. *Newsweek*.

Friedman, M. (1978, August 15). Relying on the free market, Letter to the Editor. *Times of London*.

Friedman, M. (1979, July 9). Hooray for Margaret Thatcher. *Newsweek*.

Friedman, M. (1985a, March 13). Letter to the Editor. *Haaretz* [Hebrew Newspaper]. Reproduced in Friedman, M. (1988). *Free to choose* [Hebrew Edition]. Tel Aviv: Israel Center for Social and Economic Progress and Dvir Publishing.

Friedman, M. (1985b, March 15). Judging by the record. *Jerusalem Post*.

Friedman, M. (1987a). Video interview by D. Doron and S. Plaut. Israel Center for Social and Economic Progress, Mevasseret Zion, Israel.

Friedman, M. (1987b, November 6). Liberalization: "Israel didn't go far enough". *Jerusalem Post*.

Friedman, M. *Friedman papers*. Hoover Institution, Stanford University.

Friedman, M., & Friedman, R. (1999). *Two lucky people*. Chicago: University of Chicago Press.

Gafny, A. (1977). Economic growth while reducing dependence. *Economic Quarterly, 94*, 175–185 [in Hebrew].

Galbraith, J. (1978a, August 3). Economic efficiency under democracy, Letter to the Editor. *Times* (London).

Galbraith, J. (1978b, August 20). Relying on the free market, Letter to the Editor. *Times* (London)

Galbraith, J. (1979). September seventy-nine: On professor Milton Friedman's disillusionment with the economic policy of the Likud. *Migvan, 39/40*, 28–29 [in Hebrew].

Goell, Y. (1979, January 26). A chat with the professor. *Jerusalem Post*.

Halevi, N. (1979). The exchange rate in Israel: Policy and opinion. *Revue Economique, 30*, 10–30.

Halevi, N. (1986). Perspectives on the balance of payments. In Y. Ben-Porath (Ed.), *The Israeli economy: Maturing through crises* (pp. 241–263). Cambridge, MA: Harvard University Press.

Hanoch, G., et al. (1977). The recent N.E.P. (A symposium). *Economic Quarterly, 95*, 321–343.

Har Gil, S. (1969, March 19). Nixon's friend: Admiration for Israel–in the US. *Maariv*.

International Monetary Fund Archives Catalog. Accessed February 1, 2017, from http://archivescatalog.imf.org/

Israel Television. (1977a, October 28). Special edition on the Economic Plan, Mabat [News Program in Hebrew]. Israel Broadcasting Authority Archive.

Israel Television. (1977b, October 28). Reactions at the conclusion of the Cabinet Meeting on the Economic Plan, Yoman [News Program in Hebrew]. Israel Broadcasting Authority Archive.

Jerusalem Post. (1977a, June 13). What does the Likud want? To grab the reins in order to undermine the Histadrut, Advertisement.

Jerusalem Post. (1977b, June 22). Ehrlich: Heaven forbid unemployment.

Jewish Telegraphic Agency. (1977a, March 30). IMF alarmed over Israel's economy.

Jewish Telegraphic Agency. (1977b, April 8). Rabin resigns following probe into illegal bank accounts held by him and his wife in Washington.

Jewish Telegraphic Agency. (1977c, July 21). Knesset approves fiscal measures.

Jewish Telegraphic Agency. (1977d, October 31). Abolition of currency regulations and other sweeping measures are introduced to create a free economy.

Keep, M. (2015). *Government borrowing, debt and debt interest: Historical statistics and forecasts*. House of Commons Briefing Paper #05745.

Kiviti, N. (1977, May 24). Professor Friedman: This is how I will act in Israel, *Yediot Aharonot*.

Kleiman, E. (1981). Israel: Economists in a new state. *History of Political Economy, 13*(3), 548–579.

Kleiman, E. (1986). Indexation in the labor market. In Y. Ben-Porath (Ed.), *The economy of Israel: Maturing through crises*. Cambridge, MA: Harvard University Press.

Krivine, D. (1977, June 17). No. 2 Man. *Jerusalem Post*.

Likud Party. (1977). *Election platform for the Ninth Knesset* (11 pages). Begin Heritage Center Archives [in Hebrew].

McKinnon, R. (1973). *Money and capital in economic development*. Washington: Brookings Institution.

McKinnon, R., & Mathieson, D. (1981). *How to manage a repressed economy*. Essays in International Finance #145, Princeton University, International Finance Section.

McKinnon, R. (1982). The order of economic liberalization: Lessons from Chile and Argentina. *Carnegie-Rochester Conference Series on Public Policy, 17*, 159–186.

Melnick, R., & Yashiv, E. (1996). The macroeconomic effects of financial innovation: The case of Israel. In M. Blejer et al. (Eds.), *Financial factors in economic stabilization and growth*. Cambridge: Cambridge University Press.

Meltzer, A. (2011). *Milton Friedman: Non-research activities 1976–89*, Working Paper WP56, Working Group on Economic Policy, Hoover Institution, Stanford University.

Metzer, J. (1986). The slowdown of economic growth in Israel: A passing phase or the end of the big spurt? In Y. Ben-Porath (Ed.), *The economy of Israel: Maturing through crises*. Cambridge, MA: Harvard University Press.

Meyshar, J. (1986). Investment patterns. In Y. Ben-Porath (Ed.), *The economy of Israel: Maturing through crises*. Cambridge, MA: Harvard University Press.

Michaely, M. (1983). The floating exchange rate in Israel: 1977–1980. In T. Taya & D. Bigman (Eds.), *Exchange rate and trade instability: Causes, consequences and remedies*. Cambridge, MA: Ballinger Publishing.

Michaely, M. (2007). The liberalization of Israel's foreign exchange market, 1950–2002. In N. Liviatan & H. Barkai (Eds.), *The Bank of Israel* (Vol. 2: Selected topics in Israel's monetary policy). Oxford: Oxford University Press.

Millmow, A. (2009). The transition from Keynesian to monetarist economics in Australia: Joan Robinson's 1975 visit to Australia. *History of Economics Review, 49, Winter*.

Montes, L. (2016). *Milton Friedman and his visits to Chile*, Working Paper, Universidad Adolfo Ibanez.

Nelson, E. (2009). Milton Friedman and U.K. economic policy, 1938–1979. *Federal Reserve Bank of St. Louis Review, 91*, 465–506.

Nichols, D. (1974). Some principles of inflationary finance. *Journal of Political Economy, 82*, 423–430.

New York Times. (1977, August 13). Israel is moving to make pound convert freely.

Ofner, F. (1977, July 19). What Begin's belt tightening means: He asks food, fuel cutbacks to help win renewed US aid. *Christian Science Monitor*.

Patinkin, D. *Patinkin papers*. Rubenstein Rare Book and Manuscript Library, Duke University.

Plessner, Y. (1994). *The political economy of Israel: From ideology to stagnation*. Albany: State University of New York Press.

Sargent, T., & Zeira, J. (2011). Israel 1983: A bout of unpleasant monetarist arithmetic. *Review of Economic Dynamics, 14*, 419–431.

Schiffman, D. (2014). Richard Kahn and Israeli economic policy, 1957 and 1962. *History of Economic Thought and Policy, 1*, 31–73.

Shiffer, Z. (2004). The CLA as an instrument for protecting the real wage from inflationary surprises. *Bank of Israel Review, 76*, 103–143 [in Hebrew].

State of Israel, Knesset Finance Committee. (1977). 9th Knesset, 1st Session Protocol #3, July 7. Agenda: A conversation with Prof. M. Friedman. Israel State Archives, ID number 60.0.24.369.

State of Israel, The Knesset. (1977, October 31). Divrei Haknesset (Parliamentary Record, in Hebrew) 9th Knesset, 34th session.

Sussman, O. (1992). Financial liberalization: The Israeli experience. *Oxford Economic Papers, 44*, 387–402.

Torgerson, D. (1977, May 29). New regime in Israel faces labor struggle. *Los Angeles Times*.

Tov, I. (1988). The 1977 'Economic Upheaval'—Execution of goals. *Economic Quarterly, 135/136*, 33–47 [in Hebrew].

Tzabag, S. (1995). Co-operation in the shadow of a power struggle: Israel: the Likud Governments and the Histadrut 1977–84. *Middle Eastern Studies, 31*, 849–888.

US State Department. (1977a, May 25). Meeting with Liberal MK Flomin. US Embassy in Israel to State Department. Document Number: 1977TELAV03702 (Declassified May 2009).

US State Department. (1977b, June 24). Survey of early personnel changes effected by Begin government. US Embassy in Israel to State Department. Document Number: 1977TELAV04615 (Declassified May 2009).

US State Department. (1977c, July 11). CODEL Hamilton Begin summary. US Embassy in Israel to State Department. Document Number: 1977TELAV05027 (Declassified May 2009).

US State Department. (1977d, July 14). Meshel comments on Begin and government/Histadrut Relations. US Embassy in Israel to State Department. Document Number: 1977TELAV05153 (Declassified May 2009).

Yitzhaki, S. (1986). Taxes and transfers in an inflationary decade. In Y. Ben-Porath (Ed.), *The Israeli economy: Maturing through crises*. Cambridge, MA: Harvard University Press.

Zilberfarb, B. (1991). Foreign exchange market liberalization: Anatomy of a failure. In A. Hillman (Ed.), *Markets and politicians: Politicized economic choice*. Boston: Kluwer.

Chapter 6
Economic Analysis, Advice, and Stabilization, 1972–1992: The Stein-Fischer Nexus

6.1 Economic Analysis, Advice, and Policy: Stein and Fischer

Much has been published regarding the July 1985 Israeli economic stabilization program. These writings include contemporary and retrospective accounts of the protagonists involved in its design and implementation—Israeli and American politicians and economists (Moday 1988; Berglas 1986; Bruno 1988, 1992, 1993; Fischer and Stein 1991; Peres 2015; Sharon 2015). This chapter deals with the ongoing connection between the two major economic figures—Herbert Stein and Stanley Fischer, who acted as economic advisers to the 1985 Israeli effort at stabilization—and their views of, and impact on, Israeli economic policy over the period 1972–1992. The reason for this "long-term" focus on the "Stein-Fischer nexus" is that their assessments influenced the course of economic analysis and policy *both prior to and after 1985*.

The second section of this chapter provides a brief overview of the *politico-historic setting* and concern with *reserves*, government finance and foreign economic advice in Israel over the period 1950–1953, *that set the tone for future attitudes and events*. The third section deals with the *long run* economic background that led to the 1984–1985 crisis and stabilization plan, starting in 1970 with a return to a "double-digit" inflation that characterized the years 1948–1954, accelerated by OPEC 1 and 2, and hyperinflation. The fourth section deals with the crisis of 1984–1985 and the 1985 stabilization program itself. The fifth section focuses on the outcome of the stabilization program, assessments of its success, and the input of Stein and Fischer regarding 1992 US loan guarantees. Throughout the chapter, the emphasis will be on the views of Stein and Fischer and assessments, *contemporary and retrospective*, of the stabilization program and its outcome.

D. Schiffman et al., *The Role of Economic Advisers in Israel's Economic Policy*,
DOI 10.1007/978-3-319-60682-8_6

6.2 Politico-Historic Setting

The December 1950 issue of *Commentary* published an article entitled "A Billion Dollars for Israel" (Lehrman 1950). This reported on the four-point plan developed by the Israeli Finance Ministry in 1950, which was based upon the foreign exchange requirements of Israel—not only for immigrant absorption—that reflected a projected ongoing "foreign exchange crisis until the end of 1953." The plan focused upon means of generating funds required to meet foreign exchange needs. The first point dealt with the necessity for foreign aid, consisting of US government loans and grants. By late 1950, the US was more receptive to Israel's requests for foreign aid, due to Israel's shift from "non-identification" to a strong pro-Western orientation. The second point was based upon stimulating private investment of American firms in Israel. The third point focused on philanthropy of the American Jewish community. The fourth point was the decision by the Israeli government in 1950 to eventually issue two types of dollar-denominated development bonds, albeit implementation of this would take until 1952, with resolution of the issues of tax exemption and American Jewish philanthropic funding for projects in Israel.

Two years later, in the October 1952 issue of *Commentary*, Lehrman (1952) published an article entitled "Washington comes to Israel's economic rescue." In this, he noted that between January 1949 and June 1952, the US Export-Import Bank had provided some $90 million in credits, while Congress had voted grants and earmarked funds of some $200 million, with total US assistance thus projected to reach $290 million by mid-1953. It should be recalled here that Lehrman was the author of one of the first books on the political economy of the new state (Lehrman 1951) and a recognized authority on Israel's economic development.

In his 1952 *Commentary* article, Lehrman noted that the chronic problem in Israel's economy was "her continued drastic deficiency of foreign exchange." This "foreign exchange poverty," in his words, was manifest in the fact that by the end of 1952, Israel's short-term debt to the US reached over $100 million and it was not able to meet its debt payment requirements. As a result, as noted in Chap. 2, Mikesell was sent to Israel by the US government to evaluate its foreign exchange problem and proposed a "balanced foreign exchange budget." Other measures were taken, such as compulsory loans on bank accounts and other holdings, and a capital levy, so as to get around "the poverty" of Israel's government finance, as Lehrman put it. "Foreign exchange poverty" and "the poverty of government finance" came full circle in the mid-1980s when they concomitantly brought about a crisis that eventually led to the July 1985 stabilization program.

Israel's first prime minister, Ben-Gurion, did not mince words regarding economic advisers and their advice during the country's formative years. At a June 1953 Knesset debate on the budget of the Prime Minister's Office, he criticized the recommendations of a then serving foreign adviser, Solomon Trone, and focused on the *possible* advice of the newly formed EAS—led by Oscar Gass—as *provisional* at best. He said: "Foreign experts ... were called in to advise, not to act as judges or legislators. Besides being qualified in their respective fields ... they had to have the

'Zionist spark'." The government often chose to go against expert advice; in such cases, "facts proved that we were right, for we know local needs and possibilities better" (9 June 1953).

Trone, a US-based engineer and expert in planning, had been involved before WWII in the development of electrification in Russia in the context of the Soviet 5-year plan and served as a consultant in China and Korea after the war. In 1949–1950, he was an adviser to the Indian government on coordination of regional and national planning. He authored a report critical of the Indian planning process and procedures, which became highly controversial and was shelved by the government (*Economic Weekly*, Bombay, 12 February 1950). He had been employed by the Israeli government from January 1952 and authored numerous reports on sectoral planning in Israel. In August 1952, he presented a plan to the government for investing German reparation payments and funds from other sources, totaling some $1.65 billion over 10 years (*New York Times*, 14 August 1952). A year later, according to Ben-Gurion's statement in the Knesset in June 1953, Trone had recommended "total control of production and complete economic controls—advice which the government could not accept" (*Jerusalem Post*, 9 June 1953). In the same statement, Ben-Gurion said the following regarding the EAS and Gass (as paraphrased by the *Jerusalem Post*): "… a new advisory group under Mr. Oscar Gass was here at the invitation of the government; its counsel would be heard, but not necessarily followed."

Ben-Gurion's protégé, Peres, became prime minister after the inconclusive July 1984 election. A national unity government based on rotation of the prime ministership was formed, with Peres becoming prime minister for the first period. Peres, as will be seen below, took issue with recommendations of "foreign experts" regarding how best to end Israel's hyperinflation at the time. He also expressed his lack of regard for experts in his retrospective account, when he said: "If economics professors are so smart, why aren't they millionaires?" (Peres 2015).

6.3 From "Double Digit" to "Hyperinflation": Economic Crises and Management, 1970–1984

Between 1970 and 1973, the Israeli CPI inflation rate doubled from 10% to 20% per annum. In April 1972, the new Chair of Nixon's Council of Economic Advisers, Herbert Stein, visited Israel. After extending Nixon's personal Independence Day greetings to Prime Minister Meir, Stein met with Finance Minister Sapir, Industry and Commerce Minister Bar-Lev and BOI Governor Sanbar. Stanley Fischer, then an assistant professor at the University of Chicago, was also in Israel in 1972, as a visiting senior lecturer at the Hebrew University. Interestingly enough, then, both "foreign architects" of the Israeli 1985 stabilization plan were in the country when the inflationary process, that later got out of control, took hold.

From 1948 onward, Israeli policymakers and foreign advisers were always concerned with the economic policy *triad* of prices, balance of payments/foreign currency reserves, and unemployment. High double-digit inflation characterized the first 5 years of statehood, 1948–1952. Even though an initial liberalization plan was instituted in 1952, it took until 1955 for the inflation rate to fall into the single digits.

Balance of payments and foreign reserves were also always a problem in the 1950s and 1960s. And, given the considerable *political sensitivity* of the unemployment rate, this was also problematic for Israeli politicians and *constrained* economic policy advice. The political sensitivity was emanated from the recession of 1965Q3–1967Q2, when the unemployment rate reached almost 12%, which far exceeded the 8% unemployment rate recorded in 1955, following the massive immigration of 1949–1954.

The importance of the story regarding Israel's foreign reserves between 1970 and 1984 has been somewhat overlooked in dealing with the 1985 stabilization program. Over the period 1970–1973, the level of reserves rose almost fourfold, from some $480 million to $2 billion—a result, in part, of American Jewish and other contributions to assist absorption of the *first wave* of Soviet Jewish immigration between 1968 and 1972. As a result of the 1973 war and oil price shock, however, reserves dropped back to $1.3–1.5 billion over 1974–1976 and only returned to $1.8 billion in 1977, with the beginning of peace negotiations with Egypt. Between 1978 and 1982, reserves rose from $2.8 to 4.3 billion. Moreover, the current account deficit (in $ terms) had narrowed from $2.1 to $1.4 billion over the period 1983–1984 (Bruno and Z. Sussman 1979).

However, with the economic crisis of 1983–1984—the crash of the Israeli banking system in 1983 combined with hyperinflation of 445% in 1984—reserves fell to $3.8 billion in 1983 and $3.3 billion in 1984. The implications of this continuing fall in reserves were not lost on Israeli and US politicians, economists, and foreign economic advisers, *as the level of reserves needed to cover essential imports was of considerable strategic importance.*

Regarding inflation, the story is better known. Between 1970 and the 1973 oil price shock, the economy was characterized by low double-digit inflation, but the inflation rate almost doubled between 1972 and 1973, rising to 20% in 1973, and doubled again to 40% in 1974 and 1975. While the rate fell to some 30% in 1976, a year later it was again over 40% and reached almost 50% in 1978. The oil price shock of 1979 was accompanied by a more than doubling of the inflation rate to 111% in 1979 and 133% in 1980. Inflation fell to 101% in 1981, as a result of contractionary policy and currency redenomination that affected inflationary expectations, but returned to 132% in 1982.

Economic policy *failures* were exemplified by a breakdown in the 1977 *liberalization* program, *misapplication* of supply-side and *tablita*-type measures from 1981–1982, and the 1983 banking collapse due to bank share manipulation ostensibly allowed by the government and Bank of Israel (henceforth BOI), so that hyperinflation had reached 191% in 1983, bringing about—with policy *collapse* and a high inflationary spiral—an inflation rate of 445% in 1984 (Plessner and Young 2005).

What should be recalled here is that from 1970 onward, numerous anti-inflationary measures were applied, ranging from fiscal constraint, budgetary and subsidy cuts, redenomination, attempted dollarization, and wage-price freezes, but none were able to bring inflation back to low double or single digits. As will be seen, it was a *heterodox* stabilization package combining "cold turkey" measures with an end to *monetizing* the government budget deficit—concomitantly *targeting* both hyperinflation and the reserve situation and providing the Israeli economy with *central nominal anchors* on the exchange and wage fronts—that brought inflation down from triple to double digits, but not to single digits (Bruno 1986a, 1986b, 1986c; Dornbusch et al. 1990). A *sustained* return to single-digit inflation was only achieved via *orthodox* measures such as interest rate policy, after Frenkel became Governor of the BOI in 1991 (Frenkel 1984, 1996, 1998).

6.4 Stein, Fischer, and the Growing Economic Crisis in Israel, 1982–1985

US economic aid was based on both loans and grants. Both Congress and the Administration were involved in the appropriations process, especially the department and secretary of state, who appointed economic advisers for Israel to promote the US interest. As a result, both aid and advice were politicized on multiple occasions, beginning in the early 1950s.

Stanley Fischer was more involved with the Israeli economy than Herbert Stein, but Stein was senior and was thus appointed by US Secretary of State George Schultz in 1983 to lead a panel of four American economists—Paul McCracken, Abe Siegel, Fischer, and Stein himself[1]—to assess economic measures undertaken by Israel to justify the level of economic aid, plus supplemental aid requests. As Fischer recalled in an interview with Olivier Blanchard (2005, 268): "On the occasions Herb and I traveled to Israel, we essentially had George Shultz's authority behind us. And we could say, 'The Secretary of State believes this.' As a professor, that didn't especially impress me. But when you say 'the Secretary of State believes' to a government that depends on the United States, they are not listening only to the economics."

However, most, if not all of their advice—from 1983 *until the crisis peaked in June 1985—was not applied*. For example, in April 1983, Fischer presented a paper at the Carnegie-Rochester Conference on Public Policy entitled "The economy of Israel," which was first circulated as an NBER working paper in August 1983 (Fischer 1983) and eventually published in Spring 1984 (Fischer 1984). In this paper, he outlined two alternatives for stabilization policy in Israel: (a) gradual disinflation, in which the government would accept the reality of slow real wage adjustment and (as a result)

[1] Fischer (2001a) recalled that "Abe Siegel and Paul McCracken dropped out at a relatively early stage, but Herb and I remained closely involved for years."

high real wages during the disinflation process, and (b) a "wage and macro-policy package" including a "real devaluation" and persuading organized labor "to forgo indexation temporarily," rather than "cold turkey." He noted that either choice would involve a reduction in Israel's budget deficit and stopping the printing of money to finance it (1984, 35). However, both choices were rejected back then.

In late 1983, Shultz appointed his "advisory group," and in early 1984, the first meeting took place between Shultz, his panel, and a group of Israeli officials and economists. Meetings continued up to mid-1984, but again with no outcome, because of Israeli politics and the upcoming election of July 1984. In June 1984, two key members of the Israeli group—Finance Ministry Director-General Emmanuel Sharon and BOI Director of Research Mordechai Frenkel—resigned, claiming that the government had abandoned anti-inflation policies to obtain electoral support.

Inconclusive election results led to the formation of a Labor Alignment-Likud national unity government with rotation of the office of prime minister. During 1984–1986, Peres (Labor Alignment) served as prime minister while Shamir (Likud) served as foreign minister. Moday (Likud) was appointed finance minister; by mutual agreement, Likud would hold the finance portfolio for the duration of the national unity government.[2] Peres visited Washington in October 1984, with the outcome that Schultz set up a new body, the Joint Economic Development Group (JEDG). It should be noted at this point that the JEDG still functioned as late as May 2016, focusing, among other things, on the outcome of the 1985 stabilization, the 1992 US loan guarantees to Israel, and further US loan guarantees in 2003.

According to Stein's recollections (1990, 15):

> After the Peres visit, the pace of exchanges between Washington and Jerusalem picked up greatly. Emmanuel Sharon came to Washington in November to brief us on the government's thinking. (Sharon had been brought back into the government by Peres and would be a key figure in the development of the stabilization program.) The full Israeli delegation came in December. Sharon brought to the December meeting a proposal for economic stabilization policy that Prime Minister Peres had authorized him to discuss but which Peres had not adopted. This proposal covered budget cuts, monetary restraint, devaluation, modification of the system for indexing liquid assets, and some restraint on real wages. We were unsure about whether the steps proposed were strong enough, and we were also worried about the Israeli government's ability to execute a program once it had been adopted, particularly to restrain the budget. But this proposal was much closer to what was needed than the ideas we had heard a month earlier. The proposal, however, did not get as warm a reception in Jerusalem as it had in Washington. It took six months to develop specifics and get them accepted by Mr. Peres, the cabinet, the Knesset [Israel's Parliament], and the leaders of labor and business. This had to be done by the Israelis themselves, but consultation with the Americans was continuous and, I believe, helpful.

[2]Peres and Shamir were the only ministers to rotate. The coalition agreement stipulated that any cabinet vacancy would be filled by a member of the same party. Thus, when Moday and Peres feuded in 1986, the Likud ministers arranged for Moday to swap positions with then-Justice Minister Moshe Nissim.

In his recollections, Moday wrote that in mid-November 1984, Shultz told Finance Ministry Director-General Sharon that on 19 December, he intended to present Israel's aid request to Congress. Without a clear economic plan and clarity regarding the actions being taken at that time, Shultz said that he would not request any aid at all (Moday 1988, 186).

Moday also recalled that at the conclusion of the November 1984 Washington meetings, Israel's accountant-general reported the state of his country's foreign currency reserves. The Americans were so shocked that Allen Wallis, undersecretary of state for economic affairs, sent his economic adviser Martin Bailey to meet the Israeli delegation at the airport in New York before they departed and give them "a blunt memorandum" to take back to Israel regarding the *seriousness* of the foreign reserve situation (1988, 186–187). Foreign currency reserves, measured in months of import coverage, had declined from 3 and 3.2 in 1984Q1 and 1984Q2 to 2.1 in 1984Q3. That is to say, foreign currency reserves had fallen significantly below the traditional red line of 3 months of import coverage (about $3 billion at the time) (Bank of Israel Report 1985, 232 (Table 7–25); IMF 1983, 2011, 4).

Despite what Stein recalled, in December 1984, Shultz sent a letter to Peres asserting that he would not support Israel's request for increased US aid unless a comprehensive stabilization plan was produced. Shultz advocated not only increased budget cuts but also "structural changes," such as BOI independence, so that it could curb the increase in money supply that essentially financed the budget deficit. Shultz was not impressed by the tentative plan proposed by the Israeli government, rather than the *comprehensive* stabilization policy that he deemed necessary.

In reaction to Shultz's letter, which stressed the need for *overall austerity measures*, Israeli Minister of Economics and Planning Yaacobi (Labor) was reported to have said: "the unity government knew what it faced and what it needed to do and didn't need lectures and new theories … I don't remember the US upbraiding or reprimanding Israel during all the years when the policy which brought us to our present condition was being implemented … Israel does not need moral preaching from the US" (*Jewish Telegraphic Agency*, 27 December 1984; *Chicago Tribune*, 2 Jan 1985). This contrasted sharply with his assertion in August 1984—before the formation of the Peres-led government—that a Peres-led government would adopt austerity measures, including a 10% cut in the government budget; thus, "Israel would have the 'moral authority' to ask for additional US aid" (Southerland 1984). It should be noted, however, that due to Yaacobi's public pronouncements, Moday decided to exclude Yaacobi from economic discussions relating to the Ministry of Finance (Moday 1988, 144).

According to Moday's recollections (1988, 188), US Ambassador to Israel Lewis, speaking for Secretary of State Shultz, orally presented him with a nine-point plan earlier agreed to between Sharon and the Stein-Fischer team during Sharon's November 1984 visit to Washington. These points included:

(a) Setting agreed inflation targets (government, Histadrut, industrialists association)
(b) Drafting the budget in dollar terms
(c) Passing a budget law with deviations being considered criminal offenses

(d) Enabling a change in the BOI Law prohibiting printing of money to finance the budget deficit and eliminating the deficit in the next fiscal year
(e) Managing the BOI's monetary policy according to inflation targets set within the framework of reducing the rate of increase of financial assets held by the public
(f) Adjusting shekel devaluation according to the inflation rate
(g) Reducing subsidies to the minimum required to enable policy planning
(h) Reducing directed (subsidized) credit to industry
(i) Eliminating interest on PATAM (shekel-denominated dollar-linked accounts) and prohibition of new PATAM accounts

And indeed, some of these points, especially regarding amending the Bank of Israel Law, subsidies, and PATAM accounts, later became integral parts of the 1985 stabilization program and supplementary legislation.

Moday further recalled that in March 1985 he visited Washington and New York. After he returned to Israel, he told the Israeli media that Israel would get special aid from the US and the first installment would be made available soon. Furthermore, he told the media and the public: "The Americans are not attempting to dictate [to us] an economic policy, but they have a strong hope—which we should take into consideration—that we will be wise enough to make a substantial budget cut and eliminate the indexation arrangements in the economy." What Moday did not tell the public was that Shultz had told him that Israel's anti-inflation plan, as it *then* stood, did not go far enough and would not be effective (1988, 191).

Fischer, for his part, recalled (1995, 3 note 8) that while the Treasury Department and Office of Management and Budget participated in the JEDC alongside the State Department, "Shultz took over formal control of the US role in the Israeli stabilization program at a meeting in March 1985. In that month, Shultz sent Stein and Fischer to Israel "to try to figure out what needed doing" (Fischer 1995, 6). According to Fischer, "at the end of this visit," Stein "pulled out of his pocket a list of 10 points" that became "benchmarks" for stabilization, but more about this below. Fischer went on to recall (1995, 7) that between his visit with Stein to Israel in March 1985 and the implementation of the Israeli stabilization program in July 1985, the US participants in the JEDC not only focused on "encouraging the Israeli government to stabilize" but also to ensure "that the supplementary aid was not disbursed to the Israelis before they had taken action to stabilize the economy. The problem was that the Congress was so favorably disposed towards Israel at that time, that it was difficult for the Administration to keep them from giving money to the Israelis no matter what their economic policy."

Fischer then recalled his discussions with Stein and Shultz regarding aid conditionality before their next trip to Israel in May 1985. He wrote (1995, 8): "Shultz did not like … conditionality. All along his idea had been that the Israeli government would set out a program with their own 'markers,' actions that they would set as their own conditions, so that both sides could monitor the program. Neither Herb nor I thought that this generous approach would work …" Shultz refused Stein's request to "impose conditions on the aid" and told Fischer directly that *actual* conditionality would not be imposed. When Fischer insisted on the importance of conditionality, Shultz told Fischer "you can tell [the Israelis] I will be very disappointed if they get the aid without carrying out the program" (1995, 9).

Indeed, on 21 April 1985, in a major speech at AIPAC (then the most prominent pro-Israel lobbying organization in the US), Shultz, in concise and lucid terms, outlined his views on the Israeli economic situation. He said (1985, 127): "Israel must pull itself out of its present economic trauma. And the Israeli people must do it themselves. No one can do it for them. Israel will need support as it makes the needed adjustments, and here the US can and must help. But our help will be of little avail if Israel does not take the necessary steps to cut government spending, improve productivity, open up its economy, and strengthen the mechanisms of economic policy."

In a paper dealing with the "role of the economist in society," including the role of the economist as policy adviser (2001b), Fischer wrote the following (2001b, 4):

> There are at least two important differences between policy advising and academic economics. The first is that there is a bottom line. If you are asked what impact some policy will have, it is no use replying that it all depends on the precise specification of the model. I learnt this most clearly from Herb Stein, who once asked me over a dinner in Washington in 1984 what the policy options were in Israel. I replied with a lengthy and no doubt learned analysis of the state of the economy, the role of the budget deficit, of indexation, monetary policy, the balance of policy views among the various participants—in short, a very good exam answer. When it was over, Herb asked me: "Well, but what do we want them to *do*?" That is the bottom line question for any policy adviser.
>
> The second difference is the set of constraints. The policy adviser will frequently be told that some policy proposal is not politically possible. The political objections need to be explored, for they are often less insoluble than it initially seems. But in the end, it is primarily for the politicians to judge what can and cannot be done.

Interestingly enough, Fischer's NBER working paper with Michael Bruno, dated "spring of 1984" and entitled "The inflationary process in Israel: shocks and accommodation," outlined "measures" to be taken in possible stabilization programs and the rationale for those measures. Fischer and Bruno concluded that "the program should be comprehensive and rapid" based upon "political economy, and not purely economic, grounds" as "any gradualist program in which restrictive policy … is supposed to be maintained over several years is unlikely to be followed through by the government. Hence, the conclusion that the tough medicine should be taken all at once." They suggested a "list of measures" including: (a) cutting the budget deficit, (b) freezing nominal wages, (c) fixing the exchange rate, (d) attempting to control prices, (e) real devaluation, and (f) reducing the liquidity of dollar-indexed accounts (Bruno and Fischer 1984, 36–38).

March 1985 was an eventful month regarding discussion and debate over the crisis and stabilization proposals. Stein's "Ten Points," a list of ten policy recommendations for stabilization (reproduced in Stein 1990, 15–16), originated during Stein's visit to Israel with Fischer in March 1985. Fischer (2001a) recalled:

> At the end of the visit, Herb pulled out of his pocket a ten point stabilization plan that he had jotted down on a sheet of yellow paper. The ten points were the essential elements of a stabilization program, even though they were incomplete, for instance in not sufficiently emphasizing the need for fiscal consolidation. The idea was for Sharon to take the plan privately with the prime minister and the finance minister … While the ten points are not Herb's finest prose, they were certainly written by him.

Stein's recollections regarding the origin of this document differ somewhat from Fischer's. According to Stein (1990, 15):

> In March, the State Department decided to send two of its private consultants Stanley Fischer, at the time a professor at MIT, and me, to Israel … The idea was that we could communicate more frankly than an official delegation could. Trying to clarify the issues after several days in Jerusalem, *Fischer and I made up a list of ten points for a stabilization plan* [our emphasis].[3] We did this in discussion with Sharon [the Director-General of the Finance Ministry, who had been reinstated by Peres] and wanted him to take them up with the finance minister and prime minister so that we could see what they were thinking. The list was very close to the points that Sharon had brought to Washington in December.

On 6 March 1985, Allen Wallis, Undersecretary of State for Economic Affairs, and a prominent economist in his own right, testified at a hearing before the Subcommittee on Europe and the Middle East of the House Committee on Foreign Affairs. The subject of his testimony was foreign assistance legislation for fiscal years 1985–1986. In his verbal statement, he said (1985, 205):

> In our conversations with the Israelis, we have stressed our support for their stabilization efforts. And I might say, soon after Secretary Shultz arrived and began to study the situation of the Israel economy and subsequently set up a small group working on it within the department, and still more recently, as I have mentioned, we have established a formal group. We have expressed willingness to provide extraordinary additional assistance in support of a comprehensive program that deals effectively with fundamental problems of their economy. We have made clear our view that without such a commitment, more aid simply would not help. Instead, it could perpetuate Israel's problems and create a dependency that neither of us want … We in the administration believe that further progress is necessary to eliminate the remaining structural imbalances and to put Israel back on the road to economic health. Now we commend what Israel has done to date. Our policy is to help the best way we can, but we believe Israel has not yet reached the stage in the evolution of its program where additional US aid would help. And, indeed, as I said, without further progress additional aid could actually be counterproductive. For that reason, the administration intends to continue to defer for the time being a response to Israel's request for supplemental aid.

The Chair of the Subcommittee, Rep. Lee Hamilton (D-Indiana), and other members of the Subcommittee then posed a series of questions to Wallis regarding the US stance on Israel's economic problems (1985, 214–215). Wallis was asked about the root cause of Israel's economic situation, and he replied: "It is clearly

[3]The "Ten Points" were later leaked and published in the Israeli media under Stein's name. According to Stein, this misattribution was due to the simple fact that Stein handwrote the "ten points" and Fischer then typed them into a computer, entitling them "Herb's Ten Points" (Stein 1990, 16). Initially, the leak appeared to be harmful, but over time, it helped galvanize public support for comprehensive reform. Fischer (2001a) recalled: "No sooner had we returned to the US than the list was leaked and published in the Israeli newspapers, under the title 'Herb's 10 Points.' The fact that they then appeared in the newspapers under that heading conveyed an unfortunate impression that they were being imposed on the Israelis, which contributed to an initially hostile press reaction … But, as it turned out, the leak ended up being helpful. The points were widely discussed, their shortcomings–particularly in underemphasizing the need for fiscal balance–identified, and the increased public understanding probably strengthened the government's willingness to act."

basically a political problem." Concurrent with Wallis' testimony, Schultz told the Senate Appropriations Committee's Subcommittee on Foreign Operations that the Administration would be reticent in agreeing to a specific level of aid "pending further discussion with Israel and further evolution of its stabilization program." He asserted that the US would assist "in support of a comprehensive Israeli economic program that deals efficiently with the fundamental imbalances in the Israeli economy." Shultz maintained that without such a program, "additional US assistance would not resolve Israel's economic problems but merely help perpetuate them" (*Jewish Telegraphic Agency*, 7 March 1985a).

After their return to the US, Stein and Fischer reportedly supported the proposed $1.5 billion in supplementary economic aid, if Israel was prepared to enact Stein's "Ten Points," including BOI "independence" and an end to short-term deposit indexation (Blitzer, 19 April 1985). In late April 1985, Peres sent a letter to Shultz promising a new stabilization program; Schultz received it on 20 April, a day before his address to AIPAC cited above. Schultz, who was due to visit Israel on 9 May, reportedly said that "we are looking for actions instead of promises." The Peres letter responded specifically to Stein's "Ten Points." Moreover, both Stein and Shultz were adamant in stressing that any additional aid should not be allocated prior to the enactment of necessary economic reforms by Israel. Stein, who opposed endorsement of the increased aid to Israel on 2 April by the House Foreign Affairs Committee, was quoted as saying: "A decision to provide supplemental aid before the program has been established can only weaken the sense of urgency about developing the program. Initiation of the needed program would be deferred, possibly until some future crisis" (Gwertzman, *New York Times*, 28 April 1985).

Regarding central bank independence, Peres wrote in his letter that legislation was being prepared, but he did not make any commitment regarding short-term deposit indexation, in spite of Stein's complaint that, along with the budget deficit, indexation had fueled Israel's rapid inflation. In the view of many observers, however, short-term deposit indexation was "so popular in Israel that the government would almost certainly fall if it started to tamper with it" (Kempster, *Los Angeles Times*, 29 April 1985).

During his visit to Israel in May 1985, Shultz held economic discussions with Peres and Moday. Peres told his cabinet that the increased US aid "would not be linked to any conditions," but added that Shultz and the US expected Israel to take "necessary measures" in order to save its economy (*Jewish Telegraphic Agency*, 12 May 1985b). A fortnight later, the House Appropriations Committee approved the $1.5 billion in supplemental aid for Israel. However, the chair of its Foreign Operations Subcommittee was reported to have said that the Administration could hold back the aid until the end of September 1986, to encourage Israel to implement its economic reform program (AP, 21 May 1985). And a commentary published in *The Washington Post* on 9 June was entitled "Will US dollars fix Israel's economy?" but was subtitled "Both countries may have allowed the opportunity to slip away" (Oberdorfer 1985, Washington Post, 9 June).

In his recollection of events in June 1985, Stein wrote (1990, 16): "Under Secretary Wallis led the US delegation to Israel in June. Mr. Peres was told clearly that the United States regarded the situation as grave and the need for action urgent. By the time we left Jerusalem, we felt that at least the stage was set for action. Our consultations were not the only, or the main, force leading to action. Events were compelling it. The inflation rate was soaring-as high as 1000% annual rate in some months. The shekel was selling on the black market at a 40% discount from the official rate. Exchange reserves were dwindling …"

At a weekly cabinet meeting in early June 1985, the Israeli government finally resolved to implement a comprehensive stabilization program. As one of its architects, Bruno, recalled a few months later (October 1985, 1986a, 388), Peres and Moday appointed a team of economists to come up with a workable plan to submit to the government by 30 June 1985. The team was headed by Sharon and included Bruno, Berglas, Frenkel, and Neubach. The plan they submitted was based on a "cold turkey" rather than a "gradualist" approach and was announced on 1 July 1985. Interestingly enough, Bruno also recalled (October 1985, 1986a, 388 note 6) that in July 1984 another team of Israeli economists—including Ben-Porath and Ben-Shahar—"submitted the broad outline of a very similar plan to the Prime Minister."

What brought about the decision of the Israeli government to finally implement a comprehensive stabilization program? Can it be attributed to conditionality and the threat of holding back supplementary economic aid? It should be recalled that the aid had already been approved by both the House and Senate and on 15 May 1985 by President Reagan himself. If the Israeli government had been worried about not getting additional aid, it could have implemented a stabilization program earlier in 1985. Can it be attributed to the advice of Stein and Fischer and their "Ten Points," which reflected points made by Emmanuel Sharon at a meeting with them in December 1984, as Stein noted in his retrospective (Stein 1990)? If so, why wait until June–July 1985?

Perhaps the answer lies in the fact that only in June 1985 did the government *finally* realize that the level of reserves was *critical* and posed a major risk to national security and its public standing. In other words, the Israeli decision to finally implement the 1985 stabilization program was motivated by the continuing and increasingly alarming decline in foreign currency reserves, from \$4.3 billion in 1982 to \$3.8 billion in 1983, \$3.3 billion in 1984, and \$2.6 billion in January–June 1985. Foreign currency reserves had always been seen as crucial in Israel, with the "red line" drawn at level of 3 months of imports of essential food, fuel, and raw materials (about \$3 billion at the time). As Bruno noted (1986a, 380), "By mid-1985 Israel's economic crisis reached a new high. Earlier partial attempts at stabilization had failed. In spite of a recent improvement in the trade balance, Israel was losing foreign exchange reserves very rapidly …"[4]

[4]The increase in the level of foreign reserves from \$2.6 billion in January–June 1985 to \$3.8 billion in July–December 1985, with a final level of \$3.8 billion for 1985 was a direct result of the \$1.5

And indeed, in terms of import coverage, while Israel had earlier fallen below the 3-month level, that is, between 1984Q2 and 1984Q3, prompting the "blunt memorandum" of the State Department to the Israeli government in November 1984, the fallback from 2.6 months of import coverage in 1984Q4 to 2.1 months in 1985Q1 *and only 2 months by the end of 1985Q2*, finally set off emergency alarm bells in Israel, bringing the government to implement the stabilization program in July 1985 (Bank of Israel *Annual Report* 1985, 232 (Table 7–25)).

Now, Fischer noted in his Horowitz lecture (1993, 21): "For the year before the stabilization program, Israel was completely dependent on the US Government to keep its economy afloat. In the economic sphere, at least, Israel had lost its independence. Even with its back to the wall, Israel would not take any action, even action clearly in its own long-term interest, without US pressure." He added in a footnote (1993, 21 note 18): "This pattern of behavior is not unusual; many developing countries rely on the IMF and the World Bank to pressure them to undertake policies that they know should be taken in any case."

However, while the US may have acted at the time as Israel's IMF, the adoption of a "cold turkey" stabilization program, and its implementation on 1 July 1985, was, in our view, neither the result of potential US pressure and aid conditionality nor of Fischer and Stein's advice as manifest in their "Ten Points." Rather, it was the foreign reserve statistics that spoke for themselves, indicating that a national security crisis had been reached, which could only be resolved by immediate and vigorous economic measures; words alone would not suffice (Michaely 2007).

6.5 Retrospectives on the Stabilization Program, Its Outcome, and US Loan Guarantees for Israel, 1986–1993

There are a number of retrospective accounts by Fischer and Stein regarding their impressions of the 1985 stabilization program, some of which have been cited above. However, two important assessments of the program have not received the attention they deserve. First, Dornbusch and Fischer, in an article entitled "Stopping hyperinflations past and present," wrote (1986, 30):

> By April and May 1985 … inflation was back to the 1000% per annum range. The balance of payments deficit had been reduced from its 1983 level, but foreign exchange reserves were falling rapidly, the government budget deficit was at an unsustainable level (both domestic and foreign financing were difficult to obtain) and there was a clear need for action … [here] we briefly take up the question of why the policy was so long delayed. Aside from a brief period during which the bubble inflation argument was popular, there was never much

---

billion in supplemental aid, provided in two tranches of $750 million each in 1985 and 1986. By 1986, the level of foreign reserves had risen to some $4.9 billion (Bank of Israel *Annual Reports* 1985, 1986).

> disagreement in Israel about the fundamental measures that would have to be taken to end inflation. There was, however, dispute about whether more than restrictive aggregate demand measures were needed. Some economists argued that the use of wage and price controls and agreements with the unions were doomed to failure and that attempts to use such measures only prolonged the adjustment period and made failure more likely … Others argued that heavy unemployment following cuts in demand could be avoided if wages and prices could be moved immediately to close to new equilibrium levels rather forcing changes through the Phillips curve tradeoff … The lack of action was a result of the evaluation that the costs of inflation, moderated by indexation, were less than those of the unemployment and emigration that a serious stabilization attempt would cause. The slogan was "Israel cannot afford unemployment"…

Second, in his comments on the seminal paper published by Dornbusch et al. (1990) entitled "Extreme inflation: dynamics and stabilization," Fischer made a number of crucial points for understanding Israel's 1985 stabilization program, its political context, and outcome over the period 1986–1990. His comments were *also not noticed by most economic observers at the time*, but, in retrospect, *are perhaps one of the most important assessments of the Israeli stabilization program made only a few years after its implementation and by one of its most influential proponents*. He wrote (1990, 66):

> The heterodox component was key in persuading the Israeli government to stabilize. For a long time, the fear of a massive recession had stood between the government and a stabilization program. The government was finally moved to stabilize by the argument that wage and price controls would enable the economy to move rapidly to the new noninflationary equilibrium without generating much unemployment. Despite the author's opinion of the strength of national unity government in Israel, I do not believe that it would have acted in 1985 if it had believed a major recession would follow.

He continued:

> Incidentally, to expand on the Israeli case, the reason behind the importance of heterodoxy—the government's unwillingness to confront labor—also helps account for the subsequent slow growth. The Israeli government started out with a tough program that cut real wages. But after the early success of the stabilization, wages were allowed to rise rapidly. Within six months, the average wage was back to its pre-stabilization level—and the high real wage helps account for slow growth in the next three years.

Interestingly enough, in his comments, Fischer also expressed his view of the proposed 1983 dollarization stabilization program in Israel when he wrote (1990, 67):

> … there is bound to be tremendous political opposition to dollarization, on the grounds that using a foreign money derogates from the country's sovereignty. That was the argument that forced the resignation of the finance minister in Israel who proposed dollarization to the Knesset in 1983. It has also to be recognized that dollarization is a tough way of stabilizing. A dollarizing government denies itself the advantage of printing money during the remonetization that accompanies the early stage of a stabilization program. Fiscal policy has to be correspondingly tighter than it would otherwise have been.

In order to understand Fischer's comments and the nature of the "heterodox" Israeli stabilization program he advocated in 1985, a number of issues must be briefly considered regarding types of stabilization policy. First, *orthodox* programs usually focus solely on fiscal or monetary measures, or a combination of both, while *heterodox* programs use both fiscal and monetary adjustment *and* incomes policy. When incomes policy is used in conjunction with fiscal/monetary adjustment on an equal basis, inflation can be reduced without a significant impact on real activity. And, while this is essentially what occurred in the Israeli case in 1985, as Fischer said, *the subsequent collapse in the implementation of incomes policy in the form of wage increases brought about deterioration in the outcome of the Israeli stabilization program in the years that followed* (Fischer 1987).

There is, however, an *alternate* view regarding the efficacy and reason for "success" of the *heterodox* economic stabilization policy advocated by Fischer and Stein and developed and later implemented by Bruno, first as "an influential member of the small group that developed Israel's stabilization plan during the Summer of 1985," and later "from August 1986 to August 1991 as Governor of the Bank of Israel," when "he had a major role in carrying out the plan" (Meltzer 1994, 581).

In his 1994 *Journal of Monetary Economics* review of Bruno's book entitled *Crisis, stabilization and economic reform: therapy by consensus* (1993), Meltzer noted that in Israel, "disinflation was achieved at low cost." He wrote:

> A main reason is some good luck that Bruno barely mentions. After devaluing by 20%, Israel pegged the shekel to the dollar in July 1985 just as the dollar was sharply falling against most of the world's currencies. In the first year, Israel's exchange rate fell with the dollar against its principal trading partners except the U.S … By third quarter 1986, the shekel was 15% lower against the SDR but stable against the dollar. After August 1986, Israel pegged to a basket of currencies and devalued at intervals to adjust for its higher rate of inflation … *The success of Israeli policy owes much to chance.* The compatibility of the nominal anchors for the price level and exchange rate during the first year of the program *could not have been predicted.* [The policy change that induced a shift from PATAM to shekels contributed to the stabilization.] *There was no way for the Israeli government to predict that the dollar would continue to fall sharply after the Israeli stabilization plan or that world oil prices would fall precipitously for the next year …* What remains of the case for multiple nominal anchors and heterodox policy? Not much I believe. The only clear success is Israel, *and that success owes much to good fortune* (our emphases).

Now, one of the questions raised by Dornbusch and Fischer in their 1986 evaluation of the stabilization program cited above was "why the policy was so long delayed," which they attributed to the government's fear of increasing unemployment. In his recollections, Sharon, the director-general of the Israeli Ministry of Finance, and one of the architects of the program, stated that Prime Minister Peres had put off implementation of the program from January until May 1985 so as not to affect the electoral prospects of the Labor Alignment and its candidate for secretary-general in the Histadrut election scheduled for mid-May 1985 (Sharon 2015). Once again, political-electoral considerations took precedence over economic ones.

Over the period March 1991–March 1992, there was increasing public discussion in the US regarding some $10 billion in US government guarantees, so as to enable Israel to take loans on the capital markets for the absorption of an estimated one million Soviet Jewish immigrants. For example, in March 1991 the *New York Times* reported that "a high level team of American economists—Richard McCormack,

Undersecretary of State for Economic Affairs; Herbert Stein, former Chairman of the Council of Economic Advisers, and Stanley Fischer, former Chief Economist of the World Bank—has been working in Israel under official auspices on a study of the structure of the Israeli economy," so as to perhaps find the "huge infusions of capital to take care of its new immigrants," eventually, as will be seen, in the form of an Israeli request for US loan guarantees (Silk 1991). The "official auspices" that the American trio was actually working under was the Joint Economic Development Group [JEDG] (Nasar 1991).

October 1991 saw the public reaction to the formal Israeli request for $10 billion in loan guarantees and its public advocacy by Fischer and Stein, *albeit conditional on a comprehensive economic policy reform and reconstruction program.* In an article in the *New York Times* on October 12, 1991, Fischer and Stein outlined this program. They started by saying that:

> … controversy over Israel's request for loan guarantees should drive home to the Israeli government its need to work toward real economic independence. In our personal opinion, friends of Israel should press it to develop and carry out economic reforms aimed at phasing out its dependence on U.S. financial assistance once the Soviet immigrants … are absorbed … Israel's economy is not a basket case, as critics charge, and financial assistance is not wasted on it. The failures of Israel's economic policy are not the result of socialist ideology but of political pressures and bureaucratic inertia … Its temporary need to finance investment in the huge wave of Soviet immigrants, if successful, will yield revenues that will amply justify the borrowing. If accompanied by meaningful reform, this period can help Israel achieve full economic independence and relieve it of burdens on the U.S. that bring political problems.

The program they proposed included the following economic reforms that Israel would be *required* to undertake:

(a) A medium-term budget in which the deficit would decline to zero
(b) A reduction in protection exposing industry to foreign competition
(c) Abolishment of remaining foreign exchange controls
(d) Rapid implementation of privatization
(e) Review and elimination of regulatory burdens
(f) Further reform of labor market restrictions
(g) Drastic shrinkage of government bureaucracy

They concluded by saying: "We hope the Israeli government will present its own program along these lines. We would not like to see the U.S. prescribe one for Israel. The Israelis are more capable of creating the needed program than we are."

A week after the Fischer-Stein article appeared, the third member of the original "high-level team" of US economists of the JEDG, Richard McCormack, was quoted in the *New York Times* as saying "the Israeli economy is an anomaly in the world today. It's statist when everybody else is becoming un-statist." He went on to maintain that Israel needed to "marketize" its economy by means of "selling off" state-owned and supported enterprises, "lifting restrictive labor practices and stripping away … regulation" (Nasar 1991; also see O. Sussman 1992).

On 21 February 1992, both Fischer and Stein testified before the Foreign Operations Subcommittee of the House Appropriations Committee on the subject of loan guarantees to Israel. *The most important aspect of their testimony dealt with conditionality*. After supporting Israel's request for loan guarantees and describing Israel as a "very good credit risk," Fischer (1992) went on to say "however, to reduce the risks of non-repayment to an absolute minimum, the guarantees should be made *conditional* on implementation of an Israel economic reform program and should be *tranched*—that is, handed out, provided over the course of five years on the basis of conditions that are specified in advance" [our emphasis].

Stein (1992), for his part, said:

> The effectiveness of the guarantees in furthering American and Israeli interests will depend on the economic policies that accompany the borrowing, and for the US to expect its loan guarantee to be accompanied by constructive policies is natural and proper. For the US to describe the economic policies that should accompany the loan guarantee would not be an improper imposition on the government of Israel. On the whole these policies, or at least the ones that I will suggest, are advocated by many well informed and responsible Israeli government officials as well as private students of Israel's economy. In general they follow the lines on which Israel has been moving since 1985, and conform to the intentions expressed in Israel's statements in requesting the loan guarantee. The government has not moved more rapidly in the desired direction because of political and bureaucratic obstacles. The knowledge that these policies are not only desirable in themselves, but are also the expectations of the U.S. as loan guarantor, will help to overcome these obstacles.

He went on to say that "most, but not all, of these suggestions were included in an article by Professor Fischer and me in the *New York Times* last October ... The suggested policies are in two parts, substantive and procedural. The importance of the procedural conditions should not be overlooked. In many substantial fields, the desired results cannot be specified so precisely and objectively that Israeli officials can tell exactly what is to be done and U.S. officials can tell exactly whether it has been done or not."

While Stein repeated all of the reforms set out in his article with Fischer, he added: "The government and Bank of Israel should commit themselves to the goal of reducing the rate of inflation, beginning now, and reaching international levels of 5% or less. The government of Israel should deposit 1/2 of the foreign funds it raises through the loan guarantee in the Bank of Israel to be made available for borrowing by private investors, foreign or domestic, who wish to do business in Israel." He concluded by saying "the suggestions made here are quite general. I do not think it could be otherwise at this point. That is why it is so important to strengthen Israel's mechanism for devising and implementing specific measures and the mechanism of the United States for advising on those measures and monitoring them."

Finally, after political wrangling between the US and Israel governments regarding the problem of whether the loan guarantees should cover "settlement activity" in the West Bank and Gaza, Congress authorized some $9.25 billion in loan guarantees to Israel ($10 billion reduced by about $775 million due to "settlement activity") over the 5-year period 1993–1997 (Sharp 2007, 9 (Table 2)). And indeed, the "tranches" recommended by Fischer in his 1992 Congressional testimony cited above became the model for future loan guarantees, such as that of 2003, but more about this in Chap. 7 (Sharp 2012, 23 (Table 3, note a)).

To sum up, as mentioned at the beginning of this chapter, the influence of Fischer and Stein on Israel's economy was much more than merely acting as "foreign economic advisers." Indeed, as an advisory "team" they, perhaps more than any other Israeli economist or politician, influenced the Israel economy, *for better or worse*, from 1984 onward.

References

Associated Press. (1985, May 21). Washington, DC.

Bank of Israel. (1985, May). *Annual report 1985*. Jerusalem.

Bank of Israel. (1986, May). *Annual report 1986*. Jerusalem.

Berglas, E. (1986). Defense and the economy. In Y. Ben-Porath (Ed.), *The Israeli economy: Maturing through crises*. Cambridge, MA: Harvard University Press.

Blitzer, W. (1985, April 5). US still waiting for Israeli action before approving aid. *The Jewish Exponent, 3*, 56.

Bruno, M., & Fischer, S. (1984). *The inflationary process in Israel: Shocks and accommodation* (NBER WP 1483). Cambridge, MA.

Bruno, M. (1986a). Sharp disinflation strategy: Israel 1985. *Economic Policy, 1*, 379–402 [originally published in abridged form as Bruno, M. (1985). The stabilization of the economy: The emergency plan and its initial stages [in Hebrew]. *Economic Quarterly, 126*, 207–223].

Bruno, M. (1986b). External shocks and domestic response: Macroeconomic performance, 1965–1982. In Y. Ben-Porath (Ed.), *The Israeli economy: Maturing through crises*. Cambridge, MA: Harvard University Press.

Bruno, M. (1986c). *Generating a sharp disinflation: Israel 1985* (NBER WP 1822). Cambridge, MA.

Bruno, M. (1988). *Theoretical developments in light of macroeconomic policy and empirical research* (NBER WP 2757). Cambridge MA.

Bruno, M. (1992). From sharp stabilization to growth: On the political economy of Israel's transition. *European Economic Review, 36*, 310–319.

Bruno, M. (1993). *Crisis, stabilization and economic reform: Therapy through consensus*. Oxford: Clarendon Press.

Bruno, M., & Sussman, Z. (1979). Exchange-rate flexibility, inflation and structural change: Israel under alternative regimes. *Journal of Development Economics, 6*, 483–514.

Chicago Tribune. (1985, January 2). Israel's $800 million albatross. *Editorial*.

Dornbusch, R., & Fischer, S. (1986). Stopping hyperinflations past and present. *Review of World Economics* (Welt. Archiv), *122*, 1–47 [also published as NBER WP 1810].

Dornbusch, R., et al. (1990). Extreme inflation: Dynamics and stabilization. *Brooking Papers on Economic Activity, 21*, 1–64.

Fischer, S. (1983). *The economy of Israel* (NBER WP 1190).

Fischer, S. (1984). The economy of Israel. *Carnegie-Rochester Series on Public Policy: Monetary and Fiscal Policies and Their Application, 20*, 7–52.

Fischer, S. (1987). The Israeli stabilization program, 1985–86. *American Economic Review, 77*, 275–278.

Fischer, S. (1990). Comment on Dornbusch et al. (1990). Extreme inflation: Dynamics and stabilization. *Brooking Papers on Economic Activity, 21*, 65–68.

Fischer, S. (1992, February 21). Testimony on loan guarantees to Israel, Foreign Operations Subcommittee, Appropriations Committee, US House of Representatives, Washington, DC.

Fischer, S. (1993, January 11). *Israel and her neighbors: Israeli growth, stabilization and reform.* Horowitz Lecture Series (1992) 1st Lecture. Jerusalem: Association of Banks in Israel, Hebrew University and Tel Aviv University Depts. of Economics.

Fischer, S. (1995, November). *Recollections of the United States role in the Israeli stabilization program.* International Monetary Fund.

Fischer, S. (2001a, January 6). *Remembering Herb Stein: His contributions as an economist.* Presented at American Economic Association meetings. Accessed February 1, 2017, from https://www.imf.org/external/np/speeches/2001/010601.htm

Fischer, S. (2001b, May 20). *Beyond the ivory tower: The role of the economist in society.* International Monetary Fund. (Revised).

Fischer, S. (2005). Interview with Stanley Fischer–Olivier Blanchard. In P. Samuelson & W. Barnett (Eds.), *Inside the economist's mind* (pp. 261–278). New York: Wiley.

Fischer, S., & Stein, H. (1991, October 12). Overhaul the Israeli economy. *New York Times.*

Frenkel, J. (1984). Comments on the economy of Israel. *Carnegie-Rochester Conference Series on Public Policy, 20*, 57–68.

Frenkel, J. (1996). *Israel's experience with inflation.* Federal Reserve Bank of Kansas City, Proceedings of the Economic Policy Symposium—Jackson Hole, pp. 139–146.

Frenkel, J. (1998, October 6–8). Statement, Governor of the Bank of Israel, at the Joint Annual Discussion, International Monetary Fund and World Bank Boards of Governors.

Gwertzman, B. (1985, April 28). Israel sends Shultz a plan to meet economic conditions for new aid. *New York Times.*

International Monetary Fund. (2011, April). *Assessing the need for foreign currency reserves.* Washington, DC: International Monetary Fund.

International Monetary Fund. (1983). *International financial statistics supplement on international reserves*, Supplement Series #6. Washington, D.C.

Jewish Telegraphic Agency. (1984, December 27). Shultz's letter to Peres draws fire from a cabinet minister.

Jewish Telegraphic Agency. (1985a, March 7). Reagan administration continues to demand more economic reforms from Israel before aid increase.

Jewish Telegraphic Agency. (1985b, May 12). Peres: There is "broad agreement" between Israel and the US on reviving the Mideast peace process.

Kempster, N. (1985, April 29). Peres to curb "printing-press money". *Los Angeles Times.*

Lehrman, H. (1950, December). A billion dollars for Israel. *Commentary.*

Lehrman, H. (1951). *Israel: The beginning and tomorrow.* New York: Sloane Publishing.

Lehrman, H. (1952, October). Washington comes to Israel's economic rescue. *Commentary.*

Meltzer, A. (1994). Review of Michael Bruno's crisis. Stabilization and economic reform: Therapy by consensus (1993). *Journal of Monetary Economics, 34*, 581–600.

Michaely, M. (2007). The liberalization of Israel's foreign exchange market, 1950–2002. In N. Liviatan & H. Barkai (Eds.), *The Bank of Israel* (Vol. 2: Selected topics in Israel's monetary policy). Oxford: Oxford University Press.

Moday, Y. (1988). *Eliminating the zeroes.* Tel Aviv: Yediot Aharonot Publishing [in Hebrew].

Nasar, S. (1991, October 27). Pressure grows on aid-thirsty Israel to adopt reforms. *New York Times.*

Oberdorfer, D. (1985, June 9). Will US dollars fix Israel's economy? *Washington Post.*

Peres, S. (2015, July 14). If economics professors are so smart, why aren't they millionaires? Interview with N. Strassler, *The Marker* [in Hebrew].

Plessner, Y., & Young, W. (2005). Economists, government, and economic policymaking in Israel: From "crawling peg" to "cold turkey". *History of Political Economy, 37* (Suppl. 1), 292–313.

Schultz, G. (1985, April 21). *The United States and Israel: Partners for peace and freedom.* Address before the Annual Policy Conference of AIPAC, Crystal City, VA.

Sharp, J. (2007). *US foreign aid to Israel.* Congressional Research Service Report, Washington, DC.

Sharp, J. (2012). *US foreign aid to Israel.* Congressional Research Service Report, Washington, DC.

Sharon, E. (2015, July 19). The inflation busters. Interview with M. Arloseroff, *The Marker* [in Hebrew].

Silk, L. (1991, March 15). Economic scene: Israeli blessings and burdens. *New York Times.*

Southerland, D. (1984, August 28). US poised to provide massive assistance if Israel adopts belt-tightening measures. *Christian Science Monitor.*

Stein, H. (1990). Israel's economy: Observations of an adviser. *The American Enterprise, 1*, 12–18.

Stein, H. (1992, February 21). Testimony on loan guarantees to Israel, Foreign Operations Subcommittee, Appropriations Committee, US House of Representatives, Washington, DC.

Sussman, O. (1992). Financial liberalization: The Israeli experience. *Oxford Economic Papers, 44*, 387–402.

Wallis, A. (1985, March 6). Testimony before US House of Representatives, Committee on Foreign Affairs, Subcommittee on Europe and the Middle East, pp. 204–217.

Chapter 7
Stabilization via Government Accounting Reform: The 2003 Program and Politicization of Recovery

The ostensible success of the stabilization plan of 1985 created fertile ground for a future crisis. On the one hand, the Israeli economy, which almost reached bankruptcy due to the critical decline in foreign exchange reserves and hyperinflation, had strengthened. Foreign exchange reserves started to grow (with the help of a $1.5 billion US government grant), inflation declined to low double digits, and GDP growth once again exceeded population growth.

Furthermore, the government took advantage of the spirit of reform and in the late 1980s initiated a new reform aimed at opening the local economy to competitive imports, mainly through reduced import duties. Although not all industrial sectors were exposed to reduced import duties (e.g., the duties on food imports remained high), the reform contributed significantly to the efforts to tackle inflation, increase productivity, and maintain private consumption (Zelekha 2008, 2011).

In fact, the ratio of Israeli to US GDP per capita, which declined sharply from 1975 to the crisis of 1985 (also known in Israel as the "lost decade"), returned by 1995 to its pre-crisis level (approximately two-thirds of US GDP per capita).

On the other hand, the "success" of the 1985 stabilization program lessened the need to contract and control public expenditure. Although the fear of large budget deficits remained high, the government interpreted this "success" principally as an opportunity to run expansionary budgets, that is, if tax rates would be increased as well. The problem with this policy perspective, however, is that when an exogenous shock hits the economy and puts downward pressure on government tax revenues, the immediate response will not be expenditure cuts, but rather an increase in tax rates.

D. Schiffman et al., *The Role of Economic Advisers in Israel's Economic Policy*,
DOI 10.1007/978-3-319-60682-8_7

7.1 The Crisis of 2000–2003

During the year 2000, several negative shocks hit the Israeli economy. In March 2000 the "Dot Com" collapse and NASDAQ crash significantly affected the Israeli high-tech sector. September 2000 saw the start of the second Palestinian "Intifada" (uprising) which lasted until 2003. The terror attacks especially harmed the tourism sector.[1] The events of September 2001 also took their toll on the Israeli economy; the downturn in the US economy and the concomitant impact on the European Union brought about a reduction in Israeli exports. The government tried to apply traditional expansionary fiscal policy while paying lip service to its commitment to a reasonable budget deficit. However, growth declined, negatively affecting tax revenues. The government, as noted, having been committed to a reasonable deficit, raised taxes while continuing to run an expansionary budget according to what its policymakers believed to be appropriate neo-Keynesian policy, that is to say, a supposed "balanced budget multiplier effect."

During 2000 real government expenditures rose by 4.8%, and in 2001 by about the same amount, while the nominal budget was prepared for an increase of about 7% (albeit a burst of unexpected inflation brought the real increase to only 1.4%). The top marginal income tax rate was raised from 50% to 62.5%, VAT was increased from 17% to 18%, and a new capital gains tax was introduced. The effect on the economy was quite negative. Over the period 1996–2002, which some Israeli observers called "the road to a second lost decade," real GDP grew by only 2.7% per annum, gross domestic investment fell by 1.2% per annum, labor productivity grew by only 0.2% per annum, and total factor productivity fell by 1.5% per annum.

By the end of 2002, it was obvious that the economy was again in crisis. Growth was negative for the second year in a row. Real GDP growth was −1% in both 2001 and 2002 respectively. This was accompanied by a fall in exports as noted, a rise in unemployment to some 11%, a rise in prices, and concomitantly a fall in real wages and consumption. There was a major deterioration in the quality of fiscal management: Tax revenues declined sharply and unexpectedly (the government's tax revenue forecasting model turned inaccurate); unpaid debts to government contractors equaling almost 0.4% of GDP had accumulated; and the government published financial statements that did not meet generally accepted accounting standards. Furthermore, poverty rates increased to an all-time high. The public saw policymakers as "clueless" and in desperate need of guidance. Several public offerings of government bonds in the Israeli capital market failed to attain their targets, even with high interest rates, and the government's access to international capital markets was essentially blocked. As a last resort, the Sharon government turned to the US in November 2002 and requested $8 billion in loan guarantees, plus $4 billion in military grants, to help it deal with the effects of the Second "Intifada" and the impending US invasion of Iraq. In April 2003, the US Congress authorized $9 billion in loan guarantees, to be made

[1] See also in this regard Schein (2003), who found that terrorism had much more influence on GDP than the NASDAQ.

available in three tranches over 3 years, plus $1 billion in military grants. The loan guarantees were to be reduced by the amount that the Israeli government spent on the settlement activity in the West Bank and Gaza (Sharp 2016; US Congress, Public Law 108–11).

7.2 Pre-assessment of the 2003 Economic Recovery Program by Foreign Experts and the 2003 Loan Guarantees

On 22 June 2003, John Taylor, US Undersecretary of the Treasury for International Affairs, spoke in Jerusalem to the Israel–American Chamber of Commerce on "Israel's Economic Recovery Program." Because of its importance for understanding the program and the US view of its potential efficacy, we cite Taylor's remarks here verbatim. Taylor said that:

> Finance Minister Netanyahu's economic recovery program, passed by the Knesset three weeks ago, is crucial for achieving higher productivity growth in the Israeli economy. *Under this plan the government will undertake fiscal policies and structural reforms in order to reduce government expenditures and keep the budget deficit on a downward path.* Israel's general government revenues and expenditures stand at roughly 42% and 48% of GDP respectively compared to an OECD average of 38% and 41% of GDP in 2001 … *[The]economic recovery plan therefore rightly focuses its efforts on reducing spending growth. The recent efforts to trim Israeli government ministry budgets and limit the growth of social transfers are important first steps in implementing this plan.* These efforts will reduce the government's claim on real and financial resources. In addition, the reduction in marginal tax rates will help encourage the Israeli private sector to make productivity-enhancing investments. Under this plan the top marginal tax rate will fall from 60% to 49%. This will increase the incentives to work and spur growth … In Israel, getting government out of the direct provision of commercial goods and services is a critical part of the government's plan … Boosting the privatization program will strengthen Israeli competitiveness in the global marketplace and will create generous returns to the Israeli people … I also agree … that wider financial sector reform should be a top priority for the government. A more efficient banking sector is essential to ensuring that resources are allocated to the most productive use … Recent reforms to make the pension system more market-oriented by shifting pension investments away from preferred government bonds into the regular bond and equity markets will also help to create a deeper, more liquid capital market. Labor market reforms would also boost productivity by increasing labor market participation. At only 54%, labor market participation in Israel is among the lowest in the industrialized world. These are all bold steps in the direction of restoring robust economic growth in Israel, a goal that the U.S. strongly supports. The people of the United States are providing $9 billion in loan guarantees to help the Israeli economy weather regional shocks and thereby create the conditions for the Israel government to put in place reforms that will lead to higher and sustainable growth. In negotiating the agreement, both sides agreed that the guarantees should be *linked* to progress in implementing the economic reform plan [our emphasis].

A number of important points emerge from Taylor's presentation of Israel's 2003 economic reform program. First, the program was *initiated and implemented by the Israelis themselves, along the lines advocated by Stein and Fischer from 1985 onward, and especially in the context of reforms to accompany the first loan guarantee package in 1992*, as related in Chap. 6. Second, following Fischer's "tranche" model, Taylor now advocated that disbursement of the new loan guarantees be "linked to progress" in the implementation of the 2003 economic reform program developed by Netanyahu's chief economic adviser, and subsequently accountant-general of the State of Israel, Zelekha, as will be seen below. As stated above, in 2003, Congress approved $9 billion in loan guarantees, to be provided in tranches *over 3 years*, with deductions for settlement activity. Over 2003–2005, only $4.1 billion was *actually* borrowed ($1.085 billion was deducted for settlement activity) (Sharp 2016, 26 and Table 34, p. 27). *The reason for the underutilization of the loan guarantees was, as will be seen below, the success of the 2003 economic reform program.* Congress has extended the loan guarantee program four times since 2003; thus, the Israeli government has retained (through FY 2020) the option of using the remaining loan guarantee balance of $3.814 billion. Zelekha, for one, considers the loan guarantees to be "preparations for a rainy day ... a safety net for war, natural disaster and economic crisis, which allows Israel to maintain economic stability in unstable surroundings" (quoted anonymously in Ravid 2012; cited by Sharp 2016, 26–27).

A June 2009 agreement further provided that loan tranches are not to be released automatically, but only after *written determination* of fulfillment of fiscal benchmark conditions regarding Israel's deficit and spending, and other non-fiscal criteria, as set by the Joint Economic Development Group [JEDG] (Sharp 2012, 23).

7.2.1 Theoretical Background to the 2003 Recovery Program

In the economic literature, three different approaches attempt to explain the possible outcomes of fiscal adjustments. The first is *traditional* Keynesian theory. According to this theory, fiscal expansion will increase GDP in the short term. The second is new classical theory, which took root in macroeconomic thought when the Keynesian approach failed to revive the world economy during the "stagflation" of the 1970s. New classical theory states that fiscal adjustments do not affect national output, which is determined mainly by aggregate supply, that is, the economy's ability to produce goods and services. The third approach, which attacks Keynesian theorists for neglecting the role of consumer and investor expectations, is the result of a number of significant fiscal adjustments which ended in surprising outcomes. All of them occurred in Europe during the 1980s and 1990s and brought about unique, non-Keynesian results.

The first event occurred during 1983–1986 in Denmark, which made a significant fiscal adjustment by raising taxes and decreasing government investment. The second event occurred during 1987–1989 in Ireland, which also made a significant fiscal adjustment by focusing on spending reductions, particularly social welfare transfer payments and public sector wages. Both events brought about surprising increases in economic activity and production, primarily, in each case, due to an increase in private consumption and private investment. This outcome seems to conflict with Keynesian theory, which would predict an economic slowdown. The third event occurred in Sweden during 1991–1992 in which fiscal expansion led, unexpectedly, to a sharp decrease in economic activity and production. Further challenging Keynesian assumptions was the fact that dramatic fiscal expansion in Japan during 1990s and the early 2000s—marked by an increase in government investment and a decrease in taxes—did not contribute to an increase in economic activity.

In view of these economic developments, a number of studies were carried out during the 1990s which attempted to characterize the circumstances under which the result of fiscal adjustments would *not be* Keynesian.

The conceptual foundation for most of the studies was provided by Feldstein (1982). Feldstein's assertion was that a cut in public expenditure can bring about an expansion of economic activity if the cut is perceived as signaling a future, *permanent* reduction in taxes. For example, if the government cuts government salaries, which is a current expense repeated every year, it will be able to concomitantly cut taxes, while keeping the budget deficit stable.

Giavazzi et al. (1999), following earlier work, expanded this view by asserting that contraction of the budget deficit, in turn, positively affects output via three possible transmission mechanisms. The first influences the expectations of the public regarding future tax levels and, indirectly, expected permanent income of consumers and investors. The second influences the money markets to favor the reduction of long-term interest rates, which increases market value of public capital—particularly stocks, bonds, real estate, and human capital. The third positively influences public confidence in economic stability and decreases uncertainty and risk premia. This may occur as a result of decreased inflationary expectations, decreased local long-term interest rates, or improvement in the sovereign credit rating. These three transmission mechanisms positively influence private consumption and private investment, while offsetting the direct negative Keynesian influence of the fiscal contraction. By contrast, a fiscal expansion may activate the three transmission mechanisms in the opposite direction, thereby actually causing a decrease in output.

Perotti (1997) noted that the chance of positive influence of fiscal contraction increases if the public debt is large or increasing steadily and also when the composition of the contraction strengthens public expectations regarding the decisiveness of the new policy. The European Central Bank (ECB) supported this view by noting that changing public expectations to favor future tax reduction is conditional upon the *credibility* of the new fiscal policy (European Central Bank 2001). Contraction of social welfare transfer payments, national insurance payments, and public sector wages greatly strengthens the credibility of the policy; because all three forms of spending are popular and politically difficult to cut, cutting them demonstrates the government's commitment to the policy.

Furthermore, Perotti also emphasizes the importance of favorable exchange rate developments in the success of fiscal adjustments carried out in Denmark and Ireland (substantial devaluations were carried out in both countries before the adjustments and throughout their duration, and exchange rates were kept stable afterward) as well as the implementation of disinflationary policies to assist in decreasing uncertainty and interest rates. Conversely, the two examples emphasize that credit and liquidity shortages may thwart the success of fiscal adjustments, as may have happened in Ireland in the early 1980s.

Giavazzi and Pagano (1996) emphasized the importance of the adjustment size (at least an accumulated 5% of GDP during the adjustment process) and the consistency of the new policy. Giavazzi et al. (1999) also showed, following earlier work—based on a cross section of OECD countries over the years 1970–1996—that fiscal adjustments can have *asymmetrical* and *noncontinuous* effects. In this framework, as Bertola and Drazen (1993) showed earlier, fiscal adjustments beyond a certain size create an upheaval in public expectations and consequently produce non-Keynesian effects. Furthermore, the strength of the realized non-Keynesian effects is not identical regarding expansion and contraction, and they are considerably more noticeable following a sharp contraction than after a sharp expansion. At the same time, raising taxes negatively influences output, as expected—according to Keynesian theory, in the framework of routine fiscal adjustments—but the negative influences become smaller and sometimes negligible in the framework of fiscal adjustments which extend beyond a threshold because of an offsetting increase in private consumption. Moreover, Keynesians claim that the main source of a lack of continuity in its influence is the size of the fiscal correction and its consistency, and not the size or rate of growth of the public debt.

Afonso (2001) also found a lack of symmetry and continuity in the influence of fiscal adjustments on private consumption in 15 European countries between 1970 and 1999. Specifically, he found that fiscal policy had standard Keynesian effects during routine times, but irregular fiscal adjustments had non-Keynesian effects. Concomitantly, non-Keynesian effects stand out in the framework of irregular contractions and are negligible during periods of fiscal expansions. The elasticity of public consumption with respect to private consumption during routine times is positive, and in periods of irregular fiscal adjustments, the elasticity decreases significantly.[2] A similar phenomenon was found in estimating the influence of government tax revenue in relation to private consumption with one significant difference, according to which an irregular tax increase changes the direction of influence from negative to slightly positive. When Afonso distinguished between fiscal expansions and contractions, he found that during periods of irregular fiscal contractions, the positive elasticity changes to slightly negative, and the negative

[2]These findings were contrary to the findings of Kormendi and Meguire (1990), who found that elasticity of public consumption with respect to private consumption is negative, and to the findings of Giavazzi and Pagano (1990), who found that elasticity of public consumption to output relative to private consumption to output is negative.

elasticity of government tax revenue changes to significant positive elasticity. In contrast, during periods of irregular fiscal expansion, the influence remains essentially positive and therefore Keynesian to a large extent.

In more recent research, Burger and Zagler (2008) found indications for non-Keynesian effects in the American economy in the 1990s, while de Castro (2003) presented similar findings in Spain. Giudice et al. (2007) also examined some European episodes and showed that non-Keynesian effects were achieved mainly through contraction of public expenditure and not tax increases in an output gap environment.

7.3 Critiques of Economic Policy, Circa 2002

In November 2002, Yaron Zelekha (one of the authors of this book)—after severely criticizing the expansionary fiscal policy and the quickness of the government to raise tax rates when in need of revenue—organized an economic conference at Ono Academic College in Israel. The conference panel included Deputy Governor of the Bank of Israel Dr. Meir Sokoler, former Prime Minister Netanyahu, and Zelekha himself. At the conference, Zelekha presented preliminary results of research describing non-Keynesian effects of fiscal policy in Israel (Zelekha 2010). He pointed out that the then-current Israeli economy had many characteristics that were associated in the literature with non-Keynesian effects.

Prominent in this framework were the scope of overall public expenditure and public consumption and the ratio of debt to domestic product in Israel, which in 2002 were amongst the highest in the Western world. More specifically, the characteristics that made non-Keynesian effects likely were gradual fiscal expansion, which had continued since the 1985 stabilization program; a heavy and persistent tax burden, combined with a government that was quick to increase taxes as an attempted short-term solution during times of economic distress; the large shares in public consumption of social transfers and wages, which grew almost automatically as the population grew; and, lastly, a public perception of government inefficiency and corruption. In this context, it should also be noted that in 2002, Israel's Corruption Perceptions Index ranking (compiled by Transparency International) had begun what would turn out to be a sharp deterioration, from 14th in 1996 to 18th in 2002 to 37th in 2014.

Zelekha raised the question: Had the gradual fiscal expansion from the 1985 stabilization program to 2002 created non-Keynesian effects? He answered by estimating an econometric equation for log quarterly product, which directly included public consumption and its rate of growth.[3] Public consumption, to be

[3]In addition to public consumption and its growth, the explanatory variables included: population, short- and long-term interest rates, the tax burden, world trade, Israel's export and import price indices, returns to capital and labor (with a constant to capture technological change), the level of

clear, is the part of the government budget that is spent on products and services which are included in GDP. Therefore, if the effect of public consumption on domestic product is found to be negative, it is obvious that the negative non-Keynesian effects of the total government budget are even larger. As a consequence, it may be that a policy of dealing with recession by increasing government expenditures actually made the situation worse. The results pointed to effects which went beyond even the most extreme of the aforementioned findings. In this framework the negative significant effect of any change in public consumption on domestic product stands out, and not only through irregular changes. Concurrently, it seemed that an important part of the negative influence of public consumption on domestic product existed also in the medium, and not only in the short term.

In this context, Zelekha raised serious concerns regarding the goals of fiscal policy in Israel from the 1985 stabilization program to June 2002 in general and government policy regarding the then-current crisis in particular. These emphasized decreasing the proportion of government expenditure in GDP by means of raising GDP, not by means of an absolute decrease in government expenditure. Netanyahu did not elaborate on Zelekha's presentation at the conference, except for commenting that "people should listen to what Zelekha is saying." Four months later, unexpectedly, Prime Minister Sharon, after the elections of 28 January 2003, appointed Netanyahu as the new finance minister, with the mission of "saving" the Israeli economy. Netanyahu immediately asked Zelekha to prepare the framework for a new economic policy and join him in implementing it.

The new economic policy framework which Zelekha prepared (Zelekha 2005, 2006) was directly driven by his research, that is to say, the potential for recovery and growth should be realized by means of drastic contraction of public expenditure and reduction of tax rates to match the OECD average. The goal was to encourage expectations regarding future tax cuts in order to boost private consumption.

In order to achieve this goal, Zelekha proposed three measures:

(a) A preliminary budget cut of some NIS 15 billion (at the time the budget was some NIS 200 billion and GDP NIS 550 billion), since the literature emphasized the importance of a contractionary critical mass. The budget deficit was set at 6% of GDP (instead of a projected deficit of 8–10% of GDP). The proposed budget cuts focused on social transfers and public sector salaries, since the literature also emphasized the importance of contraction implemented through earmarked, albeit politically sensitive expenditures. This was a political gamble, especially since the poverty rate had reached an all-time high. However, if the plan was to succeed, then tax cut expectations would have to be improved, private consumption boosted, growth accelerated, and employment as well as wages of low-paid workers increased, compensating for the cuts in social transfers. Successful implementation of the fiscal adjustment boosted

inflation and its standard deviation (to capture both general and inflation-related uncertainty), and a dummy variable to capture the impact of the Second "Intifada."

private consumption within 6 months, putting the 2003 deficit at 5.6% of GDP. By 2007, the deficit would fall to almost zero.

(b) A 1% spending cap—that is, a 1% cap on growth in real government expenditures; this was the first implementation of a spending cap in Israel's history. (In 2006, the cap was eased to 1.7%, and by 2009 the cap was no longer implemented.) Since the growth rate of potential GDP was 5% in real terms, this meant a significant decrease in the ratio of government expenditure to GDP. Indeed, this aim was actually achieved, so that by 2008 the ratio of government expenditure to GDP was well below the OECD average. Furthermore, the most important part of the plan was to improve the efficiency of government service provision. With the 1% spending cap and population growth of almost 2% per year, the only way to avoid permanent cuts in the level of government services was to improve the efficiency of government service provision by at least 1% per year.

(c) Contractionary monetary policy, to deal with the recent burst of inflation and instability in the foreign exchange market (which introduced great uncertainty and additional inflationary pressures). Without stabilization of inflation and inflation expectations, there would not be a recovery in consumer confidence.

However, in order to implement this plan, Netanyahu had to control the office of the accountant-general of the State of Israel (henceforth abbreviated AG), one of the most important economic positions in the government. Indeed, Netanyahu took advantage of the previous AG's resignation a few months after the elections and appointed Zelekha to this position, entrusting him with responsibility for the new economic policy program.

7.3.1 *The 2003 Economic Recovery Program and the Role of Accounting Reform*

In Israel, the AG is responsible for implementing the state budget through two channels. First, only the AG has the legal right to make financial commitments on behalf of the government, sign contracts, or approve the issuance of tenders. Second, only the AG has access to state funds; no one else is able to make payouts on behalf of the State. In addition, the AG's Office, with a staff of 3000 people, is the legal owner of all state assets.

The accounting reform aspect of the new economic plan began by dividing the government budget into new theoretical subdivisions, each one under the responsibility of a newly appointed taskforce of accountants and consultants in various fields, headed by one of the AG's senior deputies. The taskforce's mission was to present and execute a working plan to cut the budget without cutting government services—to achieve the same level of services with fewer resources. Naturally, a change had to be made in the AG's personnel and management structure by creating coherent departments for each budget subdivision and establishing new divisions and working methodologies for auditing, controls, checks and balances. Eight such divisions were established.

The first division was established for wages, pensions, and all accompanying payments, including perks such as cell phones, cars, etc. The taskforce implemented a simple supervision procedure to enforce existing law. Under the law only contracts signed by the AG's office were binding. However, politicians and government ministries had joined together in the years before 2003 to hire thousands of people illegally, raise salaries, and grant all kinds of financial subsidies to their employees, without the AG's permission. Consequently, the government never met its wage bill (i.e., the government paid wages that exceeded the wage items in its approved budget); thus, the government's wage bill was continuously growing, until it comprised 30% of the government budget. In addition to these measures, the new economic policy implemented a temporary 2-year reduction in government salaries. The new taskforce made it clear that from 1 January 2004, a contract or wage increase not approved by the AG would not be honored and charges would be instituted against any ministry director-general who signed illegal contracts. In addition, hundreds of accountants were sent to government ministries to conduct a thorough audit, to ensure that every wage contract was legal[4] and within budget.

As difficult as it is to believe, the government was deliberately avoiding the deduction of income tax from the pay slips of its employees, thus committing (in effect) the greatest act of tax evasion in the entire country! Indeed, the office that "excelled" most in this regard was the Israeli Tax Authority itself.

The second division established was for government procurement. Procurement is a business that belongs to professionals. The difference in the outcome of a tender that is well prepared can be upward of 30–50%. The difference in the outcome of a well-managed contract through its life cycle can easily be another 10–20%. Unfortunately, there was no professional government procurement agency, so every government office bought products and services for itself. Thus, the government failed to exploit the economies of scale that could be achieved via a unified purchasing program. Often, there was a lack of coordination between government ministries. Some ministries would buy excess quantities of goods (or services), while others would lack sufficient funding within their budgets to purchase the same goods.

The portion of the national budget allocated for government current purchasing (i.e., purchases not related to investments) was approximately NIS 30 billion ($7.5 billion USD), or almost 15% of total budget. However, despite this large amount, until 2003, everything related to purchasing—like other expense lines in the budget—suffered from a lack of professionalism. In fact, the situation was worse than in other areas. Over the years, purchasing had become the "private property" of

[4]To be legal, a wage contract had to meet the following conditions (among others): the employee was hired through a proper tender, the employee had the requisite qualifications, the wage adhered to the official government wage table, and all taxes were being paid.

the ministries, and their expenditures expanded accordingly. Also, it was found that illegal, improper, nontransparent waivers were used during tender procedures. Thousands of contracts worth many billions of NIS were never subjected to proper tender, and this situation had been going on for up to three decades.

Now, although purchasing is a profession with its own methodology, procedures, and tools, most of the people filling purchasing positions in government ministries lacked the requisite education and experience. Among purchasing managers, 90% lacked any professional training or academic degree; some had never worked in purchasing, having served as simple general service or logistical personnel.

Furthermore, contrary to the accepted practice in large business corporations, the government did not have a centralized purchasing authority. Thus, there was no government agency capable of performing the following essential functions: establishing a purpose-built purchasing system, transmitting accumulated experience to purchasing managers in the ministries, developing advanced tender methodologies (e.g., dynamic online tenders), establishing procedures and controlling expenses, removing needless obstacles and threshold conditions, and managing centralized tenders (for items needed by several ministries) in order to exploit economies of scale.

Third, the government did not strictly enforce separation between the agency ordering the goods and the purchasing office, which is not only essential for proper internal control but also essential for streamlining the entire purchasing procedure. Without this separation, it is difficult to maintain the proper balance between the needs of the agency ordering a system and the organization's overall need to economize. Thus, for example, the government purchases sophisticated systems but does not use them fully, because the agency that places the order is not required to reduce its expenses but only to avoid exceeding its predetermined budget. In other words, because government agencies are not rewarded for saving, but rather for remaining within their budgets, they have no incentive to adapt the systems they purchase to their needs. Instead, they purchase the most sophisticated systems possible within their budgets. When there is separation between the agency that uses the system and the agency that purchases it, the latter's only obligation is to save as much money as possible.

The third division established was for the subsidies and social transfer payment budget, which had never been audited or regulated properly. The division's staff found that over 90% of the transfers went to NGOs whose management and general expenses exceeded 50% of their incomes, and over 50% of the transfers went to NGOs whose management and general expenses exceeded 90% of their incomes. In short, 30% of government transfers never reached the needy. The division imposed new limits on the general expenses of the NGOs. In addition to auditing and new regulations, the new economic policy significantly cut subsidies and social transfers in order to incentivize work and discourage exclusive reliance on social transfer payments.

The fourth division established was for large infrastructure projects. It should be stressed that the way in which the government managed its large projects was completely "Third World." Entirely different legal documents were issued for the same tenders. Also, artificially low prices were submitted in tenders; under pressure from the winning bidders, the government would reopen signed contracts and agree to increase the price to a level that would have resulted in the loss of the tender. There was no basic know-how, no reasonable and efficient contract documents, and no reasonable risk allocation; illegal political interference was rampant.

For example, during the 1990s, the government decided that the market for electricity should be opened to competition. At the time, the market was completely controlled by the Israel Electric Company (IEC), which was notorious for its inefficiency. The government believed that if private entrepreneurs were encouraged to begin producing electricity, the IEC would have an incentive to become more efficient. The government assumed that sometime in the distant future, it might be possible to allow electricity producers to compete against each other without its intervention. It decided to begin the process by issuing a series of tenders for the construction of private power stations and grant entrepreneurs incentives and guarantees to make the opportunity more attractive for them. However, like many good government plans, it would be an understatement to say that the implementation was flawed. In the end, the state lost more than it gained.

Implementation of the plan failed in two ways. First and foremost, the government created a system of incentives and guarantees that made it worthwhile for entrepreneurs to sell most of the power they produced to the IEC, rather than to consumers. In other words, it did not create competition for the consumer's business. Second, the required power stations could only be built by multinational corporations such as Siemens and General Electric. The effective result was that rather than the IEC building power stations under direct contract with an international supplier, the government forced it to enter an agreement with the winning entrepreneur, who then contracted with the international supplier. This was counterproductive: The IEC was just as involved as before, only now there was an entrepreneur in the middle, who demanded a commission. Therefore, the price of electricity set by the "private" production tenders was necessarily more expensive than that produced directly by the notoriously inefficient IEC. The entrepreneurs then sold the expensive electricity to the IEC, which in turn pushed up the cost of electricity for all Israeli consumers. However, this was not the only shortcoming. Management of the tender was scandalous and became perhaps the most outstanding example of the substandard tender culture practiced by the government at the time. Selection of the winning bid signaled the beginning of interminable negotiations, accompanied by incessant demands by contractors to reopen signed contracts and make changes for their own benefit.

The fifth division established was the debt office. It was found that domestic government debt issues were traded via a unique system that multinational banks refused to participate in, to the good fortune of Israeli banks. When the system was changed and competition was introduced, interest on the government's $150 billion debt was cut by 30 basis points, for an annual savings of $0.5 billion in interest payments. It was also found that the government was issuing a 10-year debt in order to finance a 2-week gap in government finance (thus carrying a 5% margin on average) and that it kept a huge $5 billion uninvested cash flow with massive carrying costs and more.

The sixth division established was for asset management. For the first time in the history of Israel, the government started registering its overall assets in the government financial statements. The seventh division established was the Government Information Systems Division, which introduced an ERP (enterprise resource planning) system to support all the other reforms.

The eighth division established was the Accounting Division, which introduced annual external audits and in addition changed the Israeli Generally Accepted Government Accounting Principles (GAGAP) to International GAAP. The meaning of the reform in government accounting is inherent in the Hebrew word for an accountant (*roeh heshbon*), which is derived from the Jewish legal tradition and based on the verb root that means "to see." The most important concept in the world of accounting, "full disclosure," points in the same direction. Indeed, the purpose of accounting is to *reveal* the accounts and their significance so that the potential audience for the financial statements (which, in the case of a government, is the general public) can ascertain that the organization is being managed honestly and efficiently. The essence of the accountant's task is to observe the situation on behalf of the public and present it to them. Therefore, "looking the other way" is not an option for an accountant; anyone who turns a blind eye effectively disqualifies himself.

US Supreme Court Justice Louis Brandeis took matters one step further when he wrote, "Sunlight is said to be the best of disinfectants; electric light the most efficient policeman," that is to say, that transparency is the best gatekeeper. *The accounting reform element in the Economic Program of 2003, approved by the Israeli government in July 2004*, eventually allowed sunlight to infiltrate the darkest corners of the government's fiscal behavior; the sun's rays penetrated a system that had long been accustomed to operating in darkness.

Practically speaking, accepted government accounting practices in Israel require that financial statements include a full and complete explanation for any serious irregularities in the management of assets, obligations, and budgets. Any substantive shortcoming, missing asset, or improperly altered contract must be exposed. Any budgeted activity that was not actually implemented requires an explanation; any unlawful activity that was budgeted must be disclosed, whether it was implemented or not. Everything must be transparent and available for auditing, whether by the state comptroller, to whom copies of the complete financial statements and all related working papers must, by law, be submitted, or by the public, the media and various movements for good government. Not only are the flaws exposed and documented; critical information is disseminated regarding the rate of progress toward correcting them (or not) and the individuals responsible for their correction.

The reform itself was implemented in two stages. In the first stage, the state's balance sheet was prepared in accordance with International GAAP. This stage was completed with the publication of the financial statements for 2004 on 30 June 2005. The second stage was accomplished with preparation of the budget utilization report (the governmental equivalent of a profit and loss statement in the business sector) which was submitted with the financial statements for 2005 on 30 April 2006. Simultaneously, the schedule for translating the International GAAP from English into a binding Hebrew version was moved forward from September 30 to March 31, so they could be used for the 2006 statements, which were indeed published on 28 March 2007, as is customary in the business sector. Financial auditors for each ministry were appointed in the AG's office in order to improve the quality of the ministries' financial reporting, on which the reporting by the government as a whole is based. A Governmental Accounting Standards Board was established, including representatives from the Institute of Certified Public Accountants in Israel, the Securities Authority, and the Israel Accounting Standards Board. No longer would the AG set the accounting standards and prepare the statements on his own; the days of creative, dangerous accounting were over. The actual preparation of the statements was entrusted to external auditors who were chosen through a tender process. In 2007, the multiyear process of submitting the statements for complete external auditing was initiated.

When the 2005 statements were published, it was an important international achievement. At a time when some businesses still did not publish financial statements under GAAP, the state comptroller, the Knesset, and the entire Israeli public received, for the first time in Israel's history, trustworthy financial statements from the Government of Israel, prepared in accordance with international standards. With this step, Israel joined five leading Western nations—the US, Canada, the UK, New Zealand, and Australia—in publishing financial statements of the quality and transparency required of publicly traded companies. Israel, like the other countries named, was now far ahead of most other countries in the world, including those in the EU.

This accomplishment was widely praised by many in both Israel and abroad. Israel's representative to the international committee for establishing governmental accounting standards, International Public Sector Accounting Standards Board, immediately became an international leader in the field. Investment banks, credit rating agencies, and the IMF all commended the reform. Even the auditor of the EU complimented Israel and noted that it was now several years ahead of EU institutions.

In any case, when the reform was completed, financial statements became a highly effective economic management tool. In this context, it is important to understand that accounting includes much more than the narrow, albeit important, matter of financial reporting; it relates to all aspects of fiscal management. Although accounting is based on providing information about all types of expenses and revenue, it can also be used to better understand the overall economic substance and significance of those expenses and revenues, the processes that accompanied them, their ramifications for the government's financial management, and the consequences of its policies. For example, employment contracts signed by the government or changes in stipends or pensions are all explicated with their full actuarial significance in the financial statements.

Furthermore, accounting raises questions regarding the assets in which the government invested large sums of money. If the benefit derived from an asset is far below its cost, this must be reported and the financial statements adjusted in a way that exposes to criticism the decisionmakers who approved the initial investment. This put an end to the tradition of "white elephants." Furthermore, if the government attempts to delay critical decisions and mortgage the future of its citizens, its errors will be evident in future reports that clarify the actuarial significance of the previously concealed crisis. For example, the deferral of road maintenance expenditures requires accountants to increase the depreciation recorded for roads. No longer can politicians prettify their irresponsibility.

Therefore, these financial statements have become an important basis for evaluating the fiscal performance of the government of Israel and its financial stability. Now, government ministries and subunits had access to reliable financial information that would help them make intelligent decisions and reduce financial and budgetary risks. Furthermore, transparency of the data and consistent reporting over many years made it possible for senior civil servants, as well as ministers and Knesset members, to make year-to-year and cross-country comparisons, both while preparing the annual budget and when monitoring its implementation. This had never been possible before.

All of these reforms contributed to a better understanding of the economic and financial processes in the Israeli government and provided an incentive for government officials to prevent shortcomings before they happen or, at the very least, to redress them immediately, lest the accountants expose them to the state comptroller and the general public. In other words, the *government accounting reform led to further reforms of unprecedented importance in the behavior of both the government and politicians.*

7.3.2 The Recovery and Seeds for the Next Crisis

It took 4 years to implement accounting controls in the Israeli central government structure and to examine the thousands of contracts and hundreds of thousands of pensions and salaries. Unfortunately, little work was done on almost one hundred government companies and about 250 municipalities, where officials responsible for them strictly refused to use the measures implemented at the central government level. The successful outcome of the government accounting reform plan was a permanent savings of over $3 billion out of the $60 billion budget, all of which was allocated to finance large-scale, permanent tax cuts to stimulate economic growth[5] and to implement a coherent system of management, checks and balances (see Zelekha and Cohen 2011). In 2004, real government expenditure decreased for the

[5]The top marginal income tax rate was cut from 62.5% to 44%, the corporate tax rate was cut from 36 to 24%, and VAT was cut from 18 to 15.5%.

first time since 1985, by 1.9% (after a negligible real increase of 0.2% in 2003), although population growth was almost 2% a year. As mentioned above, a 1% spending cap was implemented (later eased to 1.7%), so that by 2008, the government expenditure share in GDP was well below the OECD average.

As a result, in 2004 Israel started its longest and strongest growth period ever (GDP per capita in US dollars rose from $18,000 in 2003 to over $30,000 in 2008, or from 49% of US GDP per capita to 62%). At the same time, the credit rating agencies raised Israel's sovereign credit rating from A− to A+.

However, Israel still had a long way to go on the road toward attaining OECD-level living standards. In addition to the work that had to be done regarding government companies and municipalities, the success of the new economic policy made politicians less inclined to risk their political support by reforming the uncompetitive structure of the local economy.

In this chapter, we first dealt with the unique characteristics of fiscal policy in Israel, from the stabilization program of 1985 up until 2002. This policy maintained one of the most inefficient public sectors in the Western world and directly led to another "lost decade" in Israel, that is to say, between 1995 and 2003, bringing about what could be called a "Great Recession" in the Israeli economy. The crisis called for a new stabilization plan, which stressed drastic contraction of public spending and of the tax burden while establishing proper norms with respect to expenditure. The severity of the crisis allowed massive implementation of government accounting reforms, along with policy reforms, with *significant results*. However, a few years after successful implementation of the economic and accounting reforms, and the resulting achievement of high growth, the core elements of the reform were abandoned, and Israel's economic situation deteriorated once again.

In 2005 Netanyahu resigned as minister of finance for political reasons and soon afterward led the opposition to Prime Minister Sharon and his successor Prime Minister Olmert. By the end of 2007 Zelekha had left office. In 2009, Netanyahu again became prime minister but abandoned the principles of the new economic policy that he himself had introduced in 2003–2004. The Israeli government's long-standing addiction to tax-and-spend policies *(in 2013, taxes almost returned to 2003 levels) and the complete abandonment of the economic reform* led to a severe deterioration in economic performance. Now, the justification for fiscal expansion in 2009 was ostensibly the potential impact of the global financial crisis (GFC) on the Israeli economy. However, it should be noted here that while the GFC affected household wealth and consumption and also the financial sector, the banking system was not affected to the extent exhibited in other countries, and there was no economic collapse. By 2015 the economy—under Netanyahu's leadership—exhibited only negligible per capita growth, and the government once again seemed helpless to deal with economic problems. *The significant difference in implementing reform, exercised by the same political leader in a crisis as compared to recovery, illustrates the problem of politicization of reform and recovery accordingly.*

References

Afonso, A. (2001). *Non-Keynesian effects of fiscal policy in the EU-15*. Working Paper, Univeridado Tecnica de Lisboa.

Bertola, G., & Drazen, A. (1993). Trigger points and budget cuts: Explaining the effects of fiscal austerity. *American Economic Review, 83*, 1170–1188.

Burger, A., & Zagler, M. (2008). US growth and budget consolidation in the 1990s: Was there a non-Keynesian effect? *International Economics and Economic Policy, 5*, 225–235.

De Castro, F. (2003). Non Keynesian effects of public expenditure in Spain. *Applied Economics Letters, 10*, 651–655.

European Central Bank. (2001, August). Fiscal policies and economic growth. *Monthly Bulletin*, pp. 39–53.

Feldstein, M. (1982). Government deficits and aggregate demand. *Journal of Monetary Economics, 9*, 1–20.

Giavazzi, F., Jappelli, T., & Pagano, M. (1999). *Searching for non-Keynesian effects of fiscal policy*. Working Paper No. 16, Center for Studies in Economics and Finance.

Giavazzi, F., & Pagano, M. (1990). Can severe fiscal contractions be expansionary? Tales of two small European countries. In O. Blanchard & S. Fischer (Eds.), *NBER macroeconomics annual*. Cambridge, MA: MIT Press.

Giavazzi, F., & Pagano, M. (1996). Non-Keynesian effects of fiscal policy changes: International evidence and the Swedish experience. *Swedish Economic Policy Review, 3*, 67–103.

Giudice, G., Turrini, A., & Veld, J. (2007). Non Keynesian fiscal adjustments? A close look at expansionary fiscal consolidations in the EU. *Open Economies Review, 18*, 613–630.

Kormendi, R., & Meguire, P. (1990). Government debt, government spending and private sector behavior: Reply and update. *American Economic Review, 80*, 604–617.

Perotti, R. (1997). *Fiscal policy when things are going badly*. Working Paper, Columbia University.

Ravid, B. (2012, January 24). U.S. to grant three-year extension of loan guarantees to Israel. *Ha'aretz*.

Schein, A. (2003). NASDAQ or Nablus: Explanations for the recent fluctuations in the Israeli economy. *Israel Affairs, 9*, 64–78.

Sharp, J. (2012). *US foreign aid to Israel*. Congressional Research Service Report, Washington, DC.

Sharp, J. (2016). *US foreign aid to Israel*. Congressional Research Service Report, Washington, DC.

Taylor, J. (2003, June 22). *Israel's Economic Recovery Program*. Speech to the Israel-American Chamber of Commerce, Jerusalem.

United States Congress. (2003, April 16). *Public Law 108–111*.

Zelekha, Y. (2005). The non Keynesian anchor of the Israeli economic policy. *Israeli Tax Quarterly, 31*, 7–18 [in Hebrew].

Zelekha, Y. (2006). Lessons of the second lost decade. *Israeli Tax Quarterly, 32*, 7–10 [in Hebrew].

Zelekha, Y. (2008). *The black guard, 2008*. Or Yehuda: Kinneret-Zmora-Bitan Publishers [in Hebrew].

Zelekha, Y. (2010). Non-Keynesian effects of fiscal expansions in Israel. *ICFAI Journal of Public Finance, 8*, 31–38.

Zelekha, Y. (2011). *Reforming consumption patterns*. Bnei Brak: Ono Academic College and Hakibbutz Hameuchad Publishers [in Hebrew].

Zelekha, Y., & Cohen, A. (2011). Supervision and control tools for the management of fiscal policy goals: Case study of Israel. *GITAM Journal of Management, 10*, 43–65.

Chapter 8
Economic Advisers and Israel's Economic Policy: Some Interim Conclusions

As presented in the chapters above, since the establishment of the State of Israel in 1948, well-known foreign economists (mostly American Jews) and Israeli economists (who were trained in the US) played an *ostensibly* decisive role as advisers in the development of Israeli economic policy. In this regard, Israel is probably the most notable example of a country—aside from the US—in which prominent academic economists have also played a role in economic policy discourse and as advisers.

Some, such as Abba Lerner and Michal Kalecki, did so in their capacity as official advisers to the Israeli government in the early years of statehood. In other instances, the individuals concerned acted principally on behalf of the US government, as was the case with Raymond Mikesell, Stanley Fischer, and Herbert Stein. In yet a third category, best illustrated by the examples of Richard Kahn and Milton Friedman, influence was manifested by the occasional entry of world-renowned economists into the Israeli discourse, partly directly and partly indirectly.

We used their contributions and economic analyses as case studies, so as to *purposively* illustrate our three possible scenarios and their related hypotheses as presented in our introduction above.

Scenario I—Crisis
In a *crisis* environment, the *policymaker's balance of interests changes*, and the *public interest may overcome any other interest.*

Scenario II—Convergence
Convergence or, better put, ad hoc convergence occurs when there is *limited difference* between the *policymaker's original policy and interests* and the *adviser's perception of the public interest.*

Scenario III—Divergence
Divergence occurs when there is *significant difference* between the *policymaker's original policy and interests* and the adviser's *perception of the public interest.*

D. Schiffman et al., *The Role of Economic Advisers in Israel's Economic Policy*,
DOI 10.1007/978-3-319-60682-8_8

The analysis of the case studies reveals that Scenario I and its related hypothesis are supported by the cases of the 1952–1953 and the 1985 economic crises in Israel. Indeed, despite the criticism levelled at the recommendations of "experts, bookkeepers, and statisticians" for dealing with Israel's 1953 foreign debt crisis, the recommendations in the 1952 Mikesell Report regarding foreign exchange budgeting *were implemented.*

During the 1985 crisis, the policy measures ("Ten Points") advocated by Stein and Fischer were implemented, for the most part, by the government, although they were *rejected* prior to the crisis itself, with other measures, such as "wage-price freezes" being attempted instead. In fact, the implementation can be easily defined as a significant success.

Furthermore, over the sample period 1948–1985, there were no other acute crises similar to that of 1985, while *outside* of the sample period, there was only one additional crisis of such magnitude, in 2003, discussed at length in Chap. 7. Although the 2003 crisis did not bring the government to approach a prominent foreign adviser for advice, it did approach an Israeli adviser to prepare a new economic policy, which was implemented for the most part. That adviser, Zelekha, was not a government official, but rather an academic adviser, and the invitation to prepare a new economic policy that contradicted the previous policy of the Ministry of Finance was unprecedented (with the exception of the 1985 crisis). This event provides additional support for Scenario I and its related hypothesis.

The analysis of the case studies reveals that Scenario II and its related hypothesis are supported in full by all three case studies *considered in their full historical contexts*. Kalecki, Lerner, and Friedman were invited by the government to advise it *after the original policy had been determined*, with Kalecki invited on an ad hoc basis, to provide justification for the extant government policy. Lerner and Friedman, for their part, were *excluded* almost immediately after it appeared that the *differences* between the government's *original policy and interests* and their *perceptions of the public interest* were, in fact, *significant*. Therefore, while at first, their advice was perceived as successful, in retrospect, it was not.

Furthermore, the analysis of the case studies reveals that Scenario III and its related hypothesis are supported in full by all four case studies, *again considered in their full historical contexts*. Kalecki, Lerner, Friedman, and Kahn failed to achieve even *limited* success, *according to their own accounts*; Friedman was not even included in the policy discussions that were ostensibly based upon his economic worldview, and the government felt the need to publicly distance itself from his advice. The support for Scenario III and its related hypothesis are even more striking when we take into account the initial ostensibly significant impact of Kalecki and Lerner. Additional support for Scenario III and its hypothesis can be seen in the fact that even the success of Stein and Fischer during the 1985 crisis only came after very similar policy prescriptions were *not* applied over 1982–1985 and in addition were partially and gradually undermined after the crisis was over and the economy was back on track.

Our data allow us to consider several sensitivity and robustness checks. First, our dataset consists of seven advisers (case studies), but dozens of policy recommendations made by these advisers. None of these many recommendations contradict our three possible scenarios and hypotheses. Second, over the years after our sample period and up to the present (1986–2016), there is no other case of a well-known international adviser taking part in Israeli economic policy discourse to contradict (or further support) our findings. However, as mentioned above, in 2003 the Israeli economy experienced an additional crisis which was of a similar magnitude to the 1985 crisis; the 2003 crisis in fact supports Scenario I and its related hypothesis.

Our findings have significant policy implications today, when many countries still suffer from the effects of the GFC. Our findings suggest that the public in these countries, as well as international organizations, should be aware of the unique "opportunity" that the *crisis* creates for the country—an opportunity to overcome vested interests in order to *maximize the implementation* of the necessary reforms before the "golden hour" passes. In addition, the public should become aware of the political *misuse* that governments make of advisers *in order to gain support for policies that were already decided upon, according to political considerations.* When interpreting our findings, however, the limitations of our dataset must be taken into account. Our dataset is limited to a single country and includes a limited number of case studies, although we did examine dozens of distinct policy recommendations. Future research should be based on a larger number of countries, advisers, and policy recommendations.

Index

D. Schiffman et al., *The Role of Economic Advisers in Israel's Economic Policy*,
DOI 10.1007/978-3-319-60682-8

MIX
Papier aus verantwortungsvollen Quellen
Paper from responsible sources
FSC® C105338

If you have any concerns about our products,
you can contact us on
ProductSafety@springernature.com

In case Publisher is established outside the EU,
the EU authorized representative is:
Springer Nature Customer Service Center GmbH
Europaplatz 3, 69115 Heidelberg, Germany

Printed by Libri Plureos GmbH
in Hamburg, Germany